Marshall W. Fishwick, PhD

Great Awakenings: Popular Religion and Popular Culture

Pre-publication
REVIEWS,
COMMENTARIES,
EVALUATIONS . . .

"**M**arshall Fishwick has written a lively, readable, amusing history of religion in America, focusing upon the leaders and invokers of the successive, perhaps cyclical, 'Great Awakenings' from Increase and Cotton Mather in colonial times to twentieth-century notables like Father Coughlin, Jim Jones, and Jerry Falwell. The author's concern is not doctrinal—terms like *orthodox* and *heterodox* are never used; he is concerned with the great movers and shakers who won immense followings, including such secular folk as Horatio Alger, promulgating the 'Fifth Gospel'–'the Gospel of Success.' Fishwick describes these colorful and, yes, successful men–and women–with wit and vividness. The reader is amused and, in the process, learns much about popular religion."

Sheldon Vanauken, MA, MLitt
Professor Emeritus of History
and Literature;
Author, *A Severe Mercy, Under the Mercy,* and *Gateway to Heaven*

"**T**his study by Professor Fishwick provides an eclectic and entertaining blend of scholarly research, personal experience, and original insight on the subject of religion in America. His sympathetic presentation of the history of our popular religiosity reminds us how deeply spiritual is the American past. Fishwick recounts the findings of his many years spent investigating the influence of secular culture upon traditional faith. Radio and television come to the fore in his saga of popular piety, which boasts a cast of flamboyant evangelists, wandering prophets, faith healers, and 'God Pumpers' of every stripe. It is the media, he argues cogently, which have worked the greatest effect upon religion in America, allowing humble pastors to rise to the rank of prophet in a world where 'salvation is won through success.' All in all, the book is an informative and interesting presentation of a much-maligned but ever-important topic."

Deland S. Anderson, PhD
*Assistant Professor of Humanities,
Virginia Polytechnic Institute
and State University*

More pre-publication
REVIEWS, COMMENTARIES, EVALUATIONS . . .

"**M**arshall Fishwick, a founding father of American popular culture studies, has written a lively, learned, and provocative history of American revivalism from the 1700s to the present. He brings historical research to bear on today's electronic revival tent, separating what is holy from what is hokey, what is prophetic from what is patently and perilously political. This is a valuable addition to the top rank of important studies of American religion."

Richard Gid Powers
Professor of History
and American Studies,
City University of New York;
Author, *Secrecy and Power:
The Life of J. Edgar Hoover*

"**O**ne of the greatest forces driving American and world societies today is undoubtedly the combination of religion-ethnicity-nationalism. Not to be aware of its potential is like going down Niagara River in a dinghy blindfolded. No one feels the forces and the threats more than Marshall Fishwick, who has been studying them for 40 years. In this book, he surveys some of the American forces and their leaders, pointing out their origins, motivations, and consequences. The picture is not rosy. Fishwick tries to be unbiased and optimistic. The result is a cogent study which is at the same time amusing. Throughout, the evaluations are energized by Professor Fishwick's inimitable style. The book is valuable information on vital subjects sparklingly written."

Ray B. Browne, PhD
*Chair, Popular Culture Department,
Bowling Green State University*

Harrington Park Press
An Imprint of The Haworth Press, Inc.

Great Awakenings
Popular Religion and Popular Culture

HAWORTH Popular Culture
Frank W. Hoffmann, PhD and William G. Bailey, MA
Senior Editors

Great Awakenings
Popular Religion and Popular Culture

Marshall W. Fishwick, PhD

Harrington Park Press
An Imprint of The Haworth Press, Inc.
New York • London • Norwood (Australia)

Published by

Harrington Park Press. an imprint of The Haworth Press. Inc.. 10 Alice Street. Binghamton. NY 13904-1580

Library of Congress Cataloging-in-Publication Data

Fishwick. Marshall William.
    Great awakenings : popular religion and popular culture / Marshall W. Fishwick.
       p.   cm.
    Includes bibliographical references (p. xxx-xxx) and index.
    ISBN 1-56023-858-5 (alk. paper).
    1. United States–Church history. 2. Revivals–United States–History. 3. Popular culture–United States. 4. Popular culture–Religious aspects–Christianity. I. Title.
BR517.F57 1994
277.3–dc20   94-20590
                                                                   CIP

For Manette and Harry Baker Adams

They have fought the good fight–
and won many a battle.

ABOUT THE AUTHOR

Marshall W. Fishwick, PhD, is Professor of Humanities and Communication Studies at Virginia Tech. He has held a number of national posts including the presidency of the Popular Culture Association, which he helped found in 1967. He has lectured widely in Europe, Africa, and Asia, has held eight Fulbright Chairs, and holds honorary degrees from Krakow University and Dhaka University. Dr. Fishwick's numerous articles and books cover such interests as poetry, history, regionalism, theology, American studies, and popular culture. His most recent books are *The Medium and the Messiah, The God Pumpers, Common Culture and the Great Tradition,* and *Go, and Catch a Falling Star: Pursuing Popular Culture.*

CONTENTS

"*[Unless America returns to] her Christian roots . . . she will continue to legalize sodomy, slaughter innocent babies, destroy the minds of her children, squander her resources and sink into oblivion.*"

–Rev. Pat Robertson

"*There is a religious war going on . . . We must take back our cities, and take back our culture, and take back our country!*"

–Patrick J. Buchanan

Preface

We are told we live in a global village, but we look out at and live in our local village. From this dust we come and to this dust we return. That is the place to start our study of popular religion in America.

On January 5, 1993 my local village (Christiansburg, VA) is charged with excitement. The Montgomery County School Board wants to change the name of two public school holidays from "Christmas" and "Easter" to "Winter" and "Spring." Pat Robertson's Christian Coalition and others of the Christian Right are indignant. A public meeting has been called to air the matter.

Nine hundred people fill the Christiansburg High School Auditorium. Law officers stand by in case matters get out of hand. The atmosphere is electric. Thirty-nine people have signed up early to speak. The first is Jim Sutphin. His position is quickly stated. "This is still a Christian nation we live in here tonight–not a religious nation, but a Christian nation." Applause breaks out. He continues. "I want all people here tonight who believe in a true living God to stand up for a moment of prayer."[1]

The audience rises to its feet. Such drama is seldom reported on national press or television. Yet it is significant. If democracy rests on the will of the people, it is at moments like this that the people's will is made manifest.[2]

Later on John LeDoux, a former navy officer and chairman of the county chapter of Christian Coalition, makes an impassioned speech. Having fought foreign enemies for 25 years he now must fight enemies at home. We are not your enemies, a university professor replies, but Americans who believe in the separation of church and state. The debate rages amidst applause, booing, and heckling. The beleaguered school board announces it will postpone its decision until a later date.

Two weeks later a new president takes office in Washington. The century's leading evangelist, Billy Graham, gives the invocation and benediction. President-elect Clinton calls on God for support, and quotes from the King James Bible. The nation is jubilant and optimistic.

One essential function of popular culture is to present morality plays to the people.[3] Once this was done at county fairs or on cathedral steps; now it is done in high school auditoriums and at political inaugurals. Like Proteus, popular religion can take on many shapes and forms. It can wax and wane, and live out cycles. But it cannot be eliminated or ignored. That is the thesis and theme of my book.

That thesis was amply illustrated later in 1993 on a bleak field outside Waco, Texas. Hundreds of federal, state, and local law enforcement officials, many more hundreds of TV crews and journalists, and millions of readers and viewers were involved. David Koresh and his Branch Davidian followers were barricaded inside their compound. On Sunday, February 28, federal agents tried to execute a search warrant at the compound. Four agents and an unknown number of cult members died in the initial gunbattle. The Great Cult Scare took over, and lasted 51 days. On April 19 the compound, having been penetrated by attack tanks, went up in flames. At least 72 cultists, including 25 children, died. We shall say more of this in a later chapter. The preliminary questions are: Are cult scares cyclical? Have others occurred, and might we expect more in the future?

The answer is easy to come by. Cults were active, and fear was pervasive, when history was still blind. Early religious documents, such as the Old Testament, demonstrate this. (Recall the worship of Baal and the Golden Calf.) Christians have rooted out cults–they prefer to call the members heretics–for 2,000 years. Many Protestants (labeled Diggers, Shakers, Quakers, and many other things) were branded "cultists," and found refuge in the New World. The famous French visitor Michel de Crèvecoeur wrote in 1782: "If any new sect spring up in Europe, it may happen that many of its professors will come and settle in America. As they bring their zeal with them, they are at liberty to make converts."[4]

And so they did. Can that liberty be denied to zealots of our century? And did not the zeal border on hysteria in the camp meetings and revivals of nineteenth-century America, where thousands ended up confessing, shrieking, speaking in tongues; and where many fell to the ground "as if slain in battle"? Barking and jerking were rampant. No one interfered. "It's a free country, ain't it?"

Some American cults blossomed into full-scale denominations, even religions. The obvious example is Mormonism. In the 1820s the Angel Moroni appeared to Joseph Smith in Upstate New York, and Mormonism began to take shape. It is now one of the fastest-growing denominations in the world. In the 1830s a Baptist preacher named William Miller announced that the Day of Judgment would occur in 1843, then in 1844. Scores of camp meetings ensued, and on October 22, 1844, thousands of Millerites gathered for the end of the world.

It didn't come. But Miller's followers lived on, calling themselves Seventh-day Adventists. It is from this group that the Davidians split in the 1960s.

Throughout history charismatic leaders appear and disappear. Who should control or restrict them? Where does liberty stop and license begin? These questions form the central thread of my book. There are no easy answers. Perhaps our wisest course is to ask the questions. That is what we shall do.

There are no citations for a number of quoted items and claims made in my book. There are several reasons for this. Many come from pamphlets and ephemeral publications that have no dates or pagination. Others are in the oral tradition, and cannot be attributed to a single source. There are folk songs and sayings which have no known author; and there are legends and claims which may well be apocryphal.

Much in popular culture escapes scholarly attribution, but carries great weight and validity. I have tried to document when I could, and use with discretion that which I couldn't. I believe this is the only way to explain *Great Awakenings*.

NOTES

1. *Roanoke Times and World News*, "Tension Over How to Name Holidays," Wednesday, January 6, 1993, sec. A, p. 2.

2. The best overview is Sydney A. Ahlstrom, *A Religious History of the American People*, 2 vols. (New York: Doubleday, 1975). Two other helpful studies are Robin Attfield, *God and the Secular* (Cardiff, Wales: University College

Press, 1978); and George M. Thomas, *Revivalism and Social Change* (Chicago: University of Chicago Press, 1989).

3. For a development of this point of view, see Marshall W. Fishwick, *Common Culture and the Great Tradition* (Westport: Greenwood, 1984).

4. J. Hector St. John [Michel de Crèvecoeur], *Letters from an American Farmer* (New York: Doubleday, 1961), p. 157. Originally published in 1782.

Prepare to meet Thy God.

Amos 4:12

And he said unto them, Go ye into all the world, and preach the gospel to every creature.

Mark 16:15

Introduction

I write of popular religion. All societies have a religion, and religion has always been popular. It always takes on the flavor and formulas of a particular culture. Not only is religion a social phenomenon, but, as Emile Durkheim observed, society is a religious phenomenon.[1] The substance of culture is religion and the form of religion is culture. Religion, Paul Tillich wrote, is whatever people take seriously.[2]

One of the cliches of our time is that the City of God has become the Secular City. Not all religious writers and thinkers have despaired of this change. Dietrich Bonhoeffer calls secularization "our coming of age."[3] At last we are free from religious dogmas and closed metaphysical systems. Instead of depending on The Almighty, we call upon The Technique to solve our secular problems. Jacques Ellul, who coined the term, says we now ignore ultimate goals and employ the practical and expedient. The crucial question is, "Does it work?" The important line is the bottom line.[4]

The Technique dominates the Western World in general, the United States in particular. Joining hands with capitalism and individualism, it has dominated many aspects of the modern world. Both superpowers, the U.S.A. and the U.S.S.R., found it equally effective in expanding their power and prestige.

The City of God and the Heavenly City sustained us for centuries, and many are reluctant to abandon them now. Secularization has confronted a formidable enemy in fundamentalism and the "old-time religion." While the influence and membership of the so-called "mainline" or liberal denominations has declined in America, that of the fundamentalists and the "religious right" has greatly expanded.[5] So has that of fundamentalists in other religions and nations around the world. Islam, Judaism, and Buddhism all bear witness to this.

They sense that world energy and interest goes to secular, not religious centers. Time-honored religious language and liturgy are losing their power; sacred scriptures are diminished or even ignored. Nonreligious forces seem to be shaping our faith, values, and cultures.[6]

These are not new complaints, especially in America. They were voiced by the first Europeans who settled our shores. Indeed, these very complaints caused our Pilgrims and Dissenters to set sail. The twentieth century is struggling with questions that have plagued us since the seventeenth century, and have plagued others for untold centuries. We are not discarding religion. Instead, we are completing a cycle.

I sing a song of cycles. Dimly perceived and seldom understood, they pace and pattern our seasons, moon, cosmos, covering the moment and the millennium. Night follows day, spring follows winter, planets repeat orbits. In our end is our beginning. Facing death, we rejoice in resurrection.

Eastern civilizations make cycles central to their thought. Hindu cycles are as short as one calendar day and night–or as long as a day and night of Brahma, 8.64 billion years. Westerners prefer linear thinking. They put lines on charts and graphs to represent reality. Our main measuring unit, the century, exists in our minds, not in nature. The decade is only a decimal position in the century; both are arbitrary intervals.

Some great western thinkers–Plato, Vico, Spengler, Toynbee, Eliot, Yeats–advance cyclical theories, but most of our thinking remains linear. The cycle I propose–that of religious revivals or awakenings in the United States–is a small item compared to various grand schemes. Yet it might throw some light not only on American religion, but on the culture as a whole.

I speak of light, not proof. Since periods and cycles are neither necessary nor self-evident, we cannot prove or predict them by any scheme yet discovered. But we can probe and ponder.

Great Awakenings seem to occur about every fifty years.[7] The first took place around the middle of the eighteenth century, powered by George Whitefield and Jonathan Edwards. It replenished a waning Puritanism and centered on the eastern seaboard. The second broke out on the frontier, involving camp meetings and circuit riders. Led by Francis Asbury, Father of American Methodism, it spanned the first half of the nineteenth century. A host of poorly educated preachers, black and white, were involved. They developed the chanted sermon and folk practices that are still with us. The second Great Awakening, like almost everything else, was changed forever by the Civil War.

The new urban industrial America needed and got a different kind of religious revival. Charles Finney was the major transitional preacher, adapting the frontier meeting to the new cities. His "laws of mind" revitalized and revamped American evangelism. For Finney, conversion was no miracle, but the predictable result of proper methods. The third Great Awakening made urban revivalism a part of popular culture. The year 1858, known as the *Annus Mirabilis* (Wonder Year) of revivalism, featured activities in all major cities, with religious and secular newspapers all over the country reporting noonday prayer meetings. The joyous camp meeting "love feast" was transferred to the city. Two national organizations–the Young Men's Christian Association (YMCA) and the U.S. Christian Commission–furthered the revival. It brought the Beechers of Boston to the fore, and allowed Dwight L. Moody to conquer Chicago and found the Moody Bible Institute. Horatio Alger, a preacher driven from his pulpit by homosexuality, made his contribution by perfecting the Fifth Gospel of Success, which has supplemented the other four. Billy Sunday gave it mass appeal and glamor. The crisis of massive immigration was weathered, and the robber barons affirmed. This Awakening leveled off during the McKinley era and the Spanish-American War.

With the twentieth century, a powerful new force–fundamentalism–fueled the fourth Great Awakening. Millions of copies of *The Fundamentals* were distributed before World War I; William Jennings Bryan emerged as the Great Commoner. Though he died the Sunday after the 1925 Scopes trial, in which he was outmaneuvered by the clever Clarence Darrow, Bryan's cause was espoused by people as different as Aimee Semple McPherson, Father Divine, and Father Coughlin. Mixing economics, politics, and theology, these "fighting angels" guided millions through the Great Depression and World War II.

The fifth Great Awakening began in the Age of Ike, when a rich, triumphant America espoused a civil religion. God could fly no higher than the American eagle. Norman Vincent Peale, Fulton J. Sheen, and Joshua Liebman brought Protestant, Catholic, and Jew back to faith, making Americans "the most religious people on earth." The radio had been a powerful religious tool since the 1920s; when television emerged in the 1950s, the Electric Church accelerated. One result was televangelism, which we shall examine in detail. This fifth Awakening has attempted, with mixed success, to get us through the crises of the Youthquake, Vietnam, and Watergate. Now, in the high-tech America of Bill Clinton, the Awakening is faltering. Despite the increase of prime-time preaching and religious theme parks, the fifth revival, like the twentieth century, is nearing its end.

These cycles are not only historic; they are also mythic. Myths, especially those connected with religious rites and beliefs, explain how things work, and why. They are the poetry of history, the foundation on which it is built.

From Puritans in somber black to televangelists in living color—they are held together by one central belief, the myth of salvation. This myth, applied to our five cycles, may provide a new angle of vision, and a new understanding of our religious heritage.

Long before and ever since the first European settlers arrived in the New World, this land has been saturated with gods, devils, and things that go bump in the night. Here, said Edward Johnson in 1630, is where the Lord will create "a new Heaven, and a new Earth, new Churches, and a new Commonwealth together." Three and a half centuries later we are still working at it.

We have used every medium, happening, and victory to laud the Messiah; we have even invented a powerful American mythology in which salvation is central. This book is about that myth: where it came from, how it functions, what it portends.

America has always been religious—but has it been Christian? What have we proclaimed? And have we practiced what we preached? Is there a cycle of salvation? Where is televangelism in the cycle?

Everything that has happened in this vast, bone-breaking land has been related to divine providence. The Creator or Mighty Spirit has not always been kind to us. The American Indians understood this, and developed a stoicism that has enabled them to survive not one but a whole series of holocausts. We may have more to learn from the aboriginals than we have to teach them. Early Europeans had to live with a god who could be both angry and vengeful. So did their progeny. On a bitter cold night in February 1675, Indians ravaged the settlement of Lancaster, Massachusetts. Mary Rowlandson, the minister's wife, supplied details:

> We had six stout dogs belonging to our garrison, but none would stir. So another time, if any Indian had come to the door, they were ready to fly upon him and tear him down. The Lord hereby would make us the more to acknowledge His hand, and to see that our help is always in Him.

The same godly sentiment echoes through American history, whether the speaker be George Washington, Abraham Lincoln, Woodrow Wilson, Franklin D. Roosevelt, or Ronald Reagan. Separation of church and state becomes paper-thin when the Lord thunders. He has chosen us to carry out His mission, and has blessed us time and again. The myth of salvation is based on that demonstrable truth. We have called upon Him, and He has listened.

The drama and the actors vary, but the myth is constant. The scene may change from Lancaster to outer space, but not the motif. *Star Wars* and *Star Trek* are new wine in old bottles. Has science fiction become the mythology of our time–hence our road to salvation? Is that why it is hard to discuss our "Star Wars defense" with the Russians in arms negotiations?

The mythology of salvation that inundates America is by no means confined to the pulpit or religious broadcast. It fills media, publications, advertisements, studios, stadiums. The "congregation" is always told that America's problems can and will be solved–if only we will subsidize, deodorize, exercise, glamorize. When life is hard, we can always find softness by squeezing a roll of Charmin toilet tissue. Let's go Krogering. Drink up–things go better with Coke. Media mythology holds that all the world's a supermarket, and all mankind merely buyers. Commercials are prepared for viewers as carefully as any young vestal or nun was ever prepared for her consecration.

Observe the highly ritualized religious performance at an annual automobile show. Colors, lights, music, the awe of the viewers, the temple priestesses (fashion models), adoring throng–are these not part of a vast public liturgy? Are not those who come–like those who use radio or television for a quick religious boost–looking for a road to happiness, even to salvation? And has not the same consumer culture that gives us automobile shows also provided McDonald's, MTV, the 700 Club, trivia games, HBO, Grand Ole Opry, and the Old Time Gospel Hour?

Though they intertwine, we shall not concentrate on secular mythology and consumerism. Our myths and cycles involve churches, preachers, and conversion. They center on five revivals, all of which start in a period of relative calm and prosperity; gain momentum with the common people; peak during a national crisis and test of will; and subside when the crisis passes. They both direct and reflect the psychic environment. God is brought forth when He is desperately needed ("Praise the Lord, and Pass the Ammunition!"), then quietly retired when things get back to normal.

I write of persons, places, and happenings that illuminate the cycles. My case will not be made like a lawyer's, or a mathematician's, in logical propositions; nor like an historian's, in chronological cadence. It will instead depend, like religion itself, on sensing the mood and measure of the people who made the revivals possible, and those who were revived. Our job is to catch the poetry of creation, the drama of salvation. We must try to catch the elation of those who spoke, and those who heard. So we must leave the prosaic world, and enter the poetic one. Recall that Shelley said the poet is the real legislator of the world. Never has religion been more glamorous, more visible, more profitable, than in our Cycle Five. But all that seems to be changing.

During the 1992 Christmas season (a time of jolly, holly, and Hollywood blockbusters) Paramount released *Leap of Faith*–a biting satire and exposé of religious revivals and faith healing. The central figure, played by Steve Martin, is a street-smart ex-con who tours the country as faith healer Jonas Nightingale. With his cynical cohorts he fleeces his "flock." He goes from town to town like a hungry lion, seeking those whom he might devour.

Opting for a happy Hollywood ending, involving a real miracle and a much-needed rain, *Leap of Faith* nevertheless makes a strong statement about popular religion in the 1990s. When someone offers you cheap grace, hold onto your wallet. Instant salvation, guided by The Technique, is a multi-million-dollar rip-off.

But there were other signs, other indications that popular religion was flourishing. During that same 1992 Christmas season, Billy Graham was flying to Russia, to conduct a crusade "To Save a Nation's Soul." Full-page ads in American newspapers listed stations where the historic crusade could be seen in the United States and Canada. Billy Graham vowed he would fill the void left when Communism collapsed. He was not the first American to make that pledge. McDonald's had already opened a giant outlet in Moscow, employing 29 cash registers. Man cannot live by bread alone–he needs a Bolshoi Mac. Again, The Technique.

Even as I analyze and criticize The Technique, I realize that scholars and critics have their own techniques, assumed rather than examined. How can a religious critic understand a religious convert, with such different premises and beliefs? Can one who isn't "born again" know what the experience is like? Can we make judgments, as Harold Bloom does in *The American Religion: The Emergence of the Post-Christian Nation*, that come from another worldview?[8]

Yet we must all seek the truth, in ways that we know and trust. There is one thing worse than pointing out that the Emperor has no clothes–and that is closing our eyes and agreeing that he does. I have tried to approach the dark and bloody ground of popular religion with open eyes and an open heart. One can do no more than that.

NOTES

1. Emile Durkheim, *Elementary Forms of Religious Life*, trans. Joseph Swain (New York: Collier, 1961). Originally published in France in 1912.

2. Paul Tillich, *The Interpretation of History* (New York: Scribner's, 1936), pp. 236f.

3. Harvey Cox, *The Secular City* (New York: Macmillan, 1965).

4. Jacques Ellul, *The Technological Society* (New York: Knopf, 1967).

5. See James D. Kennedy, *Evangelism Explosion* (Wheaton, IL: Tyndale House, 1970); and Dean M. Kelley, *Why Conservative Churches Are Growing* (New York: Harper and Row, 1977).

6. See William F. Fore, *Television and Religion: The Shaping of Faith, Values, and Culture* (Minneapolis: Augsburg, 1987), ch. 2.

7. A good summation of the cycles can be had in William G. McLoughlin, *The American Evangelicals, 1800-1900* (New York: Harper and Row, 1968).

8. Harold Bloom, *The American Religion: The Emergence of the Post-Christian Nation* (New York: Simon and Schuster, 1992). For a more objective and sympathetic view of recent developments, see Randall Balmer, *Mine Eyes Have Seen the Glory: A Journey into the Evangelical Subculture in America* (New York: Oxford, 1989).

Chapter 1

The Atlantic Seaboard Awakening

Awakenings and religious revivals have always been shaping forces of American culture. The first settlers to British North America came when the Great Puritan Awakening raged in England. Only a strong belief in God's will and guidance could cause tens of thousands to leave hearth and home and sail over uncharted seas for the "howling wilderness" full of savage beasts and beastly savages.

Their most important shared belief was that the Bible contained full and complete answers to all problems. This notion, and others such as the covenant ideal and the theory of separation of church and state, took deeper root in New England than in Old England.[1] Despite the defeat of Puritanism in England after 1688 and its splintering in America, Puritanism is still a potent force in American life, and is central to Cycle Five in the late twentieth century.[2]

Technology has changed, but not the Judeo-Christian tradition in which our religion is rooted. To miss that is to miss the central core of our spiritual pilgrimage. This core, alive today, has been transmitted from generation to generation, continuously affirmed by churches, sects, and cults; nourished by reading and rereading a standard body of literature, and hearing thundering sermons. In ancient times God made a covenant with Israel; in modern times, we insisted, with America. Emphasized for centuries, the "Chosen People" idea gained credibility and importance. This conviction of God-elected uniqueness was part of the colonies' survival apparatus. The kind of government established violated most traditional accepted European rules for successful governments. If they *were* to succeed, the Founding Fathers realized, they had to preserve the myth of God's guidance.

Names of saints and martyrs dot maps of North and South America. America was the safety valve, missionary field, haven for every religious group. No nation has ever received such a bewildering variety in such numbers: dissidents from all the Protestant sects, Judaism, and Catholicism. They were Shakers and Quakers, Pentecostals and Penitentials, Baptists and Anabaptists; Dunkers, Mennonites, and Hutterites; all kinds of Anglicans, "low and lazy, middle and hazy, high and crazy." The colonies housed the radical religious sentiments of English groups like the Ranters, Ravers, and Diggers. Turn on your television: the ranting and raving still goes on. It is the American way. It comes with the territory.

The tone of American religion is profoundly individualistic and Protestant. The Protestant Reformation, one of history's major awakenings with worldwide implications, rekindled many ideas that were ideal for the almost uninhabited American continent, there for the taking. In the sixteenth and seventeenth century, thinkers believed in the linear progress of humanity. Religious-intoxicated minds were further stimulated by confidence in progress as a universal law–one that would lead to a golden age on earth. Progress was not an accident but a necessity.

Such thinking spawned platitudes: Idleness is wicked (family motto). Hard work is salvation (family epigram). Satan finds mischief for idle hands to do (crocheted wall motto). Burning the midnight oil (compliment to a student). He's chained to this desk (compliment to a businessman). Six days shalt thou labor (Scripture). Puritan truths prevailed–and still do.

Religious tracts and novels repeating these truths have dominated American best-seller lists. The desire to hear the Christian story retold is insatiable, though exterior trimmings change. Writers who understand this–Lew Wallace, Charles Sheldon, Lloyd C. Douglas, Kathleen Norris, Frances Parkinson Keyes, and Billy Graham–have made millions.

Deep in America's democratic faith is a strong supernaturalism; we are bathed in the blood of the lamb. God is our hope and our salvation. The former British officer who led our revolution (George Washington) is remembered not only on his horse, but on his knees at Valley Forge, praying for God's support.

In this, as in most other matters, we are children of Mother Europe. Among our most valuable imports were Puritanism, Anglicanism, Catholicism, and Methodism. But people reshaped the "isms." The American preaching tradition began in seventeenth-century New England, and has remained a potent tool ever since. The founders were men like John Cotton, Thomas Hooker, and John Davenport–all Cambridge and Oxford graduates. With them began the notion that the town's minister was the person (or parson), most educated and wise. So church-oriented were the first settlements that clergymen abounded. John Cotton wrote home to England that nothing was cheap in New England but milk and ministers.

Richard Mather (1596-1669) preached in England until 1633, then moved to Massachusetts where he wrote the earliest complete work on New England theology, and helped with the *Bay Psalm Book*. His most famous son, Increase (1639-1723), published 25 books and became President of Harvard University. Even his luster paled beside that of his son Cotton (1663-1728), boy wonder of American preaching, who entered Harvard at age 12 and produced more than 450 works. Cotton's son Samuel also became a theologian and author of 20 books.

The most popular book in seventeenth-century New England was Michael Wigglesworth's terrifying epic, *The Day of Doom* (1662). Children memorized long portions of the poem, including the part about doomed unbaptized children. There was a slight concession: they could enter "the easiest room of hell."

Americans believed they were sent into the untamed wilderness to found a society in which the individual would possess all the liberty to which God thought him entitled, free from the burden of the prejudiced past, to become an inspiration and a model to the world. This conviction of mission and special providence has fostered America's religions. Edward Johnson called Massachusetts the place where the Lord will create a new Heaven. Johnson and his fellow settlers thought that God had brought them to New England for providential purposes.

To Americans, caught in the serpentine twists of late-twentieth-century global politics, the literature of seventeenth- and eighteenth-century forefathers seems too idealistic, provincial, optimistic. John Winthrop hoped that New England would be so constructed that the Lord would favor New England.

God's hand was everywhere. Pilgrims risked all for a new Haven and a new Canaan. There was abundant faith in a righteous, just God who thundered. Their faith was realistic and intolerant of evil. In times of prosperity it filled their hearts with joy; in times of scarcity, with fortitude. They were strangers in this cruel land, destined for a better one. Justice, repentance, and the pursuit of happiness were indivisible.

A tough stoicism, combined with an unquestioning faith, made the Puritans survivors. Though long gone, that early Puritan ethic is still admired. Over three centuries have passed since the Puritans' time, but their spirit still stalks the land. Consider Reaganomics and the favorite Bible verse (Proverbs 22:29) of both Cotton Mather and Ben Franklin: "Seest thou a man diligent in his work? He shall stand before kings!"

As conditions improved in the colonies, and the wilderness was gradually tamed, the rigors of a Covenant theology were relaxed. A major doctrinal revision, drafted by Richard Mather and approved by a church synod in 1662, was known as the "Half-Way Covenant." Before then church membership had required a personal experience of conversion, with children sharing in membership privileges except for the Lord's Supper. The Half-Way Covenant extended this privilege to children of second generation members, even when their parents had no experience of conversion to bring them into full communion. Good fortune and new wealth in the eighteenth century weakened further the hold of the stern democracy which had guided and monitored early settlers.

Leaders noticed with alarm that people died or went West at a faster rate than they joined the church. Some Connecticut towns were receiving only four or five new members a year.[3] In Princeton College, seedbed of Presbyterianism, there were only two professing Christian students in 1782; and at Yale, eyewitnesses reported, scholars were gambling, tippling–and who knows what else. Some read the French skeptics and took nicknames like "Rousseau" and "d'Alembert." Truth to tell, things were not much better at Fair Harvard.[4]

Clearly the power of a stern, strict, and usually angry God was diminishing as conditions improved and life got easier. Though Jonathan Edwards described the 1734 revivalistic outburst in his parish as a surprising work of God, the historian, looking back, is not surprised. William G. McLoughlin lists five categories that triggered the Atlantic Seaboard Awakening, extending from Maine to Georgia: rapid social change; the infiltration of ideas from the European Enlightenment; the lure of the western frontier and free land; changed relationships with England after the Glorious Revolution of 1688; and the advance of the Industrial Revolution, replacing the old patriarchal agrarian system with the new bourgeois capitalist system.[5] Certainly personal economic ambition was responsible for much of the social tension.

In this new climate the first Great Awakening occurred. It was an extension of the Pietism and Methodism that engulfed Mother Europe. The key figure, George Whitefield, came to Boston from England in 1740. Converted by the Wesleys, ordained in 1736, he was a reviver without equal. In cold print his sermons seem bombastic; but how did they sound, delivered from Whitefield's mighty lungs, when he was preaching an average of 40 a week? His seven trips to our shores over a ten-year period included all the colonies. He was a sensational preacher, drawing congregations of 20,000 to 30,000. He gathered up the anguish of the people, who fell into weepings and convulsions, "like persons that were hungering and thirsting after righteousness."

Whitefield, surely one of America's greatest preachers, was also a pioneer in the commercialization of religion. He reached his ever-expanding audience (most of whom he would never see face-to-face) by extensive use of the newly-popular newspapers and printing presses; and by sending advance publicity teams to herald his coming. In a new study by Frank Lambert (*"Pedlar in Divinity-"George Whitefield and the Transatlantic Revivals*, Princeton University Press, 1994) we have a carefully documented account of just how Whitefield operated, and why Benjamin Franklin said, after the revivalist's 1738 visit to Philadelphia, that "all the world was growing religious."

He was not only a Jeremiah, calling the colonists back to the Lord; Whitefield was also the father of modern mass evangelism. People like Dwight L. Moody, Billy Sunday, Billy Graham, and Pat Robertson followed behind, and in his footsteps. He casts a long shadow over our account of Great Awakenings.

Whitefield's American counterpart, Jonathan Edwards, one of eleven children, was born to a Connecticut family in 1703. Entering Yale College at age 13, Edwards converted while studying theology, and became a tutor in 1724. He preached in Boston (1731), which marks his first public appearance before the theological world. In 1737 he published *A Faithful Narrative of the Surprising Work of God*, and in 1741 delivered the most famous American sermon: "Sinners in the Hands of an Angry God." It is based on the premise that God's Covenant of Grace, though instituted even before the world was made, can become active at any time. Grace is not only free and unearned; it is undeserved. At His mere "pleasure" and by His arbitrary will, restrained by no obligation, God may declare that covenanted history is a new phase and must move toward the consummation He had planned. In reading the bitter debates Edwards had with fellow divines, we miss Edwards's insistence that the marvelous acts of grace were at every moment foreordained by the terms of the Covenant God had made. Divine history is covenanted history; it has its laws and movement just as does mundane history. Covenanted history and divine justice act only on the lives of those who are already in the Covenant, and on those whom God intends to bring into His divine way.

Edwards called to three kinds of men: the wicked, who are unredeemed beyond any possibility of restoration, yet who, in moments of God's covenanted will, may be lifted at least part way to redemption; the "natural men," who loved the earth and sensual things but whose spirits may be rejuvenated; and the redeemed, who can never be sure they are saved and who, in the immeasurable trouble this world brings to men, may suffer their feet to slide. All three could rejoice in the good news: God would pity and forgive them. They must be reborn if they would be saved. The sermon was not only a work of art: it was the foundation on which much of what has come to be known as American evangelism is based.

Before Edwards, revivalism had been an either-or polar opposite to Puritan orthodoxy. His genius was to present a both-and position. Insisting that true religion is centered on the inner man (the revivalist position) he also held that God worked though his Covenant (the orthodox position). Edwards accepted the need for first-person experience, but sheltered it under the umbrella of community. Man is, and always must be, a social animal, he insisted. Any religious experience must be subject to critical judgments. The end point is the doctrine of regeneration–how one might be born anew into the Kingdom of God.

Edward's both-and position raised theological questions that others could not answer. How could one enter the Kingdom of God unless God elected him or her? And if elected, how could a man or woman resist God? Some called this the Edwardean paradox. The popular version was put forth in an anonymous ditty:

> You can and you can't,
> You will and you won't,
> You'll be damned if you do,
> You'll be damned if you don't.

If he baffled some, Edwards fascinated and spellbound others. His courage, energy, originality, and acuteness moved hearers to the very depth of their souls. He may not have had his equal in the history of American preaching. The congregation wept, fainted, fell into convulsions as he marshalled his terrible arguments. He brought to life "the kind of hell an infinite God would arrange who was infinitely enraged against a human being who had infinitely sinned in rejecting God's infinite love."[6]

Even today the power of Edwards's metaphors and similes is irresistible. He speaks of "the bow of God's wrath bent and the arrows made ready; and it is nothing but the mere pleasure of an angry God . . . that keeps the arrow one moment from being made drunk with your blood."[7]

Edwards insisted that emotions, not intellect, were central. We seek connection with something greater than ourselves. This must be supplied by religion. God uses emotions as channels for entering and reforming the individual. God must enter, since passions untransformed are bad; the original sin is selfishness. Virtue is unselfishness. No man can achieve this virtue by himself; grace can and will save him.

Edwards had a century to test the vision of early New England Puritans; we have two centuries to test his. He has not been found lacking, and remains today the most original and compelling theologian our culture has produced. He understood the American

Dream. He saw what must happen if it were to be made into a reality. We needed a compact society of men and women whose visible lives would be marked by such beauty that they could become for our civilization its apparent good. Then the history of their lives would become the reason for a nation to resume its pilgrimage. Edwards called these men and women the people of God. If such a people does not appear, there is no covenant and no ultimate society—only an inevitable victory for the powers of darkness.

Though accounts of this first Great Awakening center on New England in general, Jonathan Edwards in particular, the impact was enormous in the Middle and Southern Colonies. However, it was not as clearly defined and focused.[8] Here religious life tended to be more fragmented and segregated. The Middle Colonies had neither an established church system (except the Anglican, in four New York counties) nor strong denominational organizations. Many of the immigrants were poor, uneducated, and conservative, unacquainted with church doctrine. The largest group were Presbyterian settlers, driven from Scotland to Ireland and then Ireland to the New World in a single generation. The first Presbyterian synod in America, founded in Philadelphia in 1717, faced a series of controversies. Only itinerant preaching and crisis conversion enabled it to survive. Various small German sects resisted acculturation, and did not grow.

The colonial South was the fortress of the Church of England, and it was not sympathetic to any emotional awakening.[9] The same landed gentry that dominated politics also ran the churches. New-light missionaries who came south from New England or the Middle Colonies found both a religious and an institutional vacuum, and in 1747 the governor of Virginia ordered all magistrates "to suppress and prohibit . . . all itinerant preachers."[10] Many of the itinerants were beaten, jailed, and fined. It would take a second, and different, kind of awakening to evangelize the South of patricians and plantations.

Despite its uneven progress and pockets of failure, the Atlantic Seaboard Awakening, which we shall call Cycle One, was of great importance. It paved the way for the separation of church and state; substituted emotion for reason in the job of conversion; produced spiritual ferment in all classes and regions; and emphasized lay participation. Many now see it as one of two concurrent revolutions: this was the spiritual, and the American Revolution was the political. They interacted in various ways. Perhaps neither would have been possible without the other. During that spiritual Revolution, however, the Calvinist fires and zeal were considerably dampened by the rise of Deism, which conceives of a God beyond the range of human experience–one who, like a master clockmaker, sets the mechanism in motion and keeps it running. This shifts the emphasis from doctrine to ethics, and enthrones science, not theology. Founding Fathers Benjamin Franklin and Thomas Jefferson were Deists; even "atheist" Tom Paine could work with them. They believed that man's free and natural intelligence would save us.

God was distant and aloof; mathematics was the universal language. Reason would replace unbridled emotion. The new motto was Voltaire's "Ecrasez l'infâme"–"Get rid of superstition and infamy."

The English colonies, in turn, would provide the world with a new model of godly government. "My country is the world," Tom Paine wrote, "my countrymen are all mankind." Jefferson believed that his generation acted "not for ourselves alone, but for the whole human race." This revolutionary generation, buoyed up by the Great Awakening, was conscious of the responsibility to provide a Christian example. The Declaration of Independence showed that its framers had an overpowering sense of its importance. They believed that they were doing something momentous. That is why they asked the judgment of "The Supreme Judge of the World" and "The protection of Divine Providence." Timothy Dwight believed the United States was "by Heaven designed, the example bright, to renovate mankind." Philip Freneau saw America as "a new Jerusalem sent down from Heaven."

Great Awakenings always involve great preaching; men such as Theodore Frelinghuysen, William Robinson, Samuel Davis, and Devereux Jarratt filled that role. They still favored the traditional nonchanted sermon, often prepared ahead of time, with logical development from sentence to sentence. This "text and context" form had served the Puritans well, as it did those who tried to rekindle the Puritan zeal. The text came from the Bible. The context was elaboration and explanation. Somewhat like a lawyer's brief, it required educated practitioners.

All this would change in that "dark and bloody ground" on the other side of the mountains. Surviving would take on new meaning; so would reviving. The muses of Europe would grow dim in the seemingly endless wilderness. Institutions would change. So would religion, and the myth of salvation. So let us head west with those hearty pioneers.

NOTES

1. Leonard I. Sweet, *The Evangelical Tradition in America* (Mercer, GA: Mercer University Press, 1984); and Alan Heimert, *Religion and the American Mind* (Cambridge, MA: Harvard University Press, 1966).

2. The best summary of Puritanism is still the anthology of Perry Miller and Thomas H. Johnson, entitled *The Puritans* (New York: American Book, 1938). Also valuable are E. S. Morgan, *The Puritan Dilemma* (Boston: Little, Brown, 1958); Darrett B. Rutman, *American Puritanism* (Philadelphia: J.B. Lippincott, 1970); Sacvan Bercovitch, *The Puritan Origins of the American Self* (New Haven: Yale University Press, 1975).

3. *Connecticut Evangelical Magazine* (1801-02): 24-27.

4. Lyman Beecher, Autobiography, *Correspondence, etc. of the Rev. Lyman Beecher* (New York: Christian, 1864), vol. 1, pp. 273f. William Ellery Channing bore witness to the worldliness at Harvard. See David P. Edgell, *William Ellery Channing: An Intellectual Portrait* (Boston: Little, Brown, 1955).

5. William G. McLoughlin, *Revivals, Awakenings, and Reform: An Essay on Religion and Social Change in America, 1607-1977* (Chicago: University of Chicago Press, 1978).

6. Frederick M. Davenport, *Primitive Traits in Religious Revivals* (New York: Macmillan, 1905), p. 108.

7. *Ibid.*, p. 112.

8. Charles H. Maxon, *The Great Awakening in the Middle Colonies* (Chicago: University of Chicago Press, 1920); and Leonard J. Trinterud, *The Forming of an American Tradition* (Philadelphia: Westminster, 1949).

9. Wesley M. Gewehr, *The Great Awakening in Virginia* (Durham: Duke University Press, 1930); and Richard L. Bushman, *The Great Awakening* (New York: Atheneum, 1970).

10. McLoughlin, *op. cit.*, pp. 89-95.

Chapter 2

The Appalachian Awakening

"We'll build our camp on this rough ground
And give old Satan another round."

–Gospel hymn

America, Emerson observed, begins west of the Alleghenies. So does my story of the second Great Awakening.[1] On the cutting edge of the frontier, life was raw and traditions were few. Anyone who preached the gospel here had to be rough and ready, appealing to the half-men half-alligators who created a new American folklore. Men who engaged in bare-knuckle fighting and eye-gougings during the week could hardly be expected to sit quietly to hear an intellectual exegesis on Sunday. New settings and sermons were required. Only the fittest people, or denominations, could survive. Out of this Darwinian drama came the first indigenous American religion–and the second Great Awakening.

Religion was only one aspect of the culture that was leaving the European model behind. The astute French visitor Michel de Crèvecoeur perceived this: "The American is a new man, and acts upon new principles. He must therefore entertain new ideas and form new opinions."[2]

And, Crèvecoeur might have added, the American must find new modes of worship. The camp met this need. A clearing in the forest, with log benches and a rude platform for the speaker, meeting grounds came alive with emotional Christianity. They came with the nineteenth century. One of the most famous, held in the summer of 1801 at Cane Ridge, Kentucky, drew a crowd estimated at between 10,000 and 25,000 at a time when the state's largest city, nearby Lexington, had 2,000. Six or seven evangelists preached at the same time from different spots. No one knows how many listeners "got the jerks." It was a watershed in American religious history.

Religion mirrors a culture; it is not always a pretty sight. To document this, read the diary of the English missionary Charles Woodmason, who toured the area in 1830. He saw and heard incredible things. Nine out of ten marriages he was asked to perform involved pregnant brides; venereal disease was almost universal, polygamy common, concubinage general. Free whiskey from rival churches turned potential congregations into mobs. Ruffians were hired to insult Woodmason, yelling, "We want no damned black-gowned sons-of-bitches out here!" And if he did persevere and hold services, what did detractors do? Scream, whoop like Indians, and set dogs (on one occasion, 57 of them) fighting under the windows where he was trying to preach. Woodmason headed home.[3]

Preachers who stayed favored coonskin over clerical collars. They adapted to the new environment, observing the ring-tailed roarers, fighting the Devil and giving him an underhold. The concept of "minister," brought over from Europe, gave way to "soul-saver." Under the Calvinists of the first Great Awakening, God was "prayed down"; now he was "worked up." Preachers had to sow the seeds and reap the harvest overnight. Two time-honored traditions were born–hell-raising and heart-breaking: fears and tears. In the South of my childhood, both still flourished. A big tent meant one of three things: a circus, a medicine show, or a religious revival. Sometimes it was hard to say which was which. Ghosts of the old camp meetings still stalk the back roads of rural America. They turn up now and again on prime-time television.

Gradually, in the Age of Jackson, an American-style religion developed, rooted in the folklife of families moving westward. It served the needs of the emotionally starved and lonely, and became the only functioning democracy for the disinherited, disenfranchised, and dispossessed. This was the Country of the Word. One day, the preachers promised, the children of the Word would find a land of milk and honey. Each person would eat of his own vine, sit under his own fig tree, and whittle on his own sticks.

The Frontier Awakening preached the religion of the Right Way, marked by swift rewards and awful punishments. Life was a hard pilgrimage, full of temptations and dangers. Hell was very hot. Still, the Right Way was not as inflexible as the old Puritanism, with mores forged upon the anvil of Jeremiah by the hammer of Calvin. Now every person stood equal with every other person before God. Those who repented would indeed be saved.

The frontier language was colorful and unforgettable. We still have some of the sermons of Moses Dissinger, who preached in Pennsylvania, then headed west for Kansas in the 1850s. This unlettered carpenter used simple graphic illustrations that everyone could grasp. "Only with the weapons the Lord has given me can I whip the devil," he explained, "even if he does come upon me on stilts as high as a three story house." Moses had no use for drunkards. "They have noses like red peppers, ears like doughnuts, bellies like barrels; they jump for the rum bottle like bullfrogs for red rags." He was thoroughly American in outlook and endeavor, in idiom, and in rhetoric.

So was the Rev. James McGready, raised on a doctrine of hard work and hard truth, filled with signs of sanctification, and licensed to preach in western Pennsylvania. He moved to Kentucky in 1798–some said he was urged to do so by an anonymous letter written in blood. He ended up in the southeastern corner of the state, known as "Rogues' Harbor." The people there were tough as hell, so McGready gave them hell. His sermons remind us of Jonathan Edwards's in Cycle One. When he described hell and its horrors, with a lake of fire and brimstone, a "very general awakening" took place.[4] Sabbath breakers were pricked to the heart. Little children cried for redemption, in the blood of Jesus, at the gates of hell.

Nor were such outbursts unusual when hallelujahs and handclaps rang out all along the American frontier. One of the best accounts is found in Peter Cartwright's *Autobiography*, published in 1956. This vivid passage proves my point:

> Drunken rowdies came to interrupt our meeting, headed by a very large drinking man . . . He cursed the jerks and all religion. Shortly afterwards he took the jerks, and started to run, but he jerked so powerfully he could not get away . . . He took out his bottle of whiskey, and swore he would drink the

damned jerks to death; but he jerked at such a rate he could not
get the bottle to his mouth. The bottle struck a sapling and was
broken to pieces . . . When he lost his whiskey he was much
enraged, and swore very profoundly, his jerks still increasing.
At length he fetched a very violent jerk, snapped his neck, fell,
and soon expired, with his mouth full of cursing and bitterness.[5]

Preaching and patriotism have seldom resulted in so much singing, stomping, and saving as in camp meetings, where people
stayed for several days. Thousands gathered for prayers, hymns,
baptisms, and weddings. Tense nerves and repressed spirits broke
loose in Jesus's name: confessing, shrieking, speaking in tongues.
People fell to the ground like men slain in battle.

Passionate sermons and howling congregations did not, of
course, originate in America. Dominican and Franciscan monks in
the Middle Ages and many Reformation preachers knew how to
arouse violent emotions; but the words and ways changed over the
centuries and across the ocean. George Whitefield was said to be
able to bring a vast audience to tears, merely by intoning the word
"Mesopotamia."

Baptists and Methodists, out of favor in New England because of
their "barking, jerking, and other primitive traits," expressed their
emotions and passion on the frontier, using what came to be called
the "Baptist whine." Feeling became the sign of conversion. A
chanted sermon evolved, with formulas, timing, and gestures that
became standardized. Popular tunes were turned into evangelical
hymns. The congregation could sing, harmonize, or shout. Emotion,
free expression, and music formed a mighty force that swept over
the land. "A white mule never dies," according to an old folk
saying in Kentucky. "When he gets real old he turns into a Baptist
preacher."

Jesus of Nazareth "came preaching," and those who followed
have been preaching ever since. Preaching, teaching, and healing
have been the keys not only to Christianity, but to other religions as
well. The four Gospels contain unassailable witness to the centrality
of preaching; Matthew is organized around Jesus's great preaching-
teaching discourse. The book of *The Acts of the Apostles* revolves

around sermons. The history of church expansion and reformation centers around its preachers, the "fighting angels." In that tradition frontier evangelists worked.

Preaching had wide appeal to blacks, who became great practitioners. Many were proselytized and converted during the second Great Awakening. Black Harry, the best-known preacher of his race, held forth on the same platform with Bishop Asbury and other founders of the Methodist Church. Black preaching, accompanied by amens and hallelujahs, created what James Weldon Johnson called "God's Trombones." We have heard them loud and clear on our own day; Leon Sullivan, Martin Luther King, Jr., and Jesse Jackson, for example. African-American gospel music is a powerful voice in contemporary Christianity.

Old-time country preachers, white and black, have perfected the chant sermon. Within the rhythmical pattern there are rises and falls, building up to a frenzied climax. The preacher then tapers off into a normal delivery at the end.

The greatest white preacher of this period, and one of the most popular in modern times, was Francis Asbury. Born in England in 1745, converted to Christianity at 16, he became a Methodist and spent much of his life evangelizing America. Despite saddle sores, boils, bronchitis, rheumatism, and ulcers he crossed what he called "my Alps, the Appalachians" 40 times. Rocks, hills, ruts, and stumps couldn't stop him. He went from strength to strength, itch to itch on the worst roads on the continent. His very survival was a miracle. Unlike many evangelists of our day, he did not end up rich for his heroic endeavors. In fact, he was penniless throughout much of his life. Once, when a friend asked him for a loan of $50, Asbury replied that he might as well have asked him for Peru.

His achievement did not involve coins but converts. This "Father of American Methodism" has a record few evangelists can equal. In the 1770s Methodists had a few hundred converts and four preachers. When he died in 1816, Asbury left behind a church with 214,000 members and over 2,000 ministers. Dedication and discipline were the keys; Christian perfectionism the slogan. Since Calvinism had won much of the East and North of this new nation, Asbury concentrated on the South. This called for a "well-disciplined army," ready to stand even physical abuse, and most of all for "order, order, good order." When both his physical and mental powers began to fail, he accepted reality without blenching. "I look back upon a martyr's life of toil, and privation, and pain; I am ready for a martyr's death."[6] Asbury's last *Journal* entry found him on the trail. Other preachers idolized him. They began services by having congregations stand and sing:

> The world, John Calvin, and Tom Paine
> May hate the Methodists in vain.
> I know the Lord will them increase
> And fill the world with Methodists.

What Asbury and men of his ilk did was to turn a part of the new nation, which was largely unchurched, into the Bible Belt. Seldom has proselytizing been so successful. "The power of God came down, and pervaded the vast assembly, and it became agitated–swelling and surging like the sea in a storm."[7]

These early pioneer preachers adapted admirably, producing the Religion of the Spiritual Choruses. Songs served many functions–invitation, "pious ejaculation," prayer, farewell–the various aspects of what salvation meant to frontier saints. Contrasting sharply with the fearful hellfire preaching, the joyful singing contributed to the frenetic quality of conversions. Conversion was central to the camp meeting, and the foundation for the spiritual choruses:

> I want to go to glory.
> We have so many trials here below,
> They say there are none in glory.

Leaders learned how to fashion word and sound into a unique formula. Saints were articulating not what religion was *supposed* to mean, but what it *did* mean. The hope of heaven replaced the burden of this world, and converts were on their way to their real home:

> And I'll sing, Hallelujah!
> And you'll sing, Hallelujah!
> And we'll sing, Hallelujah
> When we arrive at home.

Thus did old symbols take on new meaning. Frontier religion offered plain folk an alternative to an essentially closed theology. The new world that was held out to them, though expressed in the language of evangelical Protestantism, was relevant to their time and place, as is to that of today's televangelists. The power of every living religion, George Santayana noted, is in its special and surprising message and in the bias which that revelation gives to life. No sentence sums up better the power and glory of the Appalachian Awakening.

NOTES

1. There are many accounts of the second (or Frontier) Awakening, perhaps the most colorful and exciting of all the Awakenings. An early classic is Catherine M. Cleveland, *The Great Revival in the West* (Chicago: University of Chicago Press, 1916). Other major studies include Elizabeth Nottingham, *Methodism and the Frontier* (New York: Columbia University Press, 1944); Charles A. Johnson, *Frontier Camp Meeting* (Dallas: Southern Methodist University Press, 1955); Bruce D. Dickson, *And They All Sang Hallelujah* (Knoxville: University of Tennessee Press, 1974); and Donald G. Mathews, *Religion in the Old South* (Chicago: University of Chicago Press, 1977).

2. J. Hector St. John [Michel de Crèvecoeur], *Letters from an American Farmer* (New York: Doubleday, 1961), p. 157. Originally published in 1782.

3. Such crude aspects of frontier revivals were the theme of an early study by Frederick M. Davenport called *Primitive Traits in Religious Revivals* (New York: Methodist, 1902).

4. McGready's story is told by Franceway R. Cossitt, *The Life and Times of Rev. Finis Ewing, One of the Fathers and Founders of the Cumberland Presbyterian Church* (Louisville, KY: Presbyterian Press, 1853).

5. Peter Cartwright, *Autobiography*, ed. Charles L. Wallis (Nashville: Abingdon Press, 1956), pp. 134-136.

6. Francis Asbury, *Journal and Letters*, ed. Elmer T. Clark (Nashville: Abingdon, 1958); and Emery S. Bucke, ed., *History of American Methodism*, 3 vols. (Nashville: Abingdon, 1964).

7. William G. McLoughlin, *Revivals, Awakenings, and Reform: An Essay on Religion and Social Change in America, 1607-1977* (Chicago: University of Chicago Press, 1978), p. 86.

Chapter 3

The Urban Awakening

Time flies, conditions change. The frontier moved westward, but much of the religious fervor moved eastward. There is no simple explanation. A dividing line between Cycle Two and Cycle Three is hypothetical; no one knows just when and where to draw it.[1] The platitude usually used is "when revival fervor moved from the frontier to the city"; but this was merely changing frontiers. There were as many challenges and pitfalls on the city streets as on the mountain trails. Both frontiers were vital and vibrant. Was it the leadership that shifted? Just as rural preachers had dominated the first half of the century, so did city preachers dominate the second half. Evangelism may have reached its summit in the last half of the nineteenth century with the Social Gospel.[2] Having moved around the nation, it went overseas. Missionaries had their great day. Their aim was to "civilize" the heathen, rather than to spiritualize him. Instead of the church evangelizing the world, the world secularized the church.

A logical starting point for Cycle Three is 1858, the so-called *Annus Mirabilis* (Wonder Year) of urban revivalism.[3] Since the bottom had just dropped out of the economy, and panic stalked the land, somewhat cynical historians explain what happened as the acceptance of emotional mass revivalism by urban business and civic leaders seeking God's help in troubled times. If there are no atheists in foxholes, there aren't many in panics either. No wonder some contemporaries called 1858 the "Businessman's Revival." In any case, it certainly helped the fast-expanding newspapers, the so-called "penny press." The *New York Herald* and *New York Tribune* found great copy in all that went on. So did the newly established national telegraph systems. New media always bring on awakenings of vari-

ous kinds. Look at what television has done in the late twentieth
century.

But the Urban Awakening cannot be explained merely by a panic
and new technology. There was intellectual ferment throughout the
land, centering in the cities and the universities. Liberal Protestantism and various Progressive movements battled with a militant
fundamentalist revival, and changing patterns of immigration.
There was a new industrial workforce, and thousands of mill hands,
to deal with.[4] The frontier "out west" was disappearing. In 1890, it
officially closed. God moves in mysterious ways. After the Civil
War, in the not-very-United States, He moved His revivals into the
cities.

For whatever reason, or combination of reasons, there were mass
revivals and religious growth in America, both before, during, and
after the Civil War. Observers at the time called it mass hysteria, as
city after city was awakened. New York, Chicago, Boston, Albany,
Buffalo, Cincinnati, and Richmond led the way. Not only large
cities, but smaller ones and even towns were powerfully affected.
Cycle Two had been largely in the hands of Baptists and Methodists. In Cycle Three every major Protestant denomination was
drawn in. So were the Unitarians and Universalists. Two national
organizations (the YMCA and the Christian Commission) played
their part, adding to the symphony of salvation that filled the American atmosphere at a time of Reconstruction after a bloody Civil
War that nearly tore the country asunder.

Church after church reported a new mode of worship. There was
no set ritual or liturgy. Whomever the spirit called might pray,
exhort, sing, or give testimony. Distinctions of class, race, and sex
were pushed aside. Ministers and lay persons worshipped on an
equal footing. The joyous liberty of frontier "love feasts" had
somehow invaded the cities. People of all ranks and stations were
expected to be soul-winners. Intense religious feeling was matched
by an intense democratic faith. Not only churches but schools,
missions, and temperance organizations now became symbols of
that same common faith. Yet this was no "jerks and barks" revival.
Cycle Three was seldom as emotional and ecstatic as Cycle Two.
One reason for this was the enormous influence of a single man,
Charles Grandison Finney (1792-1875).[5] He, more than anyone

else, transplanted the frontier revival meeting to the newly expanding cities. In the move from the second to the third Great Awakening, he is pivotal. Although raised in the backwoods of New York state, Finney thought of entering Yale, but decided there were quicker, cheaper ways of getting what he wanted. So he taught school, read law, and sang in the local choir. Mosaic references in his law studies intrigued him and impelled him to read and study the whole Bible. Then it happened. At age 29, he was overwhelmed by mighty baptism of the Holy Ghost. Within days he had converted almost every sinner in his village.

Self-taught and motivated, Finney was licensed by the local church and started preaching in other farm hamlets. His work was so impressive that the Presbyterian Church ordained him before, he later conceded, he had even read the Westminster Confession. Confident and charismatic, he shaped his own doctrine and followed the barges to the larger towns along the Erie Canal. He talked right to the people—spoke of "skinning the unconverted shepherds" of the flock. Older pastors, noting how he filled churches, began to listen and use some of his tactics. Combining various "laws of the mind," Finney's method became archetypal for those who followed: (1) direct, exciting, colloquial preaching; (2) protracted meetings given over to preaching, prayer, and counsel from sunrise to midnight, with all other business in town closed down; (3) anxious seats at public meetings for the convicted sinners who could be singled out for special attention; (4) public prayer for the conversion of individuals by name; (5) demand for immediate decision; (6) special meetings for the anxious; (7) extensive publicity; (8) bands of trained personnel workers; (9) emotional music; and (10) the support of resident clergy.

Here was the model of the "specialized minister," the professional mass evangelist, the miracle worker who insisted (in Finney's *Lectures on Revivals of Religion*) that conversion was not a miracle, but the result of hard work. One of the most important chapters is called "How to Preach The Gospel." All preaching, he says, should be practical. The proper end of all doctrine is practice. Preaching should be direct—preached to *men*, not *about* them. It should be the language of common life, depending on words in common use. Tell stories. That is the way Jesus Christ preached—

and it is the only way to preach. Facts, real or supposed, should be used to show the truth.

Finney insisted that political activity is not antithetical to soul-saving. Indeed, to promote public and private happiness is one of the indispensable means of doing good and saving souls. His gift was popularizing doctrines for Everyman, without oversimplifying them. He didn't need to study the popular mind; he shared it. Finney spoke precisely, logically, with wit, verve, and informality. But he also used tricks of the trial lawyer. The congregation was "on trial," and those "convicted of sin" were escorted to the "anxious bench," the equivalent of the witness stand. Finney used "you," not "they," when speaking to spellbound audiences. *You* were on trial–and the case wasn't over when you left church. Individuals were pursued. Groups of volunteers swooped down on neighbor-hoods; prayer meetings were held at any and every hour. There were "inquiry sessions" after formal meetings, often hours in length. Thus did Finney marshal the kind of group pressure that came easily in frontier meetings, but was almost impossible in sprawling cities. Instead of taking the people to the frontier, he brought the frontier spirit to them.

City after city fell under his spell. Finney and his associates made the urban revival part of American popular culture. The pattern they set was closely attuned to the Jacksonian sentiments of their day: an ardent faith in progress, the benevolence of God, the dignity and worth of the common man. Popular religion was made an adjunct of popular culture.

Finney's mission was to create a universal church based upon the fundamentals of the Gospel. The millennial age was about to dawn–right here in the United States of America. Had the whole church gone to work ten years earlier, the millennium would already have come. Finney was convinced that democracy was the form of gov-ernment most approved by God. Combining legal training and religious learning, he invented suitable devices to get this message across.

Such "New Measures" got ever wider attention. In 1832 Finney began an almost continuous revival in New York City, as Minister of the Second Free Presbyterian Church. When he outgrew this–and angered conservative Presbyterians–Finney's followers built the

Broadway Tabernacle in 1834. Thus he became the first preacher to play Broadway, leaping from raw frontier villages to urban centers of financial and social power. Even before the Civil War and the era of robber barons, he lived out the rags-to-riches success story, combining emotional outbursts with sermons that resembled lawyers' briefs.

Finney stressed common sense and pressing needs. The test of truth was the number of converts. This played havoc with traditional standards of doctrine and policy and brought him into conflict with theologians of the day–including the formidable Bostonian Lyman Beecher.

The confrontation was both dramatic and historic. The Beechers of Boston looked eastward–across the Atlantic, to Mother Europe and its ancient civilization. The Finneys on the frontier looked westward, to the Mississippi and the mountains beyond. There America would create a civilization of her own.

A student of Timothy Dwight at Yale (where he heard Jonathan Edwards's grandson preach), young Lyman Beecher took avidly to Puritan doctrine and dogma. He was determined to convert "Sabbath-breakers, rum-sellers, tippling folk, infidels, and rough-scuff generally." Appalled at the methods and popularity of Charles Finney, Beecher never matched him or challenged him openly. That task was reserved for one of his own offspring–his eighth child, Henry Ward Beecher (1813-1887). Young Henry was up to the task. Everyone knew the senior Beecher was competent, but the son grew up to be spectacular–"the greatest preacher the world has seen," in the overkill of John Hay, "since St. Paul preached on Mars Hill."

Such genius was not immediately apparent. Henry had to overcome a congenital distaste for study even to graduate from Lane Theological School, where his father was president. But he tuned in to the needs of his time, and wrote *Seven Lectures to Young Men* (1844). No one knows how many young men they helped. But they did help young Beecher, who subsequently received a call to the posh Plymouth Presbyterian Church in Brooklyn, New York. He accepted. Once there, he removed the pulpit and installed a preacher's platform, which some said was as large as Plymouth Rock. Beecher wanted to be near to the congregation. He also wanted to do and say things that would bring national notoriety. Pushing aside his father's Calvinistic theology, he quickly built a radical reputation by denouncing slavery, supporting armed settlers to "Bleeding Kansas," endorsing women's rights, auctioning slaves to freedom from his pulpit, and insisting on giving freedmen the right to vote. He accepted evolution and the academic higher criticism of the Bible, and never faltered in his open admiration for successful businessmen and chauvinistic nationalism. As Henry Clay, John C. Calhoun, and Daniel Webster began to fade from the scene, Henry Ward Beecher emerged as the most popular orator in America. He held that position for over thirty years.[6]

"This Brooklyn church," James Parton wrote in *Famous Americans of Recent Times* (1867, p. 132), "is simply the most characteristic thing of America. This is the United States, the New Testament, Plymouth Rock, and the Fourth of July, all in one." What evangelist wouldn't be happy with that combination?

How Beecher got to that exalted place, fell from grace following a famous adultery scandal, and much later became seen as "a neglected hero of American history," is a complex story. What seemed damnable to the 1880s seems admissible to the 1990s: here was a man willing to "do his own thing."

Accounts of the period give conflicting views on how and why Beecher achieved such popular acclaim. Certainly it was not based on systematic theology. Beecher never wrote anything that attempted to be academic. In fact, he attacked theological systems, and the factionalism that had split Protestant America into over 150 different sects. His clearest statement came in a novel, *Norwood*, published in 1867–the first fully developed statement of Liberal Protestantism in popular fictional form. But one looks in vain for any coherent theology.

Newly rich Americans were keen on culture, mad for self-improvement. For them, Beecher became a model, an intellectual sponge, sopping up all that was new and popular in art, architecture, or literature. Through the popular press and conversations, Beecher picked up the hopes, fads, and desires of those whom he wanted to instruct and uplift. The once-puritanical nay-sayer became a yea-sayer. He left behind the bleak fears of Calvinism and preached "the ritual of a higher life, the highway upon which our thoughts are to travel toward immortality, and toward the realm of just men made perfect that they may inherit it."[7]

What Beecher was beginning to perceive and preach was the relationship between industrial progress, culture, self-improvement, natural law, and God's spiritual laws of human development. He was laying out a program for post-Civil War America. "We cannot come to the conviction of the divinity of Christ so well by the intellectual and philosophical method as we can by the spiritual and experimental method," he said.[8] But even more astonishing, considering his stern Calvinistic upbringing: "You can afford, when you have done your best, to take things easy and enjoy yourself."

Evidence strongly suggests that he began to enjoy himself with a married lady named Mrs. Elizabeth Tilton. While the case itself was moot, and the jury split, Beecher became the classic example of a pompous preacher who got caught off base. His enemies rejoiced.

When Beecher got entangled in the snares of Satan (or at least clever prosecuting lawyers), Dwight L. Moody appeared. Twenty-four years younger than Beecher, coming from the same Yankee atmosphere (he was born in Northfield, Massachusetts), Dwight left his mother's farm at age 17, went to Boston, and was converted from Unitarianism to orthodox evangelicalism. Moving to Chicago, he prospered in the shoe business, but decided in 1860 to dedicate his life to Christ. Moody worked with the Young Men's Christian Association, became president of the Chicago YMCA, and founded the Moody Church.[9]

In 1870 he joined ranks with Ira D. Sankey, a gospel hymn writer. They made extended evangelical tours of Great Britain (1873-1875 and 1881-1883), where their colorful dramatic style swept all before it. Full of confidence and capital, he founded the Chicago (now Moody) Bible Institute and taught "retailing techniques," which would help set the style and tone of twentieth-century evangelism. He favored "whirlwind campaigns," counted converts as he had once counted shoes, and kept records with "decision cards." Mathematics moved into evangelism. He planned his campaigns as carefully as the Civil War generals planned theirs, moving from prayer to Bible study to home visitation. Each city was divided into "districts," to be visited by "squads" of specially trained recruiters. This observation is not meant to impugn either his tactics or motives. His fundamental faith and mechanistic approach matched his life and his experience. Moody had no formal theological training, deplored higher criticism and evolution, and preached the literal Bible, the Second Coming, and "old fashioned gospel." In this he was prototypical.

He strongly favored various charitable works (no one has done more for the YMCA), but did not think this assured salvation, nor a better life. He believed social problems could be solved only by the regeneration of human beings, one by one. Practically speaking, that meant that the poor should be honest, sober, pious, hard-working, and obedient–a formula that so pleased employers that big money flowed into Moody's coffers. Moody was not unlike the famous Pennsylvania politician Senator Matt Quay, who admitted "I work for the people that the people work for."

Moody was born during the Jackson era. He lived through the McKinley era. The vast changes that affected the nation, going from the frontier to world power, were reflected not only in politics but also in the religious movements and methods of the time. We have, of course, mentioned only a few of the preachers. Leaving the Great Awakening and Deism behind, nineteenth-century America developed an indigenous culture to fit a vast new continent. Some European evangelists, like Francis Asbury and John Wesley, understood and adapted to this. Methodism got a hold on the land which it has never lost. That opened the door for Charles Finney, Henry Ward Beecher, and Dwight L. Moody. In these men we see the techniques, even the program, of American evangelism taking shape.

In a larger perspective, worldwide Christian evangelism peaked in the nineteenth century, as a kind of corollary to European colonialism and imperialism. If the sun never set on the British Empire, it never set on missionaries, European and American, who toiled in all parts of the globe. The Kingdom of God was given a this-worldly hue that remains today. The interpretation was tied ever more tightly to the idea of progress. Mankind has advanced, is advancing, and will advance along with the United States. Progress was not an accident but a necessity. A golden age was about to occur on earth. Be saved now, and enjoy it. Thus saith the Lord.

During what church historians call "The Great Century" Americans not only spread old religions–they brought forth new ones.

Dwight L. Moody invoking the Lord to help save wicked New York City–here depicted on the cover of *Harper's Weekly* in March 1876. (Photo courtesy of Library of Congress.)

Mother Ann Lee founded the Shakers (so called because of their special dance). Stressing poverty and chastity, this sect had 30 thriving communities before the Civil War. Another charismatic preacher, the Baptist William Miller, was wrong when he predicted the world would end between March 21, 1843 and March 21, 1844; but his followers began the Second Adventist Church anyway. Mary Baker Eddy wrote a new Bible, *The Book of Health*, and transformed it into

Christian Science. (Mark Twain disliked the name, and thought it
was like "French horn"–neither French nor a horn.) John Noyes built
a church around group marriage ("Every 'dish' free to every guest").
In contrast, George Rapp combined celibacy and communism.

But the most spectacular success came when Joseph Smith
claimed to discover the lost *Book of Mormon*, in the "burnt over"
part of western New York state, and published it in Palmyra, New
York in 1830. Unique and controversial, sanctioning polygamy,
Mormonism powered an epochal Western exodus that ended in
Utah. Today the Church of Latter Day Saints, with over 5 million
members, dominates not only Utah but a vast economic empire, the
primary dictum of which is "Believe and obey." Involved are mul-
timillion dollar holdings in real estate, agribusiness, banks, insurance companies, and a media chain of radio and television stations
stretching from Los Angeles to New York. When Mormon Ezra
Taft Benson was made Secretary of Agriculture under President
Eisenhower, he said: "This appointment means the world has come
to recognize the Church for what it is. Joseph Smith prophesied that
we would one day assume leadership in Washington." President
Reagan helped bring that about, calling the Mormon Welfare Program a model of private initiative.

What irony: the church that Joseph Smith and Brigham Young
made "far left" has gone "far right"–an ultraconservative theo-
cratic empire, a subculture of reaction. Mormons, who both helped
and anticipated the "Christian Right," not only played a major role
in defeating the Equal Rights Amendment (ERA), but excommuni-
cated Sonia Johnson when she advocated it.

While the Urban Awakening was dramatic and often explosive, it
had no central theme, no one dominating figure, no clear agenda.
The Agrarian Myth died with the Confederacy, and the Age of
Grant was also the era of the robber barons. The rise of the city,
concentration of industry, exploitation of immigrants and labor, and
materialistic philosophies made it ever harder for religion to stake a
claim that fitted the new order.[10]

If the claims varied, the new road to conversion became ever
clearer: salesmanship. Bernard Weisberger sums it up in a sentence:
"As theology grew simpler, technique became predominant."[11]
The revival became a complex ceremonial act. The next step was a

rationalization of the rite, so that the greatest number of people could be saved at the lowest possible expenditure. "Modernization" took over. Later on, as it grew and grew, we gave it other names: massification, dehumanization, McDonaldization. Gradually the heirs of Jonathan Edwards were not theologians but entertainers. As Weisberger puts it so well:

> Once, the salvation of a soul had been a miracle, recorded in God's book of life. Now, it was a nightly crowd performance, registered on cards . . . Now the revival was not even so much of a ritual as a spectator sport with religious overtones.[12]

If the old Puritan and Protestant beliefs and creeds were disappearing, new ones were taking their place. The little world of the village and clearing was giving way to skyscrapers and slums. Once the excitement was genuine; now it was manufactured by gimmicks and sound effects. Clearly the power of the old-time gospel was in peril. America needed a new gospel–and she got it. That is what we shall examine next.

NOTES

1. See William G. McLoughlin, *Revivals, Awakenings, and Reform: An Essay on Religion and Social Change in America, 1607-1977* (Chicago: University of Chicago Press, 1978), ch 1. McLoughlin holds that awakenings are essentially folk movements by which nations reshape their identity, and transform patterns of thought and action. I agree.

2. Charles H. Hopkins, *The Rise of the Social Gospel* (New Haven: Yale University Press, 1940); and Paul Carter, *The Decline and Revival of the Social Gospel* (Ithaca: Cornell University Press, 1954).

3. The events of the year are analyzed in Timothy L. Smith, *Revivalism and Social Reform* (New York: Harper, 1957). See also Aaron Abell, *The Urban Impact on American Protestantism* (Cambridge, MA: Harvard University Press, 1943).

4. Henry F. May, *Protestant Churches and Industrial America* (New York: Harper, 1949); and Liston Pope, *Millhands and Preachers* (New Haven: Yale University Press, 1942).

5. Finney's own account is preserved in his *Memoirs of Rev. Charles G. Finney Written by Himself* (New York: Harper, 1876). There are a number of biographies, of which Victor R. Erdman's *Finney Lives On* (New York: Harper, 1951) is the most reliable.

6. Paxton Hibben, *Henry Ward Beecher, An American Portrait* (New York: Harper, 1927).

7. Lyman Beecher, *Autobiography and Correspondence* of the Rev. Lyman Beecher, D.D., 2 vols. (New York: Harper, 1864) II, p. 287.

8. *Ibid.*, II, p. 299.

9. Wilbur M. Smith did *An Annotated Bibliography of Dwight L. Moody* (Chicago: University of Chicago Press, 1948) and Paul Moody wrote *My Father: An Intimate Portrait of Dwight Moody* (Boston: Houghton Mifflin, 1938). The most reliable biography is Richard E. Day, *Bush Aglow: The Life Story of Dwight L. Moody, Commoner of Northfield* (Philadelphia: Lippincott, 1936). See also James Findlay, *Dwight L. Moody* (Chicago: University of Chicago Press, 1969).

10. Aaron Abell, *The Urban Impact on American Protestantism* (Cambridge, MA: Harvard University Press, 1943); and Donald B. Meyer, *The Protestant Search for Political Realism* (Berkeley: University of California Press, 1961).

11. Bernard A. Weisberger, *They Gathered at the River: The Story of the Great Revivalists and Their Impact upon Religion in America* (Boston: Little Brown, 1958), p. 258.

12. *Ibid.*

Chapter 4

The New American Gospel

To the Four Gospels, so central to every phase and cycle of popular religion, nineteenth-century America added a fifth: the Gospel of Success. Added, not invented; for as the Greek dramatist Aeschylus had observed many centuries earlier, "Success is man's god." The theme of success, in various forms and guises, runs like a river through Western civilization. English writers like Adam Smith, "Diamond" Pitt, and Samuel Smiles were greatly admired in America. Despite all the hardships, the colonists made a success of their New World homes, and eventually formed an independent Republic. Americans came to believe that they could do anything—and indeed, they did. The concept of success moved from fact to myth.

Other cultural myths formed and flourished in this exuberant and expansionist land. The WASP (White Anglo-Saxon Protestant) was invincible; his Lady, high on her pedestal, was incorruptible; the sturdy yeoman farmer was the backbone of democracy; Manifest Destiny made conquering the continent inevitable. Westward Ho!

All these strands worked together to form what Ralph H. Gabriel calls "a national faith which, although unrecognized as such, had the power of a state religion."[1]

The famous French visitor Alexis de Tocqueville had sensed this a century earlier when he made his notes on democracy in America. "It is difficult to know from Americans' discourses," he wrote, "whether the principal object of religion is to produce eternal felicity in the other world, or prosperity in this."[2]

Success had long been the apple of America's eye. Early in the eighteenth century, writing in *Magnalia Christi Americana* suggested that the way to serve Christ in heaven is to succeed here on

39

earth. Many agreed then, and still do now. Generations of preachers and politicians agreed. Benjamin Franklin, who wrote like a Puritan but lived like a pragmatist, added an economic base to the religious. Recall his famous aphorisms: God helps those who help themselves. He that would catch fish, must venture his bait. The bird that sits is easily shot.

Popular religion and economics were fully merged in the late nineteenth century. In this Gilded Age, the era of the robber barons, Andrew Carnegie actually wrote a famous book called *The Gospel of Wealth*. It merged the cross and the dollar: this was the good news; or Gospel. Threatened by modernism, Darwinism, science, and the Higher Criticism, fundamentalists sought and found allies in capitalism. The apologists of this new combination even invented a new name for what was happening in the United States: Social Darwinism. What it boiled down to was this: everyone for him or herself, and the Devil take the hindmost.[3]

The high priest of this new popular religion was Horatio Alger (1832-1899) who reduced these ideas to a simplistic formula, marketed it in a series of best-selling potboilers, and created the Rags-to-Riches Myth.[4] His name became a metaphor for success in America. Many authors (including me) wrote about Alger, drawing from the "standard" 1928 biography by Herbert B. Mayes. Forty years later Mayes's book was exposed as a hoax with many fictitious details. Since then a new generation of scholars have set out to "demythologize" Alger and reinterpret his work. There are, they say, two Algers. The first was the Harvard-trained moralist who disapproved of the mercenary Gilded Age, the second a best-selling writer of juvenile stories about poor boys who made good. The first historical Alger wanted to be a teacher and benefactor; the second symbolic Alger has emerged as a servile acolyte genuflecting at the altar of Success. Somehow the modest achievement of the Alger hero became confused with the astounding sales success of the books. How the "first Alger" became the "second Alger" is a complex problem, not central to our concern. It is the "second Alger" who is credited (rightly or wrongly) with the Gospel of Success. We will concentrate on him.

His canonization as an American success mythmaker occurred largely after 1920, as his books declined in popularity and eventu-

ally lapsed from print. In effect, Alger's work was editorially rein-
vented to appeal to a new generation. The phrase Horatio Alger
hero was not used until 1924. The most important single factor
came in 1947 when the American Schools and Colleges Association
set up the Horatio Alger Awards, to honor living individuals who by
their own efforts pulled themselves up by their bootstraps in the
American tradition. Among the recipients of this highly-publicized
award were Dwight Eisenhower, Billy Graham, Ray Kroc, and
Ronald Reagan.

Just who was this controversial man who became a mythmaker?
Born of old Yankee stock, son of a stern Unitarian minister, Horatio,
Jr. had a strong religious bent. He learned to scorn activities leading
to mere enjoyment, and prescribed for himself generous portions of
piety. At Gates Academy and Harvard College he was called "Holy
Horatio." Indignantly Horatio changed his Harvard lodgings when
his landlady appeared in her negligee. "I might have seen her bare,
but I did not look," he wrote.[5]

Confused and unhappy, he persuaded his parents to let him journey to Paris, where he learned things which the Unitarians had
never stressed. He looked. His Paris diary contains two lines more
worthy of immortality than any in the Alger canon: "I was a fool to
have waited so long. It is not nearly so vile as I had thought."

But he was not destined to be a *bon vivant*. This well-educated
New Englander wanted a respectable niche in the cultured class.
During the Civil War (a physical disability kept him from active
duty) he wrote both juvenile and adult books designed to arouse
sympathy for the Northern war effort. In 1862 he was offered a
pulpit in an Illinois church, but declined because he wanted to stay
in Eastern society. He was proud to be elected that year to the New
England Genealogical Society; and in 1864 Alger accepted the
position as minister to the First Unitarian Church in Brewster, Massachusetts. Fifteen months later, confronted with charges of homosexuality involving boys of the church, he left town on the next
train. So his career as a preacher was short and far from sweet. Yet
he never really gave it up: his ministry merely shifted from pulpit to
pen. That is why he rates a major place among preachers. His
moralistic didactic fiction served as sermons for generations of
Americans.

After leaving Brewster, Alger faced two problems–expiation and employment. His solution was to move to New York. "I leased my pen to the boys," he later said, recalling how he began his literary career, writing juvenile books for William Adams ("Oliver Optic"). His prose was Byronic; since there were no Alps close at hand, he took refuge in the stormy metropolis. Political biographies being in demand, Alger turned out three with titles-of-the-times: *Webster: From Farm Boy to Senator, Lincoln: The Backwoods Boy,* and *Garfield: From Canal Boy to President.* He finished the last in 13 days, to get it to the publisher before Garfield died. But biography was not his medium; he needed the freedom of fiction. Alger turned out 135 novels which eventually sold at least 100 million (some estimates run to half a billion) copies.

His characters were sticks, his plots melodramatic, his coincidences laughable; yet publishers sold millions of copies. He understood the American psyche and the power of popular formula. Both his plots and tactics thrilled penniless immigrants. Consider *Paul the Peddler.* In it Paul supported his mother (a widow) and brother (an invalid) by wrapping candy which cost half a cent with a prize which cost one cent, and selling the package for a nickel. Was this not the Gospel of Success?

Alger hit his stride and perfected his formula with *Ragged Dick.* After that he told the same story with minor variations. Like a good old Protestant hymn, it only got better with repetition. Here is my parody:

> I am a sturdy lad. I know I can climb the golden ladder with only my talent and talons to sustain me. Nothing can stop me, because I have both luck and pluck. True enough, my father has been killed, and my dear mother takes in washing. As an honorable son I sell papers. Neighborhood bullies pick on me, but there's always a cheery gleam (not fostered by beer, you may be sure) in my blackened eyes when mother washes them. I know there is always room on top.
>
> I could seek better prospects; but being a sturdy lad, I cannot desert my ailing mother. Then the tide turns. One day I find a wallet which a Rich Man has dropped. Shall I keep the money, and buy mother much-needed medicine? No. Innate

honesty makes me take it to the Rich Man's house. The door is opened by his lovely blue-eyed daughter, an imperial young lady. My clean but ragged clothes bring a sneer to her thoroughbred lips; but I know she is Good Beneath, and does not understand me. Hence I love her from that moment forward–though she is Far Above Me.

As I back away from the house (she must not see the patch on the seat of my pants) her father comes in. His face lights with joy as he sees the wallet. The grin broadens as he counts the money and finds it all there. "You will be rewarded, young man," he says, taking a shiny new dime from his pocket. "I'll start you up the ladder of success." "Thank you sir, but I must stay with my sick mother." This I do, until her gallant heart gives up over the scrubbing board, and she goes to her reward. "Take Rich Man's job," she says with her dying breath. "Go up the Ladder!" Since I never disobey my mother, I take the Rich Man's job, sharpen his pencils, and hope for the best.

My chief competitor is a slick mustached fellow who wants not only the junior partnership but the boss's blonde daughter. I watch closely and discover (by pluck and luck) that he's a secret swindler. I confront him; he resists. In vain–I live clean, he smokes. So I get the credit, the promotion, and the girl. Up the ladder I go! No one can stop me now. I am a success.

Silly? Simplistic? Not to the millions who read and believed. How could a country specializing in Manifest Destiny challenge the Alger formula? And was it not confirmed daily in the newspapers and magazines? Hadn't Thomas A. Edison begun as a newsboy, Adolph S. Ochs as a printer's devil, and Andrew Carnegie as a messenger? Don't forget Phillip Armour, Jay Cooke, Jay Gould, Jim Fiske, Leland Stanford, and Cornelius Vanderbilt. (Weren't there even Stanford and Vanderbilt Universities?) Someone moving up every day, with a little pluck and luck.

Alger made no apologies for his cookie-cutter potboilers. In the open market place, his books sold and sold and sold. Not only did his heroes get ahead–so did the author. You could serve God and Mammon at the same time–his royalty checks proved it. "I should have let go," Alger admitted. "But writing in the same vein becomes a habit, like sleeping on the right side. Try to sleep on the left side and the main purpose is defeated—one stays awake." While other writers did single volumes, Alger turned out whole series—the *Ragged Dick, Tattered Tom, Brave and Bold, New World, Way to Success, Campaign, Atlantic,* and *Pacific.*

Customarily writing two books simultaneously, he sometimes got his characters mixed. Hence Grant Thornton disappears mysteriously from *Helping Himself* (chapter IX) only to pop up and thrash a bully in *Hector's Inheritance* (chapter XIII). Did Alger's readers mind? Not in the least. To them an Alger novel was as much a part of the scheme of things as state fairs, Sunday, and the Declaration of Independence. He never let them down. Even as the novel was being written, some real-life American of Alger's day would be living the legend he heralded. James B. Duke was peddling his first tobacco; Henry Ford was moving up from his job polishing steam engines; and John D. Rockefeller, after a period of unemployment, was lining up a job. Their rises reaffirmed the nation's faith in laissez-faire capitalism and in Alger. The times not only made the novels; they also justified them.

Alger accommodated to the Gilded Age. In his later novels the heroes earn far more money. In the early stories the goal tends to be a respectable middle-class career as accountant or salesman. After 1890, his heroes acquire huge fortunes—even a fiefdom. He was captivated by the stranger-than-fiction success of the Carnegies and Rockefellers. That is why *Jed the Poor-house Boy* ends up (in the 1892 novel) Sir Robert Fenwick of England, with an ancestral estate and an annual income of $25,000.

None of the peaches and cream of his books spilled over into Alger's life. There is pathos in his tipping the Astor House desk clerk to point out celebrities, or pounding the drum in newsboys' parades. A violent affair with a married woman, the antagonism of his family, and his failure to rid himself of despair, lined the face of the plump balding author. He sought refuge in the Newsboys' Lodging House for homeless youths in New York City. To the end he wrote steadily, desperately, parodying his own earlier style, writing for boys because he couldn't write for men. Finally, even the Sunday School teachers found it hard to read his little sagas with a straight face. At the century's end he died quietly in a drab dormitory room. An obituary noted that "he had been better known to the boys of thirty years ago than to the present generation." Just before his death, Alger wrote to his friend Irving Blake: "If I could come back 50 years from now probably I should feel bewildered by the newspapers in 1947." Had he come back, he could have read, in that very year, of the inauguration of the annual Horatio Alger Awards.

Those 50 years had seen the birth of a "second Alger" who met real psychic needs in a frontier nation that suddenly became a world power. If literary critics could not take his stick figures and stock types seriously, historians saw that Alger was not so much a man as a mythmaker. His influence on twentieth-century America has been so profound that it is hard to measure.

A parallel career that casts light on all this is that of Dr. George Beard, a New York neurologist active both as a physician and writer in the late nineteenth century. His most influential work was called *American Nervousness* (1881). In it he defines nervousness as "an ailment with wide political and cultural significance." Beard added to the list of legitimate medical symptoms a whole set of experiences, types of behavior, and states of mind that revitalized the Fifth Gospel and opened the floodgates for popular theology and psychology. God pumpers from Mary Baker Eddy to Robert Schuller are in his debt.

What causes America's nervousness? Beard suggested stress, noise, railroad travel, the stock market, changes in climate, overachieving; what we now call contemporary civilization, or information overload. The word he preferred, neurasthenis, is seldom heard these days. But the symptoms he uncovered are still with us.

Mind healing and self-help, endemic in twentieth-century America, are the foundation of pop psychology. The ubiquity of women is one obvious trait in the evangel of mind cure. Its most famous advocate was Mary Baker Eddy.[6] Scores of other female exponents were founders, writers, preachers, teachers, healers. Consigned to segregated delicacy, women consumed a vast literature for women, by women, about women. Only now are we beginning to look closely at the troubled souls of females, who wrote and read fatherless bestsellers, like Susan Warner's *Wide Wide World*, Eleanor Porter's *Pollyanna*, Louisa May Alcott's *Little Women*, and Kate

Wiggins's *Rebecca of Sunnybrook Farm*. Father is missing. He is inept, not a father at all (as in *Little Women),* dead, or lost. Do these novels help explain why so many women got caught up in evangelical Christianity? Do they reflect the profound influence of Dr. George Beard? And of another highly influential but little appreciated amateur theologian–a simple self-educated Yankee handyman named Phineas P. Quimby? Fascinated with spiritualism, mesmerism, and the occult, he decided to become a hypnotist. A semi-invalid, he cured himself and gained fame as a healer. One of his patients, a young woman named Mary Baker Patterson, was not only cured, but also discovered what she called the Science of divine metaphysical healing. After her first husband died in a poorhouse, she married Asa Gilbert Eddy, who died of poison. Mary Baker Eddy then lived for a number of lonely years in rented rooms where she laid the groundwork of the sect called Christian Science.

In 1875–while Alger was in his prime–Eddy published *Science and Health,* regarded by her followers as divinely inspired. Along with the Bible, it formed the Scripture of the new faith. There is only one reality: Mind, God, Good. Matter and evil are unreal. Other groups with variations of this idealism sprang up, such as New Thought Alliance and Unity. A torrent of books and magazines followed. Quimby's early focus on health was widened into promise unlimited. Ralph Waldo Trine, whose book sales for a while rivaled Alger's, wrote *In Tune with the Infinite,* which had a subtitle that summed up the American attitude towards religion: *Fullness of Peace Power Plenty.*

Not Trine but Edward Stratemeyer (1862-1930) was Alger's heir apparent. In a state of nervous prostration, and anxious to leave New York, the aging Alger sought a ghostwriter to finish his juvenile novel *Out For Business.* He found Stratemeyer an enterprising man whose stories were popular and attractive. Barely three weeks later Stratemeyer returned outlines of his projected final chapters, and the collaboration went smoothly. In the years that followed Stratemeyer and his syndicate turned out over 1,500 dime novels, retitled reprints, and revised editions.[7] No one knows the total sales figures; they must have topped 200 million copies. This library of bestsellers adapted Alger's fiction formula, blending moral heroism and economic success. My own childhood included frequent trips

into the world of Stratemeyer heroes like Tom Swift, the Rover
Boys, and the Hardy Boys. By pluck and luck–plus new technolo-
gy–they protected maidenhood, white supremacy, and Old Glory.
Tom Swift was Horatio Alger's Sturdy Lad with electric gadgets.
Like later spacey characters such as Luke Skywalker and ET, they
had what Tom Wolfe called "the right stuff."

So did Tarzan, sired by Edgar Rice Burroughs (1875-1950)–ex-
miner, rancher, and aluminum salesman. Knowing little about the
real Africa, Burroughs invented a continent where he controlled
history, genetics, and language. After selling his first piece to *All-
Story Magazine* in 1912, Burroughs wrote 24 best-selling Tarzan
novels.

Tarzan, almost literally a self-made man, grew up among the wild
animals. Instead of facing the open market, he dealt with the primordial jungle. Suckled by a female gorilla, he befriended Tantor
the elephant and feuded with Numa the lion. Leopard-women, ant-
men, white renegades, and men from Mars tried in vain to outwit
him; for Tarzan was really the son of Lord Greystoke, an English
nobleman. Here was a superb restating and repackaging of the Fifth
Gospel. Celebrating his seventieth anniversary in 1982, Tarzan had
a publication record that would make any man, woman, or ape
envious: 24 novels in 55 languages, 37 feature films, scores of
animated cartoons, and a major television series. Except for Mickey
Mouse, Tarzan is undoubtedly the best-known fictional character in
the world. Tarzan's narrative provides a large, controlling image
that gives expression to our collective hopes and dreams. The lost
Utopia and time-warp themes are there. So is the underlying order
that helps the mythic analyst arrive at the fundamental structure of
the unconscious mind.

Tarzan was not the only potential Alger hero who had a tough
childhood. Consider Dale Carnegie (1888-1955), who seems right
out of Algerland. Born on a scraggly Missouri farm in 1888, Dale
rode miles on horseback to a one-room school, studied by lamplight
after midnight, and fed pigs at 3 a.m. By pluck and luck he finished
high school–then went into the Real World to sell lard and Armour
Star bacon. He moved Onward and Upward to New York. Among
the buildings that impressed him most was Carnegie Hall. He
promptly changed his own name from the Missouri spelling of

Carnegey to Carnegie. Jobless and despondent, he contemplated suicide, just as had Alger. To the manager of New York's YMCA, who let him teach public speaking there, must go special credit for Dale's surviving. By 1916 he was able to hire Carnegie Hall for his speeches. He had a Times Square office, unusual honorary degrees, and a ghostwriter to do research on famous men.[8]

Carnegie believed Americans respected historic successes and Niagara Falls for a similar reason: cubic tons of water and cubic tons of gold are both overwhelming. *How to Win Friends and Influence People* (1937) went through 17 printings in five months. Newspapers, advertisements, radio programs, and free demonstrations popularized his method. Carnegie moved from business problems to domestic ones, dispensing marital advice with a sincerity not evident when he declared himself a bachelor so as to avoid explaining his divorce.

Sinclair Lewis defined Carnegieism as "yessing the boss and making Big Business right with God." Two key rules in *How to Win Friends and Influence People* are: "Never tell a man he is wrong," and "Get the other person saying 'Yes, yes' immediately."

Opening schools, seminars, and conferences, Carnegie was a celebrity. His death in 1955 did not stop the "yesses," and in the grim recession of the 1980s, the Carnegie methods picked up steam. Old myths die hard–they are the most enduring things cultures produce.

The myth has, of course, had its challenges and defamers. Mark Twain's classic, *The Adventures of Huckleberry Finn*, can be seen as a satire of Alger's world. Huck's life is full of complexity and bitterness; the ladder can lead to hell. The rise of the Naturalists, especially Theodore Dreiser, worked an even stronger rebuff. No happy ending here. The central protagonist in three of Dreiser's novels, Frank Cowperwood, got ahead not by returning the Rich Man's wallet but by keeping it. Life to him was nasty, brutish, and short. His formula for survival was consecrated egotism.

As a young boy Frank Cowperwood stood in front of a store window tank and watched a lobster catch and devour squid. This was the lesson of the world. The lobster ate the squid by supreme natural right. He'd be the lobster, society the squid. Dreiser's heroes liked their Darwinism raw with a little blood on it.

Equally tough and amoral were the detective heroes modeled on Dashiell Hammett's Sam Spade. His was a world of erotica and violence. In book after book the detective went through the same harrowing business. On the average he made love to three or four sexually magnetic women, consumed four or five quarts of hard liquor, smoked cartons of cigarettes, was knocked on the head, shot, and bruised in fist fights from seven to ten times–while groping his way through a dense fog. It is like the enmity between animals; there is nothing personal in it.

Another literary reaction to the Alger lad is the hero of Ernest Hemingway, who *will not* get ahead and doesn't care; to hell with you. A handsome fellow, a hunter, a lover, he is always on the move; he writes novels by day and collects women by night. Bull-fights intrigue him. Bourgeois values disgust him, and he is drawn to primitive areas, particularly Africa. Because he knows the world is a shoddy place, he takes his fun in the company of the "initi-ated." Quietly desperate, cheerfully dissipated, and highly enter-taining, he is the epitome of mobility–and in his own way, quite successful.

One way to judge the power of Alger's writing is to note those who satirized it. William Dean Howells lampooned the "success story" in *The Minister's Change, or the Apprenticeship of Lemuel Barker* (1887), Stephen Crane in *A Self-Made Man* (1899), and Scott Fitzgerald in *The Vegetable, or From President to Postman* (1922). Nathanael West wrote a parody called *A Cool Million* (1934); Gary Wills, *Nixon Agonistes* (1970), John Seelye, *Dirty Tricks; or, Nick Noxin's Natural Nobility* (1973); and William Gaddes, *JR* (1975). Behind such titles one sees the central thrust of Horatio Alger, Jr., moving from juvenile storyteller to progressive moralist to success mythmaker, and finally political ideologue. Not the texts but the context in which his books were seen motivated the changes.

The self-made man who dominated the pulpit when Alger's repu-tation was soaring was Billy Sunday, who boasted that he knew no more about theology than a jackrabbit knew about ping pong. But Lord, how the preacher and the rabbit could jump![9]

Picture a barnlike coliseum seating over 10,000, with a bare platform in the middle. Watch Billy Sunday leap forward like light-

Billy Sunday was 65 in 1927, when he struck this pose on how to deliver a sermon. He also liked to "'slide into third base" for the Lord, on stage. (Photo courtesy of Library of Congress.)

ning, Bible in hand. The Book goes on the reading desk. Soon he's leaping back and forth, in ten-foot leaps without even losing his place. In the corner is Homer Rodeheaver with God's trombone—end man for Billy's vaudeville show.

They have chatty prayers. "O Lord, remember that bald-headed banker in Syracuse? It was Syracuse, wasn't it, Rody?"

"No, Billy–Baltimore!"

"O Lord, remember that bald-headed banker in Baltimore–he raised money for you and got blood out of a turnip!" Ten thousand people are laughing, shouting, applauding. Billy is working his magic.

A stagehand brings out a huge glass jar and puts it on the platform. Billy sticks an American flag in the neck, grimaces, pulls it out. The audience knows what he means: this is a liquor bottle. Then he calls for an axe, takes off his coat, rolls up his sleeves, and with one mighty blow, smashes the bottle. People applaud wildly–even while knowing they'll stop on the way home for a beer. They love Billy Sunday. He preaches all Five Gospels: four biblical, the fifth the Gospel of Success. The *Nation* observed: Success is the one touchstone for religion; and the only success worth having is shouting thousands. Billy Sunday has the gaping crowd; therefore the Lord must be with him.[10]

The overwhelming reason Billy was so successful was his talent for dramatization. He was a great storyteller and pantomimist. No one could resist his depicting a society woman cuddling a little dog, a drunk weaving out of a saloon, a placid preacher in the pulpit. He was a dancing dervish, reproducing the jerks of the Frontier Awakening, laughing and leaping and praising the Lord. He was the "front man" of the Urban Awakening, and city after city proved it: Pittsburgh, Baltimore, Philadelphia, Los Angeles, Boston, Dallas, Detroit, Washington, New York.

It was a hard act to follow, or even imitate. Who else could pray a packed auditorium into loud laughter by saying, "Oh say, Jesus, save that man who wrote that dirty lie about me! Better take along a pair of rubber gloves and a bottle of disinfectant!"? His down-home shirt-sleeve style was a powerful weapon to win over crowds, and he used it with incredible skill. He was the ultimate defender of Jesus, womanhood, cleanliness, motherhood, hard work, and America. Put them together, and they spell "success."

The son of a brick mason, Billy was born in Ames, Iowa in 1862–the same year his father died a private in the Union Army. After four years in an orphan's home, Billy worked on a farm, became an undertaker's assistant, and entered professional baseball, playing for Pittsburgh and Chicago in the old National League. The first man who ever ran the bases in 14 seconds, he did his real running for the Lord.

Leaving baseball in 1891, ordained in the Presbyterian ministry in 1903, he was *the* American evangelist for the first third of the twentieth century. His message was clear, concise, and consistent. There could be no salvation without true repentance from all sin, and faith in Jesus Christ. Without Christ, no man is saved. With Him, no one is lost.

The message is clear. Common people flocked to hear Billy because they could understand him–and delight at his vaudeville antics. Never monotonous, Billy was a kind of human kaleidoscope. He loved one-liners, and coined them with a frequency that would have made some of our contemporary comics jealous. He said he would rather have standing room in hell than own the world and go to hell. His kind of preaching, Billy said, had warmed this cold world's heart for 2,000 years. He welcomed rivals. Trying to run a church without rivals and revivals can be done–when you can run a gasoline engine on buttermilk. There was no abstract theology or metaphysics here. He spoke right to the heart.

Teamed up with dynamic gospel hymn writer Homer A. Rodeheaver, Billy Sunday put together a "hit squad" that had no real parallels. There were advance men, associate experts, committee chairmen, choirs, parades. Enthusiasm was generally at such a fever pitch when Sunday arrived that "the battle with Satan" was already won.

Billy Sunday was a winner–and "winning" in this league meant converts for the Lord. He virtually bribed or threatened those who hesitated. At least once in each campaign, Sunday held a special meeting of campaign workers to tell them they were falling down on the job, and unless they improved, the campaign would fail. Ushers sometimes led the same man forward three or four times; a woman named Hattie Harris confessed to a Boston reporter that she had hit the trail 14 times. Still, Sunday was neither cynical nor hypocritical. "I'm calling for those who are really ready to live for Christ. Don't come if you don't mean it."

Billy Sunday was H. L. Mencken's "Calliope of Zion," playing to America. Perhaps he was shallow, like Horatio Alger. Yet both saw national needs and met them. They lived when the sweet glow of religiosity made the Fifth Gospel irresistible. Bestsellers had titles like *Elements of Success* (1848), *Success in Business* (1867), *The Secret of Success* (1873), *Successful Folk* (1878), *How to Succeed* (1882), *The Law of Success* (1883), and so on and on. Who knows where the Gospel of Success might appear next?

One voice preached that Gospel for over half a century. Norman Vincent Peale was the great-grandfather of Success Preachers.[11] He was already in mid-career when he published his bestseller, *The Power of Positive Thinking,* in 1952. Dying on December 24, 1993, he has an heir apparent in Robert Schuller, who has changed Peale's Positive Thinking to Possibility Thinking.

Born in Iowa to a devout, hard-working farm family, Robert got the call while at the plow. He studied at Western Theological Seminary and was ordained into the Dutch Reformed Church in 1950. Five years later, feeling the Westward Tilt, he migrated to Garden Grove, California. There he threw open the shutters and let the Southern California sun shine in on his psyche. As his ego basked in the warm glow of optimism, the world became a paradise of possibilities. The cross became a plus sign rather than an emblem of sacrifice. Speaking in aphorisms, Schuller bade his listeners, viewers, and readers to draw a pension from their tension, to turn their scars into stars. He practiced as well as preached the Possibility Thinker's Creed: "When faced with a mountain, I will not quit. I will keep on striving until I climb over, pass through, tunnel underneath–or simply stay and turn the mountain into a gold mine, with God's help."[12]

A clever fellow who could turn cars into pews and one-liners into books, Schuller welded California's two sacred icons (the sun and the car) into a church. He had the winning invitation: "Come as you are in the family car." Cars and cash rolled in. To his modest 1961 chapel he added the 14-story Tower of Hope in 1968. Televising his services in 1970 proved such a bonanza that in 1975 he could commission his see-through Crystal Cathedral, only a stone's throw from Disneyland. The cost was great, Schuller admitted; but "so useful and long-lived, it will be a super-bargain for everyone."

The Fifth Gospel and the Self-Made Man met in the Crystal Cathedral, 128 feet high and 415 feet long, designed by the archi-

The Reverend Robert Schuller. (Photo courtesy of Crystal Cathedral Ministries, Garden Grove, CA.)

tectural team of Philip Johnson and John Burgee and completed in 1980.

Picture this: a New World New Jerusalem, translucent and iridescent, with sunlight coming through 10,000 windows of tempered silver-colored glass, held in place by a lacelike frame of white trusses. The 90-foot doors are open, beckoning us in. Fountains shoot jets of water heavenward, and music from one of the world's largest pipe organs fills the air.

This is the Crystal Cathedral, dedicated "To the Glory of Man For the Greater Glory of God." Huge white concrete columns, the largest ever poured, hold balconies in place. Amidst the flowing fountains and exotic plants are fluttering American flags. Up front are grand military bands in full dress uniform. Feet tap to the drum beat, television cameras pan in and out, catching smiles, hugs, sliding trombones.

Out strides the Preacher in robes as blue as the California sky. Eyes twinkling, teeth glistening, he speaks words that are his trademark: "This is the day the Lord hath made . . ." This is the day, all those seated in church (or the drive-in Sanctuary) well know. On July 4 Robert Schuller will deliver his "I am the American Flag" sermon which won the Principal Award from the Freedoms Foundation and has since become a "tradition" on patriotic occasions. Adopting the persona of the flag, using exaggerated gestures and expressions, he intones, "I, the flag, have seen much. So listen and listen hard."

Starting with the bloody snow of Valley Forge, coming finally to the steaming Asian jungles, he moves on to the Brownies, Cub Scouts, Boy Scouts; to Pony and Little Leagues, Minor and Major Leagues. "Dream your dreams! Dare to believe! You can make it in America!"

Up goes Schuller's voice, out go his arms in a grand gesture–perhaps like Christ's to the multitudes on the Mount. Bands blare. Lines of flags are borne by smartly uniformed youths marching down the aisles. Suddenly a gigantic American flag descends, stretching from ceiling to floor. People gasp and clap. Super-flag in super-church! It covers and conceals the altar. Never mind, we can still see Robert Schuller; in him the cross and the flag converge.

Schuller presides over an ecclesiastical empire. In 1985 his

10,000 member congregation contributed $4 million, and his TV audience mailed in $30 million, which helped support a staff of 400. His slickly made TV programs cost $8 million annually. Schuller has stopped accepting a salary, living well off his publishing income and $15,000-a-shot lecture fees.

The best writer among televangelists, Schuller has produced 20 books, three of them bestsellers: *Tough-Minded Faith for Tender-Hearted People*; *Tough Times Don't Last, but Tough People Do*; and *The Power of Being Debt Free*. Many books, one theme: religious narcissism, coated with happy optimism. The Schuller label and by-line remains: *possibility thinking*.

Just what is it? Here is Schuller's own definition: "Possibility thinking is assuming that the ideal can become real. Possibility thinking is sifting carefully through all the alternatives and options, both real and fanciful, in the process of determining the grand objective that should be pursued."

With Schuller there are no ambiguities, no confusion. He downplays sin and centers on salvation–understandable, immediate, available. You're good, Jesus is good. Let's put the pieces together.

When asked if this is not more cultural than biblical, Schuller has a ready answer. "When I preach possibility thinking, that is biblical faith, rooted strongly in Christ. If I preach to build people's faith, I am preaching against sin. I fight sin positively."

One wonders if he has bypassed sin and settled for behavior modification; for a mask that always smiles. He would have us "buy into" a ministry the way you might choose a Laura Ashley dress or designer blue jeans. There is no agony, no *angst*. He is master of the marshmallow mood.

Nothing reflects this better than the magazine advertised and promoted by Schuller, called *Success!* With the obvious cliche logo (Nothing Succeeds Like Success), the magazine promised (at $12 for 12 issues) "a fascinating wealth of practical information to help preachers achieve more." Somehow gift subscriptions to *Success!* should be seen as a *mark* of success; for it will "mark you as very special in the eyes of your recipients." Thus does Schuller open the doors to his "kingdom."

See for yourself. Tilt West and pay a visit to the Garden. Robert

Schuller can't be as good as he looks. No one could be that good. The Man in the Light Blue Robe is our Adam, before the fall.

Fountains bubble, birds chirp, cameras focus. Sinners repent. Wonderful music comes forth from a concealed choir–is it a tape replay? The camera pans upward, catching the white cross against the azure sky. The Crystal Cathedral; heaven is near at hand.

The Rev. Robert Schuller has created the ultimate environment for retailing religion. This smiling, silver-haired man combines positive thinking and old-fashioned piety in a sweet syrup. He is a classier Norman Vincent Peale, in living color. Prime-time living!

Outside, the real world. Must we return? Is there a possibility that we too can live in the Garden? Then I see it–a sinewy seductive snake moving silently across the floor. Perhaps he too has a message for us.

NOTES

1. Ralph H. Gabriel, *The Course of American Democratic Thought* (New York: Ronald, 1940), p. 56.

2. Alexis de Tocqueville, *Democracy in America* (New York: Vintage, 1945), p. 86. Originally published in 1835.

3. See Richard Hofstadter, *Social Darwinism in American Thought* (New York: Beacon, 1955); and Robert C. Bannister, *Social Darwinism* (Philadelphia: Temple University Press, 1979).

4. Herbert B. Mayes, Alger, *A Bibliography Without a Hero* (Mendota, IL: Wayside Press, 1964), p. 89.

5. *Ibid.*

6. For an "official" biography, see Cybil Wilbur, *The Life of Mary Baker Eddy* (Boston: Christian Science, 1929). For a more candid account, see Robert Peel, *Mary Baker Eddy: The Years of Authority* (New York: Holt, Rinehart, and Winston, 1977).

7. Stratemeyer (whose personal and syndicate works were all published under pseudonyms) frequently turned out several books a year, and picked up on the popular themes of the day. In 1898, for example, while the Spanish-American War was in progress, he wrote *Under Dewey in Manila*, followed by *On to Peking–Or Old Glory in China*. When the fighting ended, he went back to the self-help genre, but kept the military flavor: *Fighting for His Own* in 1903, and *Bound to be an Electrician* in the same year. His books were published by Lee and Shepard in Boston, who prospered mightily.

8. Several books came under the "Quick and Easy" heading, but the most popular ones centered on the rich and famous. Carnegie liked catchy titles like *Little-Known Facts about Well-Known People* (New York: Blue Ribbon, 1934);

and *Highlights in the Lives of Forty Famous People* (New York: Greenberg, 1944).

9. The best biography is by W. G. McLoughlin, *Billy Sunday Was His Name* (Chicago: University of Chicago Press, 1955).

10. "Making Religion Yellow," *Nation*, June 11, 1908, p. 527.

11. Although Peale wrote a popular book called *The Art of Living* (published in New York by Abingdon-Cokesbury) as early as 1937, he didn't hit his stride until the 1950s. His all-time best seller, *The Power of Positive Thinking*, appeared in 1952. It was followed by *Faith Made Them Champions* (New York: Prentice-Hall, 1954); and *The Amazing Results of Positive Thinking* (New York: Prentice-Hall, 1959).

12. All the Schuller quotations used here and to the end of this chapter come from the "Information Package" he distributes to those who request it. The items have no date or publisher's identification.

Chapter 5

Confronting the Serpent

The serpent did beguile me.

–Eve

When it's too hot for insects in Grasshopper Valley, Tennessee, people like to sit in the shade and read the Bible. That's what George Hensley did in the August 1909 heat wave. His eyes fell on Mark 16:17: "In my name shall they cast out devils; they shall speak with new tongues; they shall take up serpents; and if they drink any deadly thing, it shall not hurt them."

These words, spoken by Jesus after the Resurrection and immediately before the Ascension, Hensley interpreted as a command he felt bound to obey. So he climbed White Oak Mountain, which rims Grasshopper Valley, and found a large rattlesnake in a rocky gap. A few days later he began his evangelical work: in a religious meeting at Sale Creek he cited the Bible texts and thrust the rattlesnake at the people for them to take up and prove their faith. They had faith, and George launched a new church.

Snake-handling is classified as a religious cult: a religion regarded as unorthodox or spurious. Often a small circle of clannish people, linked by devotion and allegiance, support a cult with all their resources, including, if necessary, their lives. The spectacular spread of cults is a characteristic of the twentieth century.[1]

Hensley had some setbacks, but he knew he was sanctified. One man, Garland Defriese, was bitten by a large rattlesnake and fell to the ground, the rattler's fangs sunk deep in his flesh. Miraculously, Garland recovered–which proved that God was merciful and Defriese was a backslider.

Hensley went on to found other churches and ordain ministers.

For 30 years the work grew without outside interference. Not until 1938 did the St. Louis *Post-Dispatch* send a reporter and photographer into the hills to cover the story. Keith Kerman, the reporter, published the earliest account of the cult.

If Kerman's story was something new, the practices he described were not. Serpent-handling and serpent worship were widespread in the early church; writers as different as Clement of Alexandria, Aronobius, Firmicus Marternus, Justin Martyr, and Plutarch all attest to it. Anthropologists found examples stretching back to prehistoric times. Brother Hensley may not have known it, but what he was doing in Grasshopper Valley flourished all over the earth.

Kerman found a meeting of about 75 men, women, and children at the Pine Mountain Church at which snakes were handled. Cymbals, tambourines, foot-stamping, and hand-clapping provided the rhythm for the worshippers who passed serpents from hand to hand while jerking violently all over their bodies. One man thrust a snake before a seated woman holding a baby; the woman smiled, and the baby gravely reached forward and touched the snake. A timberman opened the mouth of one rattler to show its intact fangs to the visitors; another man showed the scars of three bites on his hand and arm.

The men wore open-necked shirts (for no Bible text can be discovered which says Jesus or the apostles ever wore a necktie) and either pants with leather belts or bibbed and strapped overalls. The women wore dresses of polka dot, checked, or flowered cotton prints. Cosmetics, jewelry, and artificially curled hair were frowned upon as frivolous and worldly. Few of the older people could read or write, their school attendance being counted in weeks and months. Most of the younger people had had their schooling cut short in seasons when their labor was needed in the fields.

Reporter, editor, and readers were all intrigued by Hensley's cult, which has spread throughout Appalachia in the last half-century. Intensity, excitement, and courage converge. The snake does beguile us with remarkable agility and grace. We both love and loathe its flickering tongue, the fixed gaze of its lidless eyes, the slithering, undulating form of its body, the mystery of its voicelessness. No wonder snakes are prominent in creation myths, mystery cults, and as sacrificial objects; the personification of the unconscious, the instinctual layer, with all its secret, mantic, and curative powers as well as its inherent dangers which must be overcome.

In the Good Book, Jesus speaks of handling serpents. That these verses are not found in the best manuscript evidence does not bother the cult members. In dozens of rural Holiness churches, their faith in the healing and saving power of Jesus has been tested and proven without question.

I want to go and see. I drive to West Virginia and visit a Holiness Church; a friend has been there before as an observer. The small, shabby, white frame building reflects the poverty of the neighborhood and the people. It is winter; a large potbellied stove overheats the single room, mixing the smells of body odors and pine tar. There is singing; out of the mouth but from the heart. Children bang tambourines as everyone prays simultaneously. The temperature and the pitch keep rising. As the music builds to a crescendo, bodily movements become more stylized and stereotyped: paroxysms followed by swooning, furious dancing, pogo-stick jumping, swaying, and clapping. Singing ceases, but instrumental music continues in deafening cadence. Body control disappears. Individuals break from the group to dance up and down the aisle or to fall prostrate to the floor.

The "taking up of serpents" comes at the point of emotional climax. A flat box appears and a practitioner who feels "in the spirit" pulls a snake from the gnarled mass of diamondback rattlers and copperheads. Others quickly follow, sometimes holding one in each hand, passing them back and forth and allowing them to crawl over the head and upper body. The ritual is interspersed with shouting and speaking in tongues. All personal fear seems to disappear. People want to "handle one eight feet long." Has all this stunned the snakes? Why do they not bite?

Almost as suddenly as it begins, the handling stops. Serpents are returned to their boxes, and the congregation settles again into the pews. Then comes the sermon, a high-pitched stylized incantation:

Praise the Lord! Praise the Lord Hallelujah! Say it–Jesus. You can't get around th' name a' Jesus. Hallelujah! In my name shall they cast out devils. Hallelujah to God, they SHALL

speak with new tongues! Praise th' Lord! They SHALL take
up serpents. Hallelujah t' God, they SHALL take up serpents!

The search for holiness is dramatized in willingness to suffer
terrible pain or even death to get God in their lives. The support of
fellow Christians is still with them. God may not come if you don't
really pray. The person in the group who has been bitten most often
and who has suffered the most pain sits in a special place, on a
higher platform. Such people are exemplars. While the Holy Ghost
gives the power, those who have survived snake bites get recognition and praise for their faith. They have learned to cope with
anxieties by calling upon the name of Jesus and the power that he
freely offers. Support is exchanged through the laying on of hands
in healing ceremonies, group prayers, and verbal pleas–"Help him,
Lord!"

The Holy Ghost enables them not only to pick up serpents, but to
speak in tongues, preach, testify, cure diseases, cast out demons–
even to drink strychnine and lye, or use fire on their skin when the
snakes are in hibernation during the winter. They pursue holiness
above all else. "Ye shall handle serpents."[2]

They *shall*, and *do*–week after week, month after month, year
after year. They do so "in the name of Jesus"–and if they die, God
allows this to remind the living that the risk is total.

Those who have been bitten by snakes and survived have proved
they have the Holy Ghost; those bitten many times are saints.
(There are about 21 recorded deaths–no one knows how many more
have not been recorded.) Leading scholars in the field have watched
these "saints" heal wounds or even cancer; pass their hands
through fire; pick up hot coals from potbellied stoves. Apparently
they can block out pain totally. Edmund C. Gruss writes:

> One woman who attended church at Scrabble Creek experi-
> enced the stigmata as blood came out of her hands, feet, side
> and forehead. This was witnessed by all present in the church.
> She said that she had prayed that God would allow people to
> see through her body how Jesus must have suffered for them.[3]

For most of us, such an account is frightening–we wonder if it is
Jesus or Satan who is behind this kind of religion. From our per-

spective, there is much that is pathetic, even psychopathic, here. But there is something strong and primitive too–a reaching out of people to comfort one another, struggling against a hard, common fate. For these poor, restricted people, the church may be the only place they can both feel and act out their feelings. Would we deny them their mountaineer Moses, trying somehow to lead them to the promised land?

Nor are they the only group who turn to cults for succor and support. By one estimate, there are today over 2,400 groups tapping the enormous market for spiritual affirmation. Most form around self-proclaimed prophets, who give their disciples new names, clothes, even birthdays. But most of all, they give new hope. A good example is Sun Myung Moon, whose Unification Church had a membership of 2 million in 1984. Born in Korea in 1918, Moon also had mystical experiences that he passed on to cult followers. When he was 20, said Moon, He had a vision in which he was instructed by Jesus to carry out His unfinished work on earth. Having failed Himself, Jesus confided, He had been thrown out of the Trinity. Since then God had been searching for a new savior–and after all these centuries, found one in Moon. His task was to save humanity, since in God's Kingdom this poorly educated Korean would be absolute ruler and savior of mankind.

No matter how preposterous this sounds to many, it was the foundation of the Unification Church. The heart of the conversion was a group-shared messianic delusion, which many claimed brainwashed young people into becoming "Moonies." The church suffered a severe blow in 1984 when the Rev. Moon was convicted of income tax evasion and sent to jail for 18 months. But this "persecution" seemed merely to strengthen the resolve of his faithful followers.

Much more disturbing than the "Moonies" were various cults practicing hedonism, debauchery, and even Satanism. Books, films, and some rock music (the usual label was "heavy metal") seemed to be documenting, even encouraging, "way out" cults. The number for the Devil used in the Book of Revelations (666) began to appear in many places, along with other diabolic symbols–the inverted cross, goat's head, and horned satyr, for example. Yet it was not the symbolism but the actions of the groups that were most alarming. The Charles Manson murders were a fearful example. Torture, murder, mutilation, and cremation were reported in all parts of the country. A documentary, aired by ABC in May 1985, traced the alarming growth of these practices.

As terrifying as the Satanic cults are, with their probable link to scores of murders, they seldom receive concentrated national attention. Not so with a cult that went berserk in 1978. The People's Temple, an American group with land called Jonestown in Guyana, was the scene of an ambush in which an American Congressman and four others were gunned down. Then, leader Jim Jones, by persuasion or force, brought about the suicide of 913 people–before killing himself.[4]

In this most horrible bloodbath in modern cult history, children had been killed first as the bodies piled up. How could it happen?

We shall never know. Jim Jones (1931-1978), the key figure, was a speaker, not a writer. His addresses and bombastic threats confuse more than they illuminate. Once the gory facts and photographs were abroad, investigative reporters and checkbook journalists moved in. There was an endless flow of copy and broadcasts; much heat but little light. For a while, public opinion polls ranked Jonestown only behind Pearl Harbor and John Kennedy's assassination in terms of "public recognition." Now neglect has covered the episode, as dirt covered the victims. But to students of American religion, the ghosts still haunt the land.

The Temple tragedy became a media obsession, distorted and exploited. Pop records filled the airways with titles like "Guyana, Cult of the Damned" and "They Poisoned Little Children." CBS produced a two-part docudrama depicting Jones as a good man victimized and corrupted by others, mainly by women. Such partially fictionalized and sensationalized accounts reinforced myths about the Temple and created new ones.

Once it was over, everyone could and did criticize everyone else. How had Jim Jones slipped between jurisdictions? Both the House Committee on Foreign Affairs and the State Department itself criticized the handling of People's Temple. What the CIA knew was exempted from exposure. An organization called Concerned Relatives claimed to have asked the FBI for help; but FBI Director William Webster said the bureau had opened no investigation.

Hundreds of millions of dollars in claims were filed. A total of $7 million was retrieved by a court-appointed receiver. Today, the mass grave of unclaimed Jonestown victims on a hillside in Oakland, California, has only occasional visitors.

To unravel the puzzle, begin in rural Indiana, where Jim Jones was born during the Great Depression (1931). When he was three years old the family moved to Lynn, a sleepy hamlet where his father (gassed in World War I) made periodic visits to the Veterans' Hospital and shuffled every morning to the pool hall on Main Street. Feisty Mrs. Jones, who drank beer and smoked hand-rolled cigarettes, ran the family. She did seasonal work in canneries, got interested in unions, and lost her job for trying to start one. She was known as a troublemaker.

Even before he was toilet-trained, the neglected Jimmy toddled around unsupervised with a dirty face and bare bottom. Animals provided security to the little boy who wandered himself like a stray pup. "I was alienated as a child," he told a reporter years later, "and considered the trash of the neighborhood because in those days they referred to you as white trash. I fell into that category."[5] Such resentment may have been the dynamo that powered his life.

Jones drifted in and out of churches. When he tried the Gospel Tabernacle, a storefront church out on Highway 36, he met Holy Rollers–people who spoke in tongues. A female Pentecostal minister, noting Jimmy's verbal gifts (he could throw out more well-formed words per minute than most people from Lynn could read), put him in the pulpit. The crowd was delighted; but the ten-year-old boy with the cherub face began having "night terrors," in which he was pursued by a terrible snake. Insomnia plagued him for the rest of his life.

Jimmy began carrying the Bible everywhere he went. Evangelism came easy. Sometimes he would stop pedestrians on Main Street, offer salvation, and plead with them to let the Holy Spirit into their hearts. He said his father and everyone in the local pool hall were going to hell. Intelligent and ambitious, Jimmy was a voracious reader and good student. Graduating from high school with honors in 1949, he fell in love with a woman four years older than himself, went to Indiana University, and talked constantly of the Bible. Marcelline Baldwin, his new love, acted as both mother and fiancée. They established a joint bank account; she supported him. Married when Jim was 18, they lived in a small apartment, then moved to a trailer outside Bloomington.

Jim had strong views about racial and social injustice, and voiced them freely. In 1952, impressed by the Methodist social creed, Jim decided to become a minister. Two months after his decision he was student pastor at a small church in the predominately poor, white southside section of Indianapolis. It was on-the-job training, with correspondence courses to acquire standing in the Methodist Conference. Later, Jim changed his affiliation and attached himself to the Disciples of Christ. But his most important training came by constant visits to healing services, tent meetings, and revivals. He soon said, "If they can do it, I can too."

He did it. He touched people, and they fell down. The energy of the crowds shook the building amidst endless incantation. Power, control, and adulation overwhelmed him. Such a man yearns for the big time–he moved to Detroit in 1953. On his opening night, "The Kid" was up against some of the Midwest's most adept and inspirational preachers. He broke out in hives. His lips swelled. Jumping up unscheduled, he upstaged the featured evangelist. Only later did even his wife know he had taken notes and gathered bits of intelligence about the people he called up by "clairvoyance." Jones was Machiavellian from the beginning. The ends justified the means.

He not only preached; he also sold monkeys for $29 each, going from door to door to build up capital. Jones was optimistic, energetic, grandiose. His work was interracial and Pentecostal. He was on the way. In 1956 he bought an inner-city church, which he called "Wings of Deliverance." When it grew, he renamed it People's Temple. He went after people rather than money. What he wanted was total commitment–then total dependency. Like Father Divine, Jones featured a Temple soup kitchen, which served an average of 2,800 meals a month. He searched for methods to tighten, and recruiting grounds to enlarge, his organization.

Jones had an intense personal ministry especially to poor Blacks. If his demagoguery was honest, the healing was not. When he "called forth" a cancer, a trained assistant would reach down the person's throat and "bring forth" a bloodied "tumor" hidden in her handkerchief-covered hands. Eight assistants, called "the girls," gathered material for Jim Jones's revelations and assisted him with his miracle cures. Although few people recognized them, they were there at every meeting, collecting "obs" (observations) of Temple members and new prospects, sitting quietly in the congregation waiting for their cues with bits of beef brains packed in plastic bags hidden in tissues. Disguised as spinsters and black matrons, they would rise on cue out of wheelchairs or throw away their canes. They visited the ghettoes of San Francisco and Los Angeles, faces blacked with theatrical makeup, waiting for the chance to break into a prospective member's home or rummage through the garbage in search of anything at all. They would appear at a door claiming to have had car trouble, and would ask to use the phone. Once inside, they made mental notes of the house and the condition of the furniture. They would ask to use the bathroom, then search the medicine cabinet and copy the labels from prescription bottles and the brand of over-the-counter items. Only a handful of people knew anything about them. Yet they made Jim Jones's "divine insights" and revelations possible.

Why would otherwise decent young women undertake work so distasteful and deceitful? How were earlier standards of ethics and values erased from their hearts and minds? We have clues: constant activity, sleeplessness, unrelenting criticism, dizzying rhetoric, sexual harassment, the fear that anyone might be beaten at any time since the rules were always changing. If Jim Jones didn't tell them what to do, his disciples would sit motionless, feeling worth nothing."

Of course, "the girls" were resourceful. One of them, Faith Worley, was able to improve the illusions of healing by drawing from her experience with terminal cancer patients. She knew well the odor of death, and replaced the chicken guts with meat that smelled more like the real thing: beef brains aged a couple of days without refrigeration. To the vials of blood the girls—and Jim Jones—would draw from their own veins, she added heparin, an anticoagulant, before packing the blood and brains in little plastic bags. The "cancers" were stored in a locked refrigerator at Faith's house. They could be kept indefinitely.

Faith Worley first met Jim Jones in 1958, when she was eight. From age 16, Faith was kept busy in the Temple writing letters—

each in a slightly different hand, slightly different language, signed with names culled randomly from the telephone book–to senators and congressmen, urging them to vote the way Jim Jones wanted. Faith did her work earnestly. By the time she started nursing school, she was in charge of the meticulous medical records Jim Jones insisted be kept on each Temple member. He wanted blood types, medical histories, dietary information. He had to know who had diabetes, hypertension, insomnia, anxiety, depression, heart trouble, or arthritis; the better to minister to his flock.

When Faith found a job in a local hospital, she got all the medical supplies she could lay her hands on. She bought them at first, but the increasing demands were soon more than she could afford. The hospital wouldn't miss a few items from its storeroom. Faith would hardly make a dent in the supply of syringes and needles, bandages, and IV bottles; and the hospital checked the supplies of adrenaline, liquid caffeine, and nitroglycerine only to replenish them. The controlled substances–tranquilizers like Dalmane, Haldol, Quaalude; narcotics like Percodan, Demerol, and codeine were easily obtained. Stimulants presented a greater challenge. Strict record-keeping requirements make such drugs difficult to steal. Faith had to use her wits; she would wait until a patient was discharged and steal whatever was left in the bottle, then destroy the inventory sheets.

So people flocked to the Temple–lambs going to the slaughter, following the not-very-honest shepherd. People spoke of this great new prophet of God, "Father" Jim Jones. They said he knows things only God could know. He cures things only God could cure. He even raised 43 people from the dead. No one in his church ever dies!

Jones, a charismatic leader, conjured up the sexual energy of his congregation, and made it a forceful weapon. His body was an instrument used to entice and discipline; his tongue could work magic with words. There was an odd coexistence of savior and sadist, sincerity and cynicism, heroism and cowardice in this enigmatic man. Many believed he was at his best with disinherited blacks; but after all, he also sat on the platform with the First Lady of the United States, and got a "Dear Jim" letter of thanks for his evangelizing from Rosalynn Carter.

Little did she (or countless other outsiders) know that Jones flaunted himself as a heterosexual superlover. He claimed that all good socialists had to know themselves in all ways, including sexually–so they must be sodomized. His sexual encounters were frequent and frightful; he went out of his way to find male partners who had no homosexual inclinations. His endless assignations with women (married and unmarried) were explained by "the need for therapy," the reward system, and the "groupie" phenomenon. He posed as the ultimate lover, selfless and sensitive, and was seldom refused. Sometimes he forced himself on victims, justifying his acts by saying he didn't want to make them "feel guilty" about pressuring him. He claimed to have "satisfied" as many as 16 men and women in one day.

Forced to leave Indiana for sociopolitical reasons, he began the legal maneuvers that would make his enterprises rich. Before heading west for California, Jones set up a nonprofit, tax-exempt corporation to receive properties donated by church members and to manage church business. Though Jones tightly guarded his personal and church finances, he planned to hold property donated by California supporters; their homes and real estate could be held indefinitely tax-free, then sold as needed or when the real estate market was favorable. The procedure–which the Temple also would employ in a later exodus–provided another benefit: tying members financially to the Temple.

Although there were separate corporations, the distinction between church property and Jones's personal property blurred. Growing ever richer and more powerful in California, Jones saw that the money was spread around the world–especially in Switzerland, Panama, Venezuela, and Guyana.

By now he had his ruler/servant system fully operative, well funded, and fully publicized. People's Temple grew large and wealthy, attracting the favorable notice of state officials for its good works. But underneath the love and charity that the church showed to the outside world, a real cancer was growing. Megalomaniacal and paranoid, Jones gradually slipped deeper and deeper into a state bordering insanity. He "became" the Messiah–and his followers believed him. Advertisements and handbills flooded the West Coast. I have copies on file:

PASTOR JIM JONES
The most unique
PROPHETIC HEALING SERVICE!
Behold the Word made Incarnate in your midst!
God works as TUMOROUS MASSES ARE PASSED.
Before your eyes, THE CRIPPLED WALK, THE BLIND SEE!
SCORES ARE CALLED OUT OF THE AUDIENCE
And told the intimate (but never embarrassing)
details of their lives that only God could reveal!
CHRIST IS MADE REAL through the most precise
revelations and the miraculous
healing of his servant!

People and money rolled in. The Temple's air was full of gospel hymns with sentiments like this:

Something's got a hold of me (Oh, yes, indeed, I said)
Something's got a hold (got a hold) of me-ee. O–o–oh!

This "something," Pastor Jim, was not modest. "Although you know him as Father, he is also the Son and the Holy Ghost . . . the reincarnation of Jesus Christ. He is God Socialist!" The Father continued:

I want you to realize that you must be the Scripture, that any other scripture before you and the word I'm imparting is idolatry. (Yeah yeah!) Because I am freedom. I am peace. I'm Justice. I am equality. I AM GOD! (Yeah! Yeah! All right!).

And a vengeful god, at that. He never hesitated to use the belt, board, or rubber hose on those who offended him. For "bad" children, and some adults, he had the "blue-eyed monster":

It looked like an electric generator. They strapped your arms to it. Then they'd give you whatever dose Jim ordered. He did it to a lot of children. . . . I still got a scar right here. They would shock you, and it was so bad my hand was swollen up, and I couldn't move it.[6]

Slowly, news began to leak beyond the church about the beatings, the rip-offs, the coercion and humiliation, the financial extortion, and the sexual demands that Jones made on his followers. Investigations–both public and private–followed. Jones and his flock were compelled to relocate. They decided to go to Guyana, which Jim Jones promptly labeled "The Promised Land." After all, it was one of the few places on earth that was (because of isolation and heavy vegetation) safe from atomic attack.

Getting local officials to receive the group was not hard. Jones offered plenty of money, and letters of endorsement from high places–including two U.S. Congressmen. A lease for 3,824 acres of tropical hinterlands was negotiated. "The People's Temple in Guyana intends to be an agricultural mission," his news release said. "Our only interest is to produce food to help feed our hungry world in whatever way best suits the people of Guyana." Jonestown–so named by Guyanese officials–would become a model of self-sufficient communal living that would be the envy of the Third World. After all, didn't Pastor Jim have direct links to the White House and other institutions of government? On March 31, 1977, the Guyanese foreign minister announced that permission had been given to fly People's Temple members in by chartered plane.

Jim Jones moved not only people, but money. Sensing that he might never come back to America, aware of the ease of withdrawal and concealment, the Temple placed the bulk of its money in Panamanian and Swiss banks, often in numbered accounts, or in the names of longtime but low-ranking members who almost certainly never would quit.

Here is an example of how the church sought to disguise its assets and to keep money moving: the Panama account under Associacion Evangelica de las Americas first was transferred to Associacion Religiosa por San Pedro, another front religious corporation. Then the funds were shifted to a numbered account, and later put under the name of Esther Mueller, Jones's longtime housekeeper. In October 1978, seven time-deposits ranging from $200,000 to $1.6 million would be transferred to the name of Annie McGowan, another elderly Temple member. The amounts in Temple accounts varied from nearly nothing to millions of dollars.

Isolated in his jungle bastion, ever more threatened by events and revelations in the United States, the Father grew more and more paranoid. He saw himself and his people as sacrificial lambs; scapegoats. He thought the system was out to get him:

> We've reached out to everyone who is oppressed, and that is what is bothering them. We've organized poor people and given them a voice. The system doesn't mind corporate power for the ruling elite, but for the first time we've given corporate power to the little man and that's an unforgivable sin. And that's the whole problem in a nutshell.[7]

But the "whole problem," as events would soon show, was not that simple. Jim Jones never gave power to anyone. He kept grabbing it until he had absolute power—which corrupted him absolutely.

Several years earlier, Father became preoccupied with what he saw as the ultimate ritual of apostolic faith: mass suicide by poisoning. He had already experimented with chemicals that would murder uncooperative members without leaving any traces.

Because of the shroud of secrecy drawn over the whole move, resettlement, and life in Guyana, no one can be sure of just what took place. Former members remaining in California, called "Concerned Relatives," gathered enough evidence to arouse official response and cause magazines like *New West* and the *Mendocino Grapevine* to publish shocking exposés. Soon, law suits against Jones and the People's Temple surfaced, charging fraud, false imprisonment, and assault. *People's Forum,* the cult's official organ, lashed back hysterically, using such headlines as this:

> Blackmail, Bribes, False Testimony, Faceless Accusers and Media Manipulation Try to Destroy People's Temple!

As stories and tensions mounted, Congressman Leo Ryan of California sent a telegram to Jones announcing his intention to visit and see first hand what was going on. NBC became interested in the trip. The final act of the tragedy was about to be played out. Jones had decided that the only way out was to kill the intruders, then achieve happiness by mass suicide.

How did he come to this position, both politically and theologically? Because he owned private property in a foreign land, he was far more protected from "U.S. agents and killers" than he would have been in California. He had accumulated millions of dollars, and the spell he had worked over so many was intact. Whatever else he was, Jim Jones was a survivor. Why the sudden turnabout?

Jones's own reply was published in the January 1978 number of *People's Forum*, p. 3:

> I expect to die for my beliefs. In these days you don't have to be as great a man as Martin Luther King to die for taking a stand. I am not about to be used as an excuse to bring hardship down on the people of the United States.

President Jimmy Carter received letters supporting Jones from a number of prominent people (including radical Angela Davis and San Francisco Supervisor Harvey Milk). Each member of Congress got a letter from Pamela Moton in Jonestown, complaining of "harassment by several agencies of the U.S. government," and closing with a blunt warning: "I can say without hesitation that we are devoted to a decision that it is better even to die than to be constantly harassed from one continent to another."

Die they did–by the Father's order, backed up by poison and pistols. The man who had spent most of his years pumping God ended up pumping cyanide. The immediate cause was the decision of Congressman Leo Ryan and his party to fly to Guyana and investigate–a decision that cost them their lives. Events followed with lightning swiftness. While the Congressman and his party were being murdered, the Father was preparing his flock for the next world, while the choir sang: "Because of Him this world has hope again!"

The Father on his throne was telling everyone how to die: "Take the potion like they used to in ancient Greece, and step over quietly. You're not committing suicide–it's a revolutionary act. There's no way we can survive."

Meanwhile his medical staff was preparing "the potion"–tubs of Fla-vor-Aid, heavily laced with potassium cyanide. Three tubs were used. Hypodermic needles were filled, as were paper cups. Large syringes and small squeeze bottles were loaded. Security guards patrolled the pavilion with guns. No one dared run. No one would pass through alive.

Stanley Clayton, one of the few who escaped, remembered details:

> I seen mothers who volunteered their babies to go. I seen nurses went to different babies and pulled the babies from their mothers' arms, and poured stuff down babies' throats. As he hurried the others through, pastor Jim said, "They're not crying from pain. It's just a little bitter-tasting."[8]

Parents and grandparents screamed hysterically as children died. The doomed convulsed, twitched, gagged. Others vomited, screamed, bled. A woman grabbed the microphone. "This is something we can all rejoice about," she said. "Jim Jones has suffered and suffered. He is our only God!" The "only God" was reduced to only one word as he herded the victims forward: "Quickly. Quickly. Quickly. Quickly."[9]

Those who held back were jabbed with needles. Just before the reel-to-reel tape ran out (the source of much of this material), Jones made his own final statement: "We've set an example for others. One thousand people who say: we don't like the way the world is." His estimate was not far off; 913 died that night.[10]

Stanley Clayton, meanwhile, slipped off into the bush, having got past the last security guards by saying, "I was instructed to count security guards." It worked. He lived.

Jim Jones did not. His brains and skull were blown away by a single shot. Some think he had an escape plan, but was murdered at the last minute. Others believe he committed suicide. There are no living eye-witnesses; we will never know the truth about his death.

But there are some things we do know, and should not allow ourselves to forget. James Warren Jones was a Protestant minister, and his Temple was part of a mainstream American denomination, Disciples of Christ. He was at various times defended, applauded, and rewarded not only by his own but by other "respectable" religious denominations. He received distinguished religious awards, and to the end maintained religious affiliations. If John Donne was right when he said (in *Meditation XVII*) that no man is an island, but is a piece of the continent, then Jim Jones was part of the "continent" of the American church.

If Jonestown was a descent into hell, we must admit it was a hell of misplaced idealism. Since the suicides in Jonestown, other "suicide missions," in all parts of the world, have occurred. The most widely publicized and discussed in the United States occurred outside Waco, Texas. After a bloody shoot-out on February 28, 1993, a 51-day siege of the Branch Davidian compound took place, under the intense scrutiny of a first-class media blitz. Suddenly popular religion was front-page news, as journalists, commentators, and experts closed in for the kill. The whole scene took on the aspect of a Greek drama, with the chorus shouting, "Who is to blame?"

The drama became a chilling tragedy when the cult members were incinerated by an uncontrollable fire started several hours after FBI agents, using an armored vehicle, knocked holes in the compound and piped in tear gas.

Professor Robert Coles of Harvard University suggested that we suffer not from a rash of cults but a plague of experts. "God save us from them all," he wrote in the *New York Times* on April 25, 1993, "from so-called experts. They descend on every tragedy–the psychiatric experts, the religious experts, the mediation experts, all of them shrieking, 'If you had only listened to me!' They suffer from the great delusion of our times, that social scientists will deliver us from irrational madness."

An example of that madness surfaced when the media tried to figure the "cost" of the Waco affair. Reporters from the *Houston Chronicle* set the figure at $6.6 million–by including per diem allowances, overtime, and helicopters. The Governor's Office, speaking for the Texas National Guard, added $300,000 to $400,000, and other claims came in. What about the "cost" to those who suffered and died–and mourned the dead? Can faith be converted into dollars? When does religion become not a sweet refuge, but a fortress of merciless hatred?

News stories come and go, but cults are always with us. Some estimates say there are 2,500 in the United States. As we approach the millennium–2000 A.D.–how many will emerge, where and why? And will not such movements emerge when the so-called mainline churches are in disarray and retreat?

Scholars write of movements, but human beings feel pain, one at a time. Consider Freddy Lewis, who lost 27 relatives at Jonestown–including his wife and seven children. When I talked to him on

March 10, 1990, after all these years, he told me he still pays frequent visits to the mass grave in Oakland, California. What can scholars say to Freddy Lewis?

NOTES

1. See Walter R. Martin, *The Kingdom of the Cults* (Grand Rapids, MI: Zondervan, 1976). Other important studies are I. M. Lewis, *Religion in Context: Cults and Charisma* (New York: Cambridge University Press, 1986); and Rodney Stark, *The Future of Religion: Secularization, Revival, and Cult Formation* (Berkeley: University of California Press, 1985).

2. There is a whole literature on this subject. The best single source is Weston LaBarre, *They Shall Take Up Serpents: Psychology of the Southern Snake-Handling Cult* (New York: Schocken, 1969). See also Balaji Mundkar, *The Cult of the Serpent* (Albany: State University of New York Press, 1983).

3. See Edmond C. Gruss, *Cult and the Occult* (Phillipsburg, NJ: Presbyterian, 1980), p. 82. See also Steve Allen, *Beloved Son: A Story of the Jesus Cults* (Indianapolis: Bobbs-Merrill, 1982).

4. Judith M. Weightman, *Making Sense of the Jonestown Suicides: A Sociological History of the People's Temple* (New York: Mellen, 1983).

5. See Stephen C. Rose, *Jesus and Jim Jones* (New York: Pilgrim, 1979), p. 44.

6. See Ken Levi, *Violence and Religious Commitment: Jim Jones' People's Temple Movement* (University Park: Penn State University Press, 1982), p. 118.

7. Rose, *op. cit.*, p. 223.

8. Recorded on a reel-to-reel tape and summarized in Stephen C. Rose's *Jesus and Jim Jones*.

9. *Ibid.*

10. *Ibid.*

Chapter 6

The Modernist Awakening

Everything nailed down is coming loose.

–*Marc Connelly,*
Green Pastures *(1930)*

Having visited the 1900 Paris Exhibition, Henry Adams wrote his famous essay on "The Dynamo and the Virgin." He sensed that a revolutionary age was beginning. Traditional values, symbolized by the Virgin Mary, would be outmoded. The best parallel Adams could think of was the revolution in 31 A.D., when Constantine accepted the cross of Christianity for the Roman Empire. Once more new forces were at work in the Western World–occult, super-sensual, irrational. They were, Adams believed, "a revelation of mysterious energy like that of the cross . . . immediate modes of the divine substance."

A few years later Albert Einstein put forth his theory of relativity, supplanting the Newtonian worldview, which had been accepted for generations. Scientists rejected forever the "clock mechanism" model of the universe and the rigid axioms of static physics. Both time and motion were relative to the observer; causality was replaced by purpose, product by process. Suddenly we were adrift on a strange sea–not only stranger than we could know, perhaps stranger than we could imagine.

Henry May tries to catch the enormous impact of these new ideas in *The End of American Innocence.* "Everybody knows that at some point in the twentieth century," he writes, "America went through a cultural revolution. Glance at a family album, or pick up a book or magazine dated, say, 1907. You will find yourself in a completely vanished world."[1]

It had started to vanish, in fact, in the late nineteenth century, with the invention of the phonograph (1877), the incandescent light bulb (1879), synthetic fiber (1883), the Kodak box camera (1888), the Diesel engine (1892), the Ford car (1893), and the radio and movie camera (1895). There was much to confirm the remark of Charles Peguy, in 1913, that the world had changed less since the time of Jesus Christ than it had in the last 30 years. How would the people who preached the Gospel of Jesus Christ, and believed the Bible to be "the word of God," react to all this?

No aspect of our lives was more affected than religion. Churches were split down the middle. Some determined to advance with this brave new world, and became liberals. Others determined to fight errors and heresies to the end–Armageddon–and became fundamentalists, Pentecostals, or charismatics. But those who renounced the new godless devices were quick to adopt them to their own ends. So effective was the Old Time Gospel on television that a new word came into prominence–televangelism.

If a single word was at the center of this fierce and bitter struggle, it was "modernism." What emerged from the spectacular growth of scientific and technical discovery was the sense of an accelerated rate of change. "One could feel present at the end of one kind of history," Robert Hughes writes, "and the start of another, whose emblem was the Machine, many-armed and infinitely various."[2]

Louis Kampf points out that "new" and "modern" are old notions, but never have people felt so driven by irreversible forces as they have in this century.[3] And it was the first quarter of the twentieth century, Kampf claims, that established the categories within which most of the modernist phenomena fall.

In theology, modernism attempts to accommodate traditional teachings to contemporary thought, and especially to devalue traditional supernatural elements. But to the popular mind in America, this effort has failed more often than it has succeeded. True enough, Sinclair Lewis, H. L. Mencken, and the "smart set" have ridiculed the fundamentalists and the Bible Belt; the 1925 Scopes trial (known as "the monkey trial") seemed to make evolution the winner over revelation. But one should not be too sure of this. Glance at the bumper stickers as you speed down the interstates. They hardly proclaim what was called a few years ago "the death of God."

Consider these messages, which I noted in a single day while visiting a highly successful revival service:

> I'm into God
> Smile, Jesus Loves You
> Died 4U2
> Don't Get Caught Dead Without Jesus
> Jesus Already Made My Day
> Jesus on Board
> Jesus is Awesome
> Beam Me Up, Jesus!

We must go back over a century to understand what the modernist struggle is about, and why it has never been resolved.

The key to the controversy appeared in 1870, when Charles Darwin published *The Descent of Man* with the hypothesis that evolution explains our origin and development. By 1900 scientists and theologians were proclaiming that a belief in evolution strengthened their faith, bolstered by the findings of geology, genetics, anthropology, and comparative religion. Higher criticism brought the Bible under new scrutiny and suggested new meaning. Those who believed in a reinterpretation of Christianity in accordance with the modern worldview became known as liberals. Otherwise, they claimed, Christianity could not be relevant to the modern believer.

Such thinking sent shock waves throughout the conservative Christian world. They believed we were giving up our birthright—playing into the hands of Satan himself. Back to the Bible, back to fundamentals! That is the cry that fostered what came to be called, in the 1980s, the Radical Right.

We have for so long linked radical to the left that we forget the Latin origin: *radix*, root. That which is radical springs from the roots or foundation; is fundamental or basic. Fundamentalists are surely the radicals of our time.

They are the "true believers." As Eric Hoffer points out in a book by that title, they are also masters of religio-fiction–the art of turning practical purposes into religious causes. This is the cutting edge of their newly discovered power.

No one expected it. For years–especially since the monkey trial, fundamentalism was a source of amusement, condescension, even contempt. Intellectuals quote H. L. Mencken on the subject. He was savage and Swiftian, and when William Jennings Bryan died he gloated, "We got the son-of-a-bitch!" After-dinner speakers on the best circuits did not hesitate to define fundamentalism as little fun, much damn, and absolutely no mentalism.

In the reign of Reagan, fundamentalists sat on the right hand and waged war against the left. They had the votes, the vigor, and the technology to fight on many fronts–and win. Who's laughing now?

Once a subculture of believers, they are fast becoming a counter-culture of behaviors. Writers like Jeffrey Hadden (*The Gathering Storm in the Churches*) and Richard Neuhaus (*Time Toward Home*) predicted this a decade ago, but few agreed.[4] Future historians may well say that the rise of a new Christian right (dramatized by the election of a born-again, Baptist, Sunday-school-teacher President in 1976) and the decline of liberalism were crucial.

The time has passed when we can dismiss the "bellowing Baptists" (to quote Mencken again) as "charlatans, mountebanks, peasants come home from the barnyard." We must face squarely the questions that their new prominence raises. Is this a fad, trend, or movement? Wherein lies its force and leadership? Why do many of us who have considered ourselves life-long friends of the humanities appear as "the enemy?" Just who, in Radical Right parlance, are the liberal secular humanists, evangelicals, fundamentalists, and charismatics? Why is the Supreme Court denounced for forbidding school prayers, and condoning abortion? What does it mean to be "born again"? When we make a "decision for Christ," just what are we deciding? Are there parallels with the Radical Right in Islam? When and how do "decisions" come from a creative act of the spirit?

While dramatic changes in American politics and economics have been fully analyzed, those in religion are often ridiculed or ignored. Elitists in universities and seminaries seldom speak the language of revivalists and itinerant preachers, being more concerned with homiletics, Christology, phenomenology, and semiotics. They concentrate on exegesis and comparative analysis. Many still hold to H. L. Mencken's outmoded concepts of the Bible Belt and Sinclair Lewis's stereotypic *Elmer Gantry*. Times change. We need a new map of American religion. In addition to the mainline and ethnic churches and sects, it must include the evangelical, fundamental, Pentecostal, charismatic, and cultic. With such a map we might know much more about the Radical Right and how it bolsters the New Conservatism.

Many mapmakers have found the task formidable. As early as 1854, Phillip Schaff concluded that the United States offers a motley sample of all church history. Eighty years later, Dietrich Bonhoeffer observed, "It has been granted to the Americans less than to any other nation on earth to realize the visible unity of the Church of God."

If our churches lack unity, they have never lacked authority and appeal. G. K. Chesterton said ours is a nation with the soul of a church. He was wise enough not to say just what that church believed. Like a rainbow, it has many colors, hues, combinations; some fade even as one tries to describe them. Theology in America–or anywhere else–is not so much a collection of creeds and doctrines as a continuous activity in which a struggling community tries to find its identity and test its faithfulness. We must assume that is what invigorates and motivates the Radical (or New) Right.[5]

They also have a common enemy: the liberals, who have strayed from the truth and who worship false gods. The word itself (from Latin *liber*, meaning free) suggests the ample, open, unconfined. Originally it meant suitable for a freeman, an idea which lingers in terms like *liberal* arts or *liberal* education. Liberal implies tolerance of others' views; open-mindedness to ideas that challenge the status quo and established traditions. For many of us born and raised from 1930 to 1980, liberalism was "the American Way."

While liberalism has dominated twentieth-century America, an earlier flowering came in the eighteenth century with the Enlightenment and Deism. Thomas Jefferson was a shining light. He did not mind if his neighbor thought there were 20 gods or no God; since it neither picked his pocket nor broke his leg. Placing heavy emphasis on reason, liberals feared both the dogmatic and the miraculous, convinced that natural processes and common sense were the best guides. Specifically, in the nineteenth century, they championed the Social Gospel, freedom from theological domination by creeds and religious hierarchies, and openness in doctrine. Theirs was the religion of Jesus–not the religion about Jesus which theologians stressed. Jefferson extracted only the words of Jesus, and assembled them in what is called the *Jefferson Bible.*

This was a Christ *in,* not *above* culture; the stress was on moral improvement. Optimistic about human destiny, liberals believed that if you gave people the light they would find their way.[6]

Essentially, liberalism was an attitude rather than a credo. The liberal was one who had a controlling passion for reality, kept an open mind toward the world, believed in the comprehensive nature and range of the true church, and trusted in truth rather than in authority and force. Leaders in the vanguard of liberal theology, which cut across the major denominations, included William Newton Clarke, George A. Gordon, Phillips Brooks, and later, Shailer Mathews, Walter Rauschenbusch, and Harry Emerson Fosdick. Fosdick, the founding minister of Riverside Church in New York City, popularized liberalism and its beliefs. His successor is William Sloan Coffin. The religious influence of this school infiltrated the colleges and seminaries of America, made its impact on the thinking of denominational officials, and took root in the mission fields.

This was for decades the outlook of the educated, the elite, and leadership. Liberals dominated much of our national life and politics from Teddy Roosevelt to Franklin Roosevelt and beyond. In the 1970s the Christian Right began to assert itself on a number of issues, with considerable force. Spokesmen began to develop a plan to "save" America–and to elect those who agreed. Leaders included Bill Bright (founder and president of Campus Crusade for Christ) and John B. Conlan (Republican Congressman from Arizona). With the backing of rich, conservative businessmen, they created new enterprises, like Third Century Publishers, and revitalized others, like Christian Freedom Foundation. Religion was tied in with political, economic, and military programs–the model for much that would follow.

The major challenge to liberalism came first from the evangelicals–a tree with ancient roots that has blossomed in modern Europe and America. "Evangelical," from the Greek word *evangelion* (the evangel, or good news) characterizes the good news that the original apostles proclaimed, and the gospel writers (or Evangelists) recorded.

The term *evangelical* has had different meanings in divergent cultures and epochs. Since the Reformation it has applied mainly to Protestants, who claim to base their teaching preeminently on the Gospel. There are three major theological tenets: (1) The full authority of Scriptures in matters of faith and practice; (2) the necessity of personal faith in Jesus Christ as Savior and Lord (conversion); and (3) the urgency of seeking the conversion of sinful men and women to Christ (evangelism). "Evangelical" is a comprehensive term referring to that group of believers who accept the absolute authority of the Bible, have been converted to Christ (are born again), and who share their faith with others.

If we think of "right" as pointing to the rigid, unbending, and literal, then fundamentalists are to the right of evangelicals. That is why many fundamentalists rejected President Jimmy Carter, who was proudly evangelical. In fact, the year of his election, 1976, was widely heralded as "The Year of the Evangelical." The highly regarded pollster George Gallup, Jr. reported in that year that one-third of adult Americans claimed to have had a dramatic religious experience; eight out of ten believed Jesus to be divine; 65 million believed the Bible to be inerrant; and half that number thought God had created Adam and Eve to be the parents of the human race.

Carl F. H. Henry, who founded *Christianity Today* in 1956 and edited *Basic Christian Doctrine* in 1962, is widely regarded as evangelism's leading theologian. He defines an evangelical as

> one who believes the evangel. The Good News is that the Holy Spirit gives spiritual life to all who repent and receive divine salvation proffered in the incarnate, crucified and risen Redeemer. The Christian message is what the inspired Scriptures teach—no more, no less—and an evangelical's life is governed by the scriptural revelation of God and His purposes.[7]

However we define them, the evangelicals have always flourished on this soil—before and after the United States came into existence. Among their best-known systematic theologians are Charles Hodge (1797-1878), William G. T. Shedd (1820-1894), Augustus H. Strong (1836-1921), Franz Pieper (1852-1931), and Louis Berkhof (1873-1957). Carl F. H. Henry (born in 1913) has published his six-volume, 3,030-page *God, Revelation, and Author-*

ity–the group's most substantial volume. Also impressive is Henry's understanding and acceptance of new media. Evangelicals, he says, must inspire the mass media "to picture-window evangelical realities to the restive world. . . . We must be ready to launch Christian satellites or lease time on those already orbiting."

Such statements led to the term "evangelical chic." In the Reagan Years, evangelicals had constant media coverage, fast-growing churches, highly visible campus and youth ministries, and expanding colleges and seminaries. Scores of publishing houses and hundreds of evangelical radio stations and TV stations were established in the 1980s and early 1990s. Sales of Bibles and books have boomed. Numerous conversion stories have been related by people in the public eye–"twice born" celebrities such as former White House hatchet man Charles Colson, Jeb and Gail Magruder, Johnny Cash, television's "Galloping Gourmet" Graham Kerr, former Black Panther leader Eldridge Cleaver, a large number of athletes, Malcolm Muggeridge, Jimmy Carter, and Ronald Reagan. These conversion stories have caught the eye of mainline Protestants, Roman Catholics, and secular reporters. Many of the nation's great churches are now evangelical.

By 1983, according to a Gallup poll, six in ten Americans gave evangelicals a "highly favorable" rating. While the four denominations that epitomize the cultured Protestant Establishment–United Methodist, United Presbyterian, Episcopal, and United Church of Christ (Congregational)–suffered a net loss of 2.7 million members in the 1980s, the Southern Baptist Convention alone gained nearly 2 million and is now the nation's largest Protestant body (18 million). For several years the fundamental wing has been in control, and maintained its power in the 1985 denominational conventions. While conservatives were long ignored by outsiders, they now are on the upswing. They flourish because institutions give them the visibility of denominational headquarters, colleges, seminaries, publishing houses, periodicals. Ecumenical Protestants have lost the prominence they enjoyed for two or three generations, and conservatives appear by contrast to prosper. Evangelicals are modifying their traditional style and approach while still affirming the doctrines at the heart of Christianity. They now make up a substantial part of the American population.

If evangelism set the "cultural pattern" during the 1980s, there are at least three major subcultures that gained strength and made maximum use of electronic media: fundamentalists, charismatics, and neo-evangelicals. Of the three, the fundamentalists were most aggressive and expansive in the mid-1980s.

The basic Latin root, *fundamentum*, means a foundation or basis; that which is essential. Religions, like buildings, need *foundations* on which to stand. Hence the fundamentalists are the "strict constructionists" of evangelicism. They trace their American beginnings to a series of Niagara Conferences which met annually from 1875 to 1901. This led in turn to the writing of *The Fundamentals*, a set of 12 booklets, each about 125 pages, setting the theological issues of the day from a conservative standpoint by prominent scholars from the United States, Canada, and Great Britain. Through the generosity of Lyman and Milton Stewart, these booklets were sent, over a five-year period (1910-1915), to 3 million people. Every pastor, evangelist missionary, theology professor, theology student, Sunday school superintendent, and YMCA and YWCA secretary in the English-speaking world whose address could be obtained received a copy. The significance of *The Fundamentals* was twofold. Initially, a great interdenominational witness was achieved with firm conviction and considerable intellectual power. The project also created a kind of entente between two incompatible conservative elements: a denominational, seminary-oriented group and a Bible institute group (i.e., Moody Bible Institute and the Bible Institute of Los Angeles). Despite differing theological interpretations of various passages of Scripture, the authors of *The Fundamentals*, reflecting these two groups, were generally united on belief in the Bible's literal inerrancy. The dissemination of *The Fundamentals* marks the beginning of fundamentalism as a major movement.

With it came a new outburst of millenarianism—the belief in Christ's physical return, to be followed by His literal reign on earth for 1,000 years. Frequently the distinction is made between premillennialists and postmillennialists. Premillennialists believe that the second coming of Christ will take place before the millennium. This interpretation presupposes a degeneration of society until Jesus returns to establish His kingdom. Postmillennialists of the twentieth century are those who believe that the second coming of Christ will occur after the millennium, and will be the result of the Christianization of the world without miraculous intervention.

Five dogmas are central in the fundamentalist literature: (1) the verbal inspiration of the Bible; (2) the virgin birth of Christ; (3) Christ's atonement for our sins; (4) His bodily resurrection and; (5) His second coming.[8] This position can be separated from conservatism–a Protestant movement which upholds the inspired content of the entire Bible, but has come slowly to accept some basic conclusions of scholars' Higher Criticism. Conservatism produced theologians of the stature of J. Gresham Machen (1881-1937), for many years a professor of Greek New Testament at Princeton Theological Seminary. Conservatism has not been a major factor in recent years.

More and more people now tend to associate fundamentalists with the Radical Right–deeply rooted in dogmatic, witch-hunting, intolerant Protestant fundamentalism. There is much overlapping of membership, leadership, activities, and resources between some fundamental churches and groups like the John Birch Society and the Anti-Communist Leadership Schools.

Since evangelist and fundamentalist are the two most used (and overused) words in contemporary religious writing, we might ask, just how do they differ? It is impossible to give a precise answer because of the many and imprecise groups, definitions, and assertions. Both movements proclaim full allegiance to the Bible as "the Word of God." But fundamentalists resist modern critical attempts to study or revise the Bible, while evangelists generally try to take seriously the claims of recent scholarly study and discovery. Their common enemy is what they call "liberal secular humanism"; but they also fight each other. The evangelical Carl Henry, says he believes that the great flaw in fundamentalism is not so much its reactionary spirit as its spirit of lovelessness. There is an irony here. The more fundamentalists stress separation from apostasy as a theme, the more the spirit of lovelessness seems to prevail. Often they merely attack organizations and personalities.

Another highly vocal component or subculture within evangelism is the charismatic renewal. The root word, *charisma*, is Greek for divine gift. Antecedents include many of the older Pentecostal groups, such as the Assembly of God and Church of God. Both emphasized "speaking in tongues." Charismatics (who now find their main strength in the middle class) tend to be orthodox in belief, are born-again Christians, and witness to their faith. Their religious identity, however, is not centered so much on the defense of doctrinal formulations as on the experience and testimony that precede doctrine. The charismatic experience–most often seen as subsequent to conversion–is termed *baptism* in the Holy Spirit (after the pattern in the book of Acts), by which a believer, in the course of prayer, is "filled with the Spirit" and receives one or more of the spiritual gifts mentioned by Paul in I Corinthians 12-14 and elsewhere in the New Testament. Charismatics usually feel that the ability to "speak in tongues" as a prayer language (one of the gifts cited and practiced by Paul) is the best evidence of spirit baptism. Other prominent gifts emphasized within charismatic renewal include divine healing and prophecy.

While the older Pentecostals set up their own churches, today's charismatics tend to stay inside historic denominations and attempt to renew their power. One outstanding example is St. Paul's Episcopal Church in Darien, Connecticut. Led by the Rev. Everett L. Fullam, the church has grown so fast that services are now held in the local high school. The stress here, and in all such churches, is on exuberance and conversion.

Fundamentalism, like most American religious groups, has a tendency to splinter. Education, affluence, and a new lifestyle tend to change religious beliefs and practices. Thus a mobile minority of the stricter fundamentalists broke away in the 1940s, rejecting what they perceived in the older "bedrock fundamentalism" as theological and cultural excesses–anti-intellectualism, sectarianism, social unconcern, and an almost complete repudiation of the values of the wider society. The term neo-evangelical has generally been replaced by the more historic and inclusive designation, evangelical. These evangelicals created their own distinctive subculture and lifestyle; and to the American public at large, they are *the* evangelicals. Although I shall refer to both the charismatics and the older fundamentalists, attention will be directed primarily to the neo-evangelicals of the more comprehensive movement–its changing theology, leadership, and patterns of behavior.

Liberalism, evangelism, and fundamentalism–like God Himself, these currents do not stand still. They move, change, and churn, like the face of the deep. They are loaded not only with meaning but with emotion.

As religious groups contended for power, two colorful fundamentalists achieved national status and notoriety. William Jennings Bryan (1860-1925) and Billy Sunday (1862-1935) were near-contemporaries in the Age of Transition. Willie and Billy (as they were known to their friends) were as great a pair of spellbinders as the nation ever saw; yet they both lived to see the fundamental values they lived by discarded and discredited. Now, half a century later, fundamentalism is alive and well and filling the airwaves. So in a real sense, their souls go marching on.[9]

True enough, Willie and Billy were easy to parody. Neither claimed to be theologians. Billy Sunday boasted that he knew no more about theology than a jackrabbit knew about ping-pong. But this Calliope of Zion (Mencken's nickname for Sunday) was unforgettable on the platform. A professional baseball player turned revivalist, he slid into home plate for Jesus. He had a unique talent for dramatization, and regularly skipped, ran, walked, bounced, slid, and gyrated around the stage. He hated the "bastard theory of evolution" and the "deodorized and disinfected sermons" of mainline churches, and insisted that Christianity and patriotism are synonymous, just as hell and traitor are synonymous. His bizarre antics were popular during the war years; but by 1930, Sunday could no longer find enough people to fill his dirt-floor tabernacles. Behind his vaudeville routine was the rough-and-ready frontier life that was gone forever. Now other voices would have to carry the fifth Great Awakening forward, and fight the sins of the modern world.

William Jennings Bryan, born in rural Illinois in 1860, came to be known as the Great Commoner. He was a perennial candidate for the presidency, reaching his zenith in what came to be called the "Cross of Gold" speech: "You shall not press down upon the brow of labor this crown of thorns, you shall not crucify mankind on a cross of gold."

He lost to William McKinley, but continued to be his party's standard-bearer for 20 years. Having served as Woodrow Wilson's Secretary of State, he resigned and funnelled his enormous charisma and popularity into religion. Fundamentalism's major defender, he became the butt of ridicule and scorn at the Scopes trial in 1925, and died five days after its conclusion.

Even conceding that Bryan got a bad press, and is not the buffoon that Mencken pictures, he is easy to laugh at. An unrelenting foe of overdrinking, he was himself the victim of overeating. In photographs he looks like Jackie Gleason, or Hardy of Laurel and Hardy, larding the lean earth. His favorite snack was radishes, which he carried in a pith helmet for instant consumption. "I am fond of radishes," he liked to say. "I eat radishes in the morning; I eat radishes at noon; I eat radishes at night; I like radishes."

And the people liked Bryan, rooted in old-time rural America, Bible thumping and Bible quoting, daring the modern world to discard him. Finally it did.

New and powerful voices took over. Three of the leading ones were a black cult leader from the Deep South, a Roman Catholic priest from the Midwest, and a woman evangelist transplanted from Canada. They kept the fundamentalist Messiah alive, and carried the myth of salvation to millions. Father Divine, Father Coughlin, and Aimee Semple McPherson deserve special scrutiny and comment.

No more incredible preacher has walked this land than George Baker, self-proclaimed Father Divine. Known to thousands as God on earth, this Messiah (like many others) was more anxious to obscure his past than to clarify it. Even now it is hard to separate fact from fiction.[10]

The son of illiterate, black South Carolina sharecroppers, Baker had an obscure beginning. His probable birth date was 1880. A fellow preacher who knew Baker before he became God, Saint John The Vine Hickerson, later recorded that Baker moved to Baltimore in 1899, where he worked as a gardener for 50 cents a day. He became the disciple of the mulatto minister Samuel Morris, who insisted he was the Father Eternal and called himself Father Jehova. Baker was his assistant for several years, mastered his rhetoric, then moved North to start a church of his own.

Why did Baker's Peace Mission Movement take hold, and carry him to national prominence? Charisma and talent were important; but the crisis in the black church, which the Depression mercilessly exposed to the urban poor, was decisive. "For lack of leadership," the black historian Carter Woodson wrote in 1931, "the Negro church has no program except saving souls from hell–when conditions against which the church should fight are keeping the Negroes in hell."

George Baker–now Father Divine–had a program, which he launched in Harlem in 1933. Half of the black families there were on relief, and almost all of them were tired, hungry, and sick. They needed a savior–and got one.

Father Divine became the symbol of the new progressive spirit of the Negro church. An uncanny sense of timing prompted him to become the activist-reformer, offering free meals and jobs to needy guests. By the early 1930s, bands of disciples were forming throughout the ghettoes, anxious to have their spiritual emptiness filled by Divine. He organized his disciples–now known collectively as the Peace Mission–into a tight-knit set of religious cooperatives, highly responsive to Father's every command. He was a one-man Great Awakening, and soon had the largest, most cohesive movement in the northern ghettoes.

Those who passed him off as a cult leader underestimated his skill at adapting to changing communal needs. He had the money, following, and executive ability to put his extraordinary claims to work: "I am a Negro and God dwells in me. You are a Negro and you are like unto me. Therefore you are superior to white." This was a startling claim for a squat, completely bald man who was barely five feet tall. But does God not come in the most insignificant, the most illiterate, the most downtrodden of the children of men? "Do you see the mystery?" he asked his followers.

"So true, Lord, so true!" they shouted in response.

How did Father Divine attain his glory? How did this man born in a squalid shanty end up as God? This was his astonishing answer: "I was combusted one day in 1900 on the corner of Seventh Avenue and 134th Street in Harlem." He had another mystical answer: "Before Abraham was, I am."

Why did so many, black and white, follow him? Again, he had a remarkable answer, as Sara Harris records in *Father Divine*: "I am their life's substance. I am their energy and ambition! They recognize my deity as that which was in the imaginary heaven, and if they can only get a word with me, they feel they are in heaven!"[10]

More importantly, they were well fed. At huge banquet tables, they could eat, drink, sing their hearts out, stomp, clap, and repeat little ditties:

Just to look at you,
Wish I was in heaven ten thousand years
Just to look at you.

How did he pay for such feasts and buy up vast properties in and out of Harlem? By having true followers put all their money and labor into "Divine Peace Mission Movement Cooperatives," meeting rigid regulations imposed by Father. No one took out any profits. They must turn their bodies and minds over to God for His use.

With his money the Father created jobs. In old Harlem lofts, stores, and abandoned factories he started stores, barbershops, restaurants, boarding houses. His critics called it "chain store religion"; Father called it "God Incorporated." Between 1933 and 1937, Father Divine became Harlem's chief housing agent, with enterprises in New Jersey, Connecticut, and Maryland. Members of legitimate churches and storefront churches, black and white, joined him. He was not teaching far-off heaven or hell, but God right here, right now. If God is at hand, then heaven is at hand. Enjoy!

Father Divine knew what many leaders have known over the ages: to get a lot you must ask a lot. He demanded literally everything of the faithful. They must renounce the outside world and all their previous lives. If they had families, they either brought them into the movement or renounced them completely. Within the movement ties of kinship were not acknowledged. Relatives regarded one another simply as sisters and brothers, even if they were mothers and sons. Members received a small allowance for room and board in the movement's lodging houses and a few dollars for incidentals. They also got new names–Sweet Angel, Love Blessing, Beautiful Peace, or even Universal Vocabulary.

Nothing with negative or evil overtones was allowed. So no "Hellos"–that suggested hell. No Amsterdam Avenue–use Amsterbless. This, plus Father Divine's thaumaturgical healings of everything from corns to cancer, gave his ministry a special ambience. So did his secretaries, 26 young girls, half of them white and half

black, who were "nuns dedicated to live for God and God alone."
There was a special poem that the secretaries had to repeat:

> You've got to make a hundred
> Ninety-nine and a half won't do
> And if you make a hundred
> Father will have made it–not you.

This elite corps wore red jackets with large Vs for virginity
emblazoned on the pockets. "The Sweets," the truest virgins of
Father Divine's movement, took a solemn oath:

> To make every word we speak real and true.
> To ask not of another, but ask only of You;
> To let nothing ever break us apart;
> To keep you forever, the Sweet of our heart;
> To be by all these things united forever
> To You–this is the Sweets' sincerest endeavor!

They even had their own Ten Commandments, one of which held
they would "never, no, never condemn or find fault with anything
our Savior may say or do." This led some skeptics to wonder if the
Father might set aside celibacy–since divinities don't live by the
same rules as mere mortals. In many ancient cultures, and in more
recent Hinduism, cult prostitution was a highly esteemed form of
religious observance, as was incestuous marriage between royal
brothers and sisters. What is forbidden behavior in the profane
sphere becomes sacred and obligatory conduct when its practitioners are divine or operating in the realm of the holy. Even if Father
Divine had in fact been wallowing in promiscuity, he may still be
said to have been following a code of conduct appropriate for a god.

Yet all this showmanship (carried to a tragic extreme later on by
the cult leader Jim Jones) should not obscure Divine's understanding of the times in which he lived. Robert Weisbrot, in *Father
Divine and the Struggle for Racial Equality* (1983), describes him
as one of those rare cult figures who derived his greatest sense of
power from helping to shape society according to his ideas of justice. He was for integration, equal rights, and economic cooperation
long before they became popular issues for most Americans.

From all accounts he was a powerful preacher, quick of mind and movement, shooting out clipped words that flew like bullets. In the manner of black Southern preachers, he encouraged shouted responses, and repeated time and again his famous punch line: "Peace! It is truly wonderful!" When he preached, ecstasy reigned among the poor, the racially outcast, and the troubled in spirit. No wonder many of them knew with deepest conviction that this was the Kingdom of Heaven on earth.

Father Divine got a poor press even at the peak of his power. Most of the accounts mirror the cynicism and condescension of the white-dominated era towards blacks. So did the biographies. Robert A. Parker's *The Incredible Messiah: The Deification of Father Divine* presents him as a petty tyrant who aped the fascist leaders then menacing Europe; a demagogue who liked high living. John Hoshor's *God in a Rolls-Royce: The Rise of Father Divine, Madman, Menace, or Messiah* (1936) tends to burlesque blacks and trivialize Divine's achievements. Sara Harris's *Father Divine* (1953) focuses on alleged sexual pathologies of Peace Mission disciples and rumors of Divine's sexual indiscretions. She mixes fascination with sarcasm, and settles for gossip instead of analysis.[10] Just what did George Baker stand for?

The Father Divine Peace Mission Movement represented a withdrawal from the logic and mores of everyday American life into a utopian world governed by a divinity, asceticism, and a leader whose behavior stood in dramatic opposition to the expectations of white Christianity.

Father Divine was no racist. Whatever resentment he felt about white America was muted. Some of his wealthiest supporters were white, and he proclaimed a deracialized America. His main point was not that he was black, but that he was divine.

Because he considered himself God, he lived accordingly, to devotees' delight. To the great frustration of the Internal Revenue Service, however, he was never proven to have possessed any personal wealth. He lived on the largess of his followers and in and through the chain of cooperative restaurants, lodging houses, and other enterprises that the movement held in the followers' names.

After 1940 the aging Father Divine began to lose his charisma and appeal. The Peace Mission evolved from a spontaneous mass movement to a formal sect supporting an elaborate bureaucracy. The catalyst behind his conservative shift was a bitter court fight, brought on in 1937 when a former follower sued for money allegedly kept illegally by Father Divine. When the New York court ruled in her favor, Father Divine realized this opened the floodgates for many other law suits. The weary cult leader decided to incorporate several key Peace Missions with officers and trustees, and to leave New York permanently so as to avoid the state's courts. Living in Philadelphia, isolated from the heart of his Harlem-based movement, he was in effect retired. One brief return to fame came in 1946, when he married a beautiful 21-year-old white disciple called Sweet Angel. Embarrassing questions were raised. Why, after years of forbidding disciples to marry, had he now wed? Why did he choose a new convert, nearly 50 years his junior?

Living now in bourgeois respectability, God did not choose to answer. Other black leaders, like Adam Clayton Powell, Jr., Leon Sullivan, and "Prophet Jones" came to pay homage to the elder statesman. Because of failing health he seldom travelled after 1950, enjoying his 32-room mansion on "the mount of the house of the Lord." As Cycle Four wound down and a post-war America moved into the Age of Eisenhower, the religious leader who had typified the first half of the century, with its lingering Depression, enjoyed his garden-filled estate. One of the last acts of the aging divinity was to write to President Lyndon Johnson, congratulating him on introducing civil rights legislation and the Voting Rights Act in 1965. By then, a new religious revival was well under way, and positive thinking had gripped the land. A few months later, the man who insisted he was God left his earth.

*   *   *

How then can one summarize modernism, as a concept and as an Awakening? Most writers think of it as setting the tone for the twentieth century and the Progressive Era before World War I. Gathering strength from America's new world position after 1920, modernism stressed "the three Ps"–Pep, Progress, and Prosperity. Teddy Roosevelt set the stage and a later Roosevelt (Franklin D.) picked up the optimistic tone after the Great Depression with his New Deal.

Franklin Roosevelt guided us through World War II, into a period of unprecedented power and abundance. The 1960s saw the development of a counterculture, and massive disillusionment, epitomized by the war in Vietnam. Then followed Watergate, President Nixon's resignation, racial tension, and the steady accumulation of an unmanageable national debt.

Norman Rockwell's idyllic America never existed–but throughout much of the twentieth century, one could imagine that it might have. Not so after the tarnishing of the American Dream as the century neared its close. Observers sought new labels. We were entering a post-Protestant, postmodern, even posthistorical era.

Learned scholars and theologians have found it hard to sort out and summarize how men and women related to God in the Age of Modernism. One of the most famous scholars, John Macquarrie, published his ponderous *Twentieth Century Religious Thought*, describing such categories as absolute idealism, pluralistic personal idealism, phenomenology, ontology, Ritschlianism, and neo-Thomism.[11] These terms meant little to those who preached and practiced popular religion. They still sang hymns like "What a Friend We Have in Jesus," "The Old Rugged Cross," "Onward Christian Soldiers," and "Amazing Grace." The Great Divide among twentieth-century American Christians might be labeled "inclusive vs. exclusive." The inclusive churches (including those called mainline) tended to be liberal, open to change, and anxious to include new interpretations. For them truth came in many forms, and they believed that one must respect others who have different insights. They tended to exalt the role of women (including ordination), racial equality, and environmentalism. Their key phrase was positive affirmation.

The exclusive churches, generally thought of as conservative, tended to resist change and to question new interpretations. For them secular humanism was an enemy, and challenging old dogmas was the work of the Devil. By its very structure, Roman Catholicism is exclusive, endorsing the Doctrine of Infallibility. Many Protestant groups, such as those Southern Baptists believing in the inerrant truth of the Bible, were just as exclusive. The Church of Christ allowed no instrumental music, and Seventh-day Adventists insisted that Saturday is the real Sabbath. Their key phrase was negative judgment.[12]

The evangelicals, less scripture-bound, continued the process of personal conversion and commitment central to earlier Awakenings. They believed in spreading the Good News (Gospel) of salvation through Jesus Christ. Some groups, such as the Mormons, even required a mandatory missionary period for their youth, who go throughout the world. Other evangelical groups include the Disciples, Jehovah's Witnesses, and the televangelists. The evangelical mainstream has broadened over the years. It is in a real sense the successor to the fundamentalist movement; but as David H. Watt points out, "It is also drawing increasingly on conservative Protestantism that was never fundamentalist."[13] Popular journals like *Time* and *Newsweek* proclaimed 1976 "The Year of the Evangelicals." By then, televangelism was becoming a force to be reckoned with in American politics.

The charismatics continued to stress the operation of the Holy Spirit and the superrational. Appealing to the lower middle class and group fervor, charismatic services tended to be extravagant and exuberant. So did those of the Pentecostals, such as the Church of God and Assembly of God. They were not political, and "bore witness" to their faith in oral testimonies. Theirs was the ecstasy of "speaking in tongues."

No one can sure just how many people belonged to these various groups and subgroups; but it is certain that there were millions of Americans never swayed by modernism in the twentieth century. Many turned their backs on the new technologies and theories and chose the Old Rugged Cross. Some combined the two, and powered a new religious revival–the Electronic Awakening. Turning from the meeting house to mass media, they added a new dimension to our religious history. We turn to that now.[14]

NOTES

1. Henry May, *The End of American Innocence* (New York: Knopf, 1959), p. 3. May's later book is also helpful here: *Ideas, Faiths, and Feelings: Essays on American Intellectual and Religious History, 1952-1982* (New York: Oxford University Press, 1983).

2. Robert Hughes, *The Shock of the New* (New York: Knopf, 1988), p. 15.

3. Louis Kampf, *On Modernism: The Prospects for Literature and Freedom* (Boston: M.I.T. Press, 1971), p. 3.

4. The best summaries of this period, with full bibliographical references, are by George M. Marsden: *Fundamentalism and American Culture: The Shaping of Twentieth Century Evangelicalism, 1870-1925* (New York: Oxford University Press, 1980); and *Evangelicalism and Modern America* (Grand Rapids, MI: Eerdmans, 1988). Another excellent source is Jeffrey K. Hadden, whose books include *Prime Time Preachers* (Nashville: Addison, 1981); and *Televangelism: Power and Politics on God's Frontier* (New York: Holt, 1988).

5. The most comprehensive summary is Matthew C. Moen, *The Transformation of the Christian Right* (Tuscaloosa: University of Alabama Press, 1992). See also Ferenc Szasz, *The Divided Mind of American Protestantism, 1880-1930* (Tuscaloosa: University of Alabama Press, 1982).

6. This idea is fully developed by H. Richard Niebuhr, *Christ and Culture* (New York: Harper and Row, 1951).

7. Carl F. H. Henry, *God, Revelation and Authority* (Waco, TX: Word, 1976-1983), vol. 1, p. 23.

8. James I. Packer, *Fundamentalism and the Word of God* (Grand Rapids, MI: Eerdmans, 1958), ch. 2.

9. William Jennings Bryan, *The Memoirs of William Jennings Bryan by Himself and His Wife* (Port Washington, NY: Kennikat, 1971), p. 67. The book was issued in 1925 by John C. Winston, Philadelphia.

10. See Sara Harris, *Father Divine* (New York: Collier, 1971); Keith V. Erickson, "Black Messiah: The Father Divine Peace Mission Movement," *Quarterly Journal of Speech*, 63 (December 1977); and Kenneth E. Burnham, *God Comes to America* (Boston: Lambeth, 1978).

11. John Macquarrie, *Twentieth Century Religious Thought* (New York: Harper and Row, 1963). The topics named here are listed in the table of contents.

12. The best set of documents tracing the history of American Christianity is H. S. Smith, Robert Handy, and L. A. Loetscher, *American Christianity*, 2 vols. (New York: Scribner's, 1960). The most comprehensive and readable single volume is by Sydney E. Ahlstrom, *A Religious History of the American People* (New Haven: Yale University Press, 1972).

13. David H. Watt, *A Transforming Faith: Explorations of Twentieth-Century American Evangelicalism* (New Brunswick, NJ: Rutgers University Press, 1991), p. 161.

14. See Anthony F. C. Wallace, "Revitalization Movements," *American Anthropology*, 58 (1956): 264-281; and William F. Fore, *Television and Religion: The Shaping of Faith, Values, and Culture* (Minneapolis: Augsburg, 1987).

Chapter 7

Civil Religion

God, guts, and guns–they made America.

–bumper sticker

We dropped the A-bomb on Hiroshima in August 1945. Many have long believed that the Creator speaks to man. This time He thundered.

Years later we can't capture the elation and triumph of that momentous day. Having won a two-ocean war, America was the unchallenged superpower. GIs could come home and our influence could go abroad. The American Century was about to begin.

For years all signals were go. The economy retooled. Having won his crusade in Europe, Eisenhower returned to lead one in Washington. Exports, babies, and Bibles boomed. The American dream was becoming a reality. Christians were confident that their revival would be as spectacular in its own way as was that of the recovery. Having won the crusade for democracy, we could launch one for Christ.

We had "Praised the Lord and Passed the Ammunition" with marked success. Unity, dedication, and sacrifice had paid off. The forces of evil (that is, our enemies) had been vanquished. Now was the time to replay the whole drama at home.

Because this euphoria of the 1950s would vanish in the 1960s, and even theologians would wonder if God was dead, it is important to look at the background of Cycle Five, with its spectacular achievements at mid-century. We need to reread such documents as Barbara Ward's *Report to Europe on America* (1952, p. 86). "We don't need polls or statistics to confirm what we can so easily see," she wrote, "the walls of new churches rising in town and countryside wherever we went." Being a historian, she saw many old ingredients in the new attitudes. Puritanism, patriotism, and prosperity had combined to make a powerful brew. This had been the case in each of the four Great Awakenings, and cycles, that had preceded the one underway in the 1950s. Other triumphant generals–Washington, Jackson, Grant, Teddy Roosevelt (who was in fact a rough-riding colonel)–had preceded Eisenhower. Does winning wars set off religious revivals? And does losing them (our first experience came with Vietnam) bring on talk of Armageddon?

For all its pluralism and diversity, American culture has deep enduring themes and beliefs which are central to our self-image and our actions. Despite many changing circumstances, for example, our American religion soars with the eagle. Can it reach heaven?

The flight is swift and high-minded. We came here to build a New England, complete with a New Canaan. That fostered a Fifth Gospel, centering on success and self-made men. When the Gospel was extended beyond individuals to the nation, civil religion came into play, along with patriotism and chauvinism. What has it done to Christianity?

The term "civil religion" first appeared in Jean Jacques Rousseau's *The Social Contract* (1762). The state, he asserted, could only endorse God's existence, the punishment of vice, and the exclusion of religious intolerance. The United States concurred, and put the separation of church and state in the Constitution's First Amendment. The acknowledged public deity is related more to law and order, than to love and salvation. This God (mentioned four times in our Declaration of Independence) is intensely involved in history–especially ours. And thereby hangs the tale.

The United States is (or at least thinks it is) the most religious nation on earth. We love God, and like to think the attraction is mutual. Over 95% of our citizens say they believe in God–double that of most European countries. But is it God we really revere? A person without a church is not badly handicapped; but a person without a country has no identity or mobility. In the United States, the nation may be the bearer and object of religion.[1]

Patriotism, one might reply, is not religion. We have a semantic problem–what is a religion? The use of symbols, rituals, holidays, and media have created an American civil religion–there is no other word for it. Admittedly, it is neither sectarian nor in any specific sense Christian. But it is central to our belief system and our understanding of the cosmos, reflecting both our private and public views. Nor is that system of which we speak simply "religion in general." While generality is seen as a virtue, America's civil creed is specific enough. Because of this specificity, civil religion is saved from empty platitudes and serves as a genuine vehicle of national self-understanding.

The vehicle had to be built from the ground up. Being a new nation with old memories, we had no indigenous body of traditional imagery to draw from and certainly didn't want what had been left behind in Europe. American Indians were cast aside as barbaric and inappropriate for symbolic use until they finally surfaced on one-cent pieces toward the end of the nineteenth century (after they were no longer a serious threat to anyone.) Neither the Pilgrims, huddled on their New England rocks as self-conscious Protestants, nor the Cavaliers, building plantations on more hospitable land, thought of themselves as a "race" or a "nation." From the first our condensed and contrived symbols have been in conflict. The cross and the flag are dissimilar icons. Which do we follow in moments of peril? In times of triumph? If they make demands, which do we heed? Can a Roman Catholic, a Jew, or an agnostic preside over Protestant America?

The centerpiece for civil religion has been the Bible with the exodus theme; our Liberty Bell has its quotation from Moses. Our own Moses was George Washington, who freed us from the British yoke and was apotheosized even before he died. Civil religion grew with the nation, a product of the same culture. We succeeded in mixing Puritanism, patriotism, and prosperity into a powerful brew. The separate colonies formed one nation, under God.

Then we expanded our civil religion. Nineteenth-century writers like Emerson, Thoreau, and Melville added new elements—especially transcendentalism. The Civil War, with casualties far exceeding those undergone by Americans in any war before or since, transformed civil religion. Now death and rebirth entered the formula, symbolized in the life and death of Abraham Lincoln. Nowhere is it stated more vividly than in the Gettysburg Address, part of the Lincolnian "New Testament" among the civil scriptures.

Robert Lowell notes the insistent use of birth images in the speech explicitly devoted to "these honored dead": "brought forth," "conceived," "created," "a new birth of freedom." The Gettysburg Address is a symbolic and sacramental act. Its verbal quality is resonance combined with a logical, prosaic brevity. In his words, Lincoln symbolically died, just as the Union soldiers really died—and as he himself was soon really to die.

Much was made of Lincoln's recurring dreams. The legend arose that he had received warnings of his impending death. Lincoln was elevated to the status of a demigod; a divine agent or a *theios aner* (divine man). Identification with the Christian mythos of one sacrificially slain made this apotheosis easier. On the one hand, Lincoln was the American Christ; on the other, our indigenous King Arthur—absent but not destroyed. We also got a new Judas, John Wilkes Booth. Civil religion was a double winner.

With the Christian archetype in the background, Lincoln, our martyred president, was linked to the war dead, who "gave the last full measure of devotion." The theme of sacrifice was indelibly written into the script. Memorial Day integrated local communities into the national cult, just as the Fourth of July had done years before.

Primary vehicles for perpetuating these things were the public schools and schoolbooks. These books, of which the graded *Readers* of William Holmes McGuffey were the most successful, self-consciously set about not only to produce universal literacy but also to provide the new generation of readers with values that would equip them to deal with growing up American.

The basic attitudes were evangelical and ethnocentric. McGuffey's works were mild in this regard. While they strongly emphasized such Protestant attitudes as the work ethic, temperance, and special providences, they refrained from the excesses of racism and nationalism that were characteristic of many other works. Their collective purpose was to provide young people not simply with functional skills but with an entire world picture—a cosmos—religious in essence and Protestant in emphasis.

Popular songs helped, too. "America" was written by a Baptist minister, Samuel Francis Smith. Julia Ward Howe's "Battle Hymn of the Republic" was full of strong Old Testament imagery. The less militant "America the Beautiful" was written by an English professor at Wellesley College–a Congregationalist well-immersed in civil religion and love of the land. These songs remain popular–almost sacred–today.

We have always drawn heavily from biblical archetypes: exodus, promised land, chosen people, born again, covenant, sacrifice, rebirth. Working with them, America has produced its own sacred heroes, places, and events; its own solemn symbols and rituals. Most Americans–including theologians and preachers–have blessed the secular and sacred as an organic unit.

Civil religion can be misused. Look how the "American Israel" theme helped justify the shameful treatment of American Indians and immigrants; how the American Legion ideology has branded numerous nonconformists or liberals "Reds" or "Communists." The way the John Birch Society interprets patriotism must make early American patriots turn over in their graves.

Many critics of religion, the "American Way," or American Shintoism, are really talking about civil religion. They find much to criticize. Yet civil religion, at its best, points to transcendent religious reality as seen in or revealed through the American experience. Like all religions, it has suffered various deformations and distortions. At its best, it has neither been so general as to lack incisive relevance nor so particular as to place society above universal human values. The leaders of the church may not have represented a higher truth or vision than those (like Lincoln, Roosevelt, and Kennedy) who used the language of nationalism.

Unremitting pressure from civil religion helped find a partial solution for our greatest domestic problem, the treatment of minorities. It remains to be seen how relevant it can become for our role in the world at large, and whether we can effectually stand for the revolutionary beliefs for which our forebears fought.

Civil religion has reached its third "Time of Trial." The first, in the eighteenth century, wrestled with the question of independence; whether we should or could run our own affairs in our own way. The second was over the issue of slavery, which in turn was only one aspect of the larger problem of the full institutionalization of democracy. This we are still far from solving though we have had some successes. We have been overtaken by a third: the problem of responsible and acceptable action in a revolutionary world which wants many of the things which we have–in abundance. How do we quell the Revolution of Rising Expectations?

In providing answers to this question, and strategies for our continuing supremacy, Billy Graham became the archetypal twentieth-century American evangelist. How did he see American history?

God had given America victory over the British, the French, the Mexicans, and the Germans twice in one century. But in Korea, things went awry. Sin must have been moving in the camp, subversion in the land. Regarding sin and subversion as the same phenomenon, Billy Graham sought to persuade every American to confess his or her sin. America's prestige was at stake; so was God's. Subversion of America was a sin against God, and sin (as defined by his evangelical faith) was subversion. Sensing the mood of the times, Graham played a key role in civil religion. Graham's main appeal was to mainline churches. He had less to say to the immigrant-ethnic background churches. Not all Americans found this useful. Groups that have an explicit theological concern, orthodox, neo-orthodox, or liberal, found their theologies at odds with Graham's. So did the ill-defined, though numerous and influential, religions of the disinherited, the many Holiness, Pentecostal, and millenarian sects of the socially and culturally submerged. Their "peculiar" outlook was frequently still too vital and all-absorbing to be easily subordinated to some common faith.

How can our culture become more religious yet more secular at the same time? Many observed it, but could not fully explain it. The paradox is there, and we cannot dismiss it by suppressing one or the other side of the apparent contradiction. We can't write off the new religiousness as shallow emotionalism, escapism, or pretense. The people who join churches, take part in crusades, send their children to church schools, and identify themselves in religious terms are not fools or hypocrites. They are usually honest, solemn people who take their religion seriously.

The widespread secularism of America, in which religion is made to provide the sanctification and dynamic for goals and values otherwise established, is difficult for Europeans to understand. In Europe the confrontation between secularism and religion tends to be more explicit and well defined. In the United States hostility or demonstrative indifference to religion is a minor and manageable force. America's secularism is found within the churches themselves.

This may have bothered some theologians, but not President Eisenhower. To Ike both World War II and his presidential campaign were crusades. He was called upon to fight against corruption at home, and "Godless Communism" abroad. Knowing this, Americans could chant: "I like Ike." "The things that make us proud to be Americans," he said, "are of the soul and of the spirit."

Ike was both the Olympian conqueror and the man next door. His friendly smile and good intentions were part of our psychic landscape. When things went wrong, he was not to blame. Everyone knew he meant well. The same tactic worked a generation later for Ronald Reagan. This is why they had such enormous appeal to religious groups–even though neither of them had strong church connections. They represented the national piety that surrounds the presidential office and was particularly strong in the 1950s–the soft nationalism that knows there is a domain of the common and good and American that is more important than all the "things that divide us."

John Gunther, a pop writer who understood the Pop President, wrote a popular book entitled *Eisenhower: The Man and Symbol*, in which he noted that theory irritated Ike.[2] He believed in first things first; in short, he believed in civil religion. No wonder we liked Ike.

Who were Ike's counterparts in the pulpit? Norman Vincent Peale, a Methodist preacher specializing in "positive thinking," and writing best-selling, euphoric self-help books; Bishop Fulton J. Sheen, a highly literate Roman Catholic priest, and "Angel of the Airways"; and Billy Graham, a dynamic Presbyterian revivalist with lots of charisma. Religion spilled over into Hollywood. Bible "spectacles" with Hedy Lamarr as Delilah and Rita Hayworth as Salome filled movie houses across the land. Cecil B. DeMille parted the Red Sea and explored Moses's love life in even bigger "spectacles." As for books, one out of every ten bought in America was religious. There was a rash of pop tunes, all "plugging" some spiritual truism or celebrating faith. Jukeboxes, radios, and television sets spewed forth religious ditties.

In 1900, 36% of the total American population was churched.

That number reached 49% in 1940, 60% in 1955. Thus, while it took four decades to increase the church-affiliated population from one-third to one-half, only 15 years were required to go from one-half to three-fifths of a rapidly expanding general population.

Religion under these circumstances tends to be compressed into arranged stereotypes and formulas of the mass media. It is "salable" religion, clearly and candidly cut to fit the requirements of ratings, box offices, and newsstand sales. A large part of it is under commercial rather than churchly auspices. It does not challenge, offend, or disturb. It is "useful" in fulfilling already established secular purposes.

The central theme of the popular revival is self-help. The American emphasis upon the technical is applied to the problems of spirit and soul. Religious writers, as they constantly explain, teach the "formulas," "the methods," the "secrets" by which the self may succeed. They do not suggest that religion might challenge the goals given the self. Religion is a source of techniques by which these goals might be more effectively realized. The correlation between spiritually induced power and worldly success is complete. By practicing the right spiritual techniques, one achieves greater income, fame, and position–in a word, success.

That is why there was no real difference between Eisenhower's prayer breakfasts, Billy Graham's engineering of mass consent, Norman Vincent Peale's positive thinking, Fulton J. Sheen's equating Christianity with Americanism, Rabbi Joshua L. Liebman's *Peace of Mind*, and various anticommunist crusades feeding upon McCarthyism, Korea, and Cold War.

American religion became less theological and liturgical, more chauvinistic and materialistic. Paul Tillich, a leading Protestant theologian, thought the revival was accompanied by loss in the dimension of depth. Perhaps the "Return to Religion" was nothing but a desperate and futile attempt to regain what had been lost. Our growth was horizontal, not vertical. The power of depth is most present in those who are aware of the loss–and are striving to regain it.

There was diminishing power of depth even in death–as Jessica Mitford's *The American Way of Death* showed. Following Evelyn Waugh's *The Loved Ones* and Ralph Hancock's *The Forest Lawn Story*, Mitford showed that deep human mourning was giving way to funeral directing. Avoidance and evasion took over, along with sympathy cards: bland, sentimental, shallow. One word seldom if ever used was *death*–let alone corpse, grave, worms, or decay. The sting had been removed.

It is one thing to read about the "American way of death," and another to live through it, as I did when my parents died. Numb with grief, one must walk through the neon-lit casket supermarket, starting with a bronze model reminiscent of the Pharaohs, with a salesman murmuring, "For those who *really* care . . .", looking down to the dimmer end, where the "cheap" gray caskets await–presumably for those who don't care. No need to go through the excruciating details. All told, we have commercialized grief and invented what Mark Twain called "a mean little ten-cent heaven about the size of Rhode Island."

Civil religion took over most of our national holidays–Independence Day, Memorial Day, Labor Day, the birthdays of Washington, Lincoln, and Martin Luther King. Thanksgiving involved less and less thanking and more and more eating. Both the turkey and the turkey-consumers were stuffed; how best to forget one's gluttony and relax? Watch a televised football game, of course. Easter remained religious for many, although new bonnets, rabbits, and egg rolls (including a well-publicized one on the White House lawn) increased. Christmas was tied up in an orgy of getting and spending. Staggering home from the mall, millions of Americans watched reruns of *White Christmas*, which became a church service at home in front of the tube. Bing Crosby's version of the title song is still the best-selling recording by a solo artist. Despite the title, the movie isn't religious at all. A group of former soldiers rally their buddies to save the postwar ski lodge of their old commander. Finally young girls dressed in fairy-princess costumes dance a ballet in front of a Christmas tree. The cast is drawn from all faiths (Bing Crosby was a Roman Catholic, Danny Kaye a Jew). Anyone is welcome, since there is no Christian doctrine or ritual. Even Frosty the Snowman or Rudolph the Red-Nosed Reindeer would feel at home. "The Man Upstairs" would understand.

But the zenith of the "chumminess cult" was reached when God became, in Jane Russell's inimitable phrase, "a livin' Doll." What relation has this kind of deity to the biblical God Who confronts sinful man as an enemy before He meets repentant man as a savior? Is this He of Whom we are told, "It is a fearful thing to fall into the hands of the living God" (Hebrews 10:31)?

So the dream of the New Israel and the Promised Land continued; we still sought the new order (*novus ordo seculorum*), the divinely sanctioned new beginning, different from and superior to the institutions of the Old World. This conviction, emerging out of American history, was nourished into the present century. The New World had to be new if it was to be anything at all. This conviction still remains in American life, hardly shaken by the new shape of the world and the Youthquake of the 1960s which seemed for a while to be destroying the old morality and everything the fundamentalists stood for.

Indeed, the American Century was fast turning into the American nightmare. Bloody assassinations (including President Kennedy, his brother Robert, and Martin Luther King, Jr.) shook our whole society. The counterculture turned sour, and became the Woodstock Nation. The pinprick that was Vietnam became an infection, then a cancer. A very un-American motto filled the air: "Hell no, I won't go."

Hippies and yippies scorned the religion which they considered part of the Establishment. Instead of Christianity they turned to astrology, witchcraft, cults, kinky sex, and reincarnation. Tired of conformity and consumerism, they dropped out and tuned in.

Youth culture found new idols in India's Ravi Shankar, the Maharishi, and various Eastern cults. One outspoken critic was India's Gita Mehta, who noted that while the West marketed Coca-Cola, the East peddled Karma Cola. (Karma means soul or spirit). "Give them games and riddles," he advised fellow Indians. "Tell them to beat each other, make love, do whatever comes into their heads."

One of the popular imports, Zen Buddhism, made converts of Jack Kerouac, Gary Snyder, and Alan Watts. Robert Pirsig's *Zen and the Art of Motorcycle Maintenance* was a bestseller. Then came scientology, Silva Mind Control, EST (Erhard Seminars Training) and other self-actualization techniques. Cycle Five was more than a Christian revival–it took in the whole world.

The American occult fostered its own "glamor elite." Louise Huebner became official witch of Los Angeles county while Sybil

Leek promoted her *Diary of a Witch*. There was also a booking agent for Soul Travel (Paul Twitchel) and a rector of the Church of Satan (Anton LaVey). Bands of saffron-robed followers of Hare Krishna gyrated on street corners as cymbals tinkled or sought donations in airports. Others ran away from home to join the Moonies (followers of Sun Myung Moon). Itinerant gurus gave various reasons for coming to our shores. Swami Sivanda, for example, found British Columbia a bit cold for meditation.

Jesus was far from forgotten. He became *Jesus Christ Superstar* and worked his *Godspell* on Broadway. The media was fascinated with Jesus Freaks, Jesus Trippers, and Street Christians. Jesus was "in"–merchants and hucksters made the most of it. Then the hysteria faded like flowers in the Flower Children's hands; discarded by a consumer society that wants a thrill every season and a Messiah every Monday.

The famous 1969 pilgrimage to Woodstock in upstate New York was the turning point. It was a modern Children's Crusade run amok. By the mid-1970s, after the chilling experience of Watergate, the nation sought new directions and leaders. Jimmy Carter became president in 1976.

The first president with an evangelical church connection since Garfield, he and his family powered fundamentalism's greatest prominence since the Scopes trial. Yet Carter was too liberal, too pragmatic for the New Religious Right. He was moral, sincere, hard-working; but he seemed unable to cope with mounting problems and inflation, and lost the religious following he once had. The new conservative choice was Ronald Reagan. He too got into the Oval Office–and stayed. He brought new people and a new attitude toward government; he definitely favored frontier virtues and old-time religion. Those who belonged to a subculture, the fundamentalists, began to form a counterculture. They had money, machines, and muscle; and they knew how to use them.

No one should underestimate their dreams, and determination to turn them into reality. Their ability to unseat politicians on all levels is well documented. Some of them even want to change the landscape. In 1982 Pierre Bedard announced that (with the Lord's help) he was going to turn a vast stretch of the Florida swampland into a theme park called "God's World." Everything would be state of the art. The domain would throb with "vivid color and thundering audio" and would feature a daily reenactment of the burning of Sodom and Gomorrah. One dared not ask who would be committed to the righteous flames.

That the American eagle flew over highly religious people long before the Europeans came is a fact that most of us tend to ignore. Native Indian culture was rich in origin myths, ritual cycles, and deep insights. Many of them still live, with the Navaho, Pueblo, Hopi, and other Indian tribes. Still other people living outside the European mythology–Africans, with immense symbolism and ritual–were forced to participate in the Euro-American dream. They were not paid performers, but slaves. This is the theme of Robert Bellah's book *The Broken Covenant: American Civil Religion on Trial* (1975). The trial continues. Much of the evidence is unexamined, and new material accumulates daily. No one knows what the outcome will be.[3]

The cutting edge of the civil religion argument is the First Amendment to the Constitution, assuring the separation of state and church. During the decades in which fundamentalists showed no political concern, and bland Protestantism prevailed in the White House, the tension was minimal. The candidacy, then election, of a Roman Catholic lit the fires. When John F. Kennedy ran for president in 1960, there were widespread Protestant predictions that if elected he would not keep the proper separation of church and state. In Houston, he responded to specific questions–whether he would send an ambassador to the Vatican, support financial aid for parochial schools, endorse school prayer, or reduce foreign aid because of the recipient's population control practices. He rejected all these propositions. Some 20 years later, President Ronald Reagan adopted every one of them.

Greatly heartened by Reagan's stance, fundamentalists hoped to reverse certain "liberal" decisions of the past decade affirming the church-state separation.[4] On June 5, 1985, the Supreme Court reaffirmed its insistence that government must pursue a course of complete neutrality toward religion, striking down an Alabama law allowing for a period of "meditation or voluntary prayer." The decision was clearly a victory for the pro-civil liberties advocates, and a setback for the fundamentalists. Jerry Falwell promptly labeled the decision as discriminatory and hypocritical: "The court seems to be telling Americans, an overwhelming majority of whom want the return of voluntary prayer to public schools, that a dose of herpes is to be tolerated, but a dose of God is not."[5]

Simultaneously Pat Robertson, president and founder of Christian Broadcasting Network, urged his flock to "continue their struggle to secure an interpretation of the First Amendment which accords with American history . . ."[6] At the time this decision was handed down by the court, 25 states had "moments of silence" laws.

One thing is sure: fundamentalists will never be silent again. Perhaps they have, as Jerry Falwell claims, hijacked the jumbo jet of evangelism. Certainly they have made billboards out of a million car bumpers, which have stickers reading: Honk If You Love Jesus; God Bless America; and God, Guns and Guts–They Made America. American flags wave in the church, and God's name is invoked whenever lawmakers meet. It was also invoked in the White House, by the conservative, God-fearing Reagan who in 1984 carried the largest number of electoral votes in the nation's history.

Although many of the policies of the country changed with the election of the more liberal Democrat Bill Clinton to the presidency in 1992, the emphasis on religion and the struggles over separation of church and state continued. Some even thought that the Christian Coalition was gaining power and prestige.

Have the new conservatism and the new religious right converged? How will this affect both our civil religion and our Christianity? If the tide of religiosity is rising, how high will it rise, and what will it wash away? The one thing we can say about the future is that anything we say now may be wrong.

NOTES

1. The classic book on this topic is Will Herberg, *Protestant, Catholic, Jew* (New York: Garden City, 1955). His other major book for our purposes is entitled *On Academic Freedom* (Washington: American Enterprise Institute, 1971).

2. Gunther reflects well the attitudes of this period, in his long series of best-sellers. See especially *Inside USA* (New York: Harper and Bros., 1947).

3. Bellah continued his work in this field, and published *Habits of the Heart* (Berkeley: University of California Press, 1985). The book has been widely read and praised.

4. This was the origin of what the media came to call the "New Religious Right." See Robert C. Liebman and Robert Wuthnow, eds., *The New Christian Right: Mobilization and Legitimation* (New York: Aldine, 1983).

5. See the Roanoke-*Times*, June 7, 1985, p. 3.

6. Since Pat Robertson has his own television network, many of his pronouncements are made on air. For a discussion of his interpretation of the First Amendment, see his book entitled *America's Dates with Destiny* (New York: Nelson, 1986), chapter 3. He extends his views to a global scale in *The New World Order* (New York: G. K. Hall, 1992).

Chapter 8

Secular Salvation

One need not go to church to be "saved." America has made salvation the Siamese twin of consumerism. You need only eat, dress, and smell right to "make it." How do you learn about all these things? From the media–so that each medium is in its own way our mentor. Electrified, computerized, and televised, we are programmed for our own special salvation.

Ancient Sparta was a military state, ancient Israel a religious state, modern England an industrial state. The United States became the world's first media state. Media have become many things: the message, the money, the monster, the Messiah. Our very atmosphere has become a mediatmosphere.

Everyman has become Everyfan. In *Everyman*, the medieval English morality play, the hero is a Christian trying to face the hardships and temptations of that time. His hope and salvation is the church, and organized religion. In our day, organized sports have, for many, replaced organized religion. The medium of television, our indoor chapel, seems to confirm this. We see game after game, sport after sport, in and out of season. One baseball game takes more telecast time than a year's reporting on the United Nations by all major networks combined.

Being imperially big business–up from thousands to millions of bucks–sport has turned to technology (like all major corporations) to maximize profits: astroturf, springier pole vault poles, in-helmet football radios, computerized scouting, and rabbit baseballs. Why not? Put your money where your heart is. Sport smacks of divinity.[1]

Sports as ritual, opiate, obsession, yes. But religion? That depends on definitions. If religion is whatever we consider ultimately important (as Paul Tillich held) consider this true tale: recently the

Denver Broncos had a bad day and fumbled seven times against the Chicago Bears. One fan–Everyfan–couldn't stand it. "I have been a Broncos fan since they got organized," he scribbled in his suicide note. "I can't stand it any more." Then he shot himself in the head–a splendid example of ultimate commitment. "In God we trust" has been replaced by "We're Number One." Are superstars, coaches, or bowl games surrogate "God pumpers?" Sports are well on the way to being the largest single waking activity of modern life. Half the American population watches bowl games over New Year's.

Sports in modern America has become so gigantic an enterprise that no one can keep up with all aspects of it–or even with sports literature. More than half a century ago, the philosopher Max Scheler noted the growth, and wondered if we saw it in the proper context: "Scarcely an international phenomenon deserves social and psychological study as does sport," he wrote in 1927. "Sports has grown immeasurably in scope and social importance, but its meaning has received little serious attention."[2]

Sports have infiltrated–perhaps dominated–American education, and form a separate subculture when they become "big time." When two teams–often two towns, states, or nations–"clash," we revert to primitive tribalism. Not only boxing, but ice hockey, wrestling, soccer, and football have become blood sports. On all levels there is elaborate ritualism (songs, yells, marches, masks, animal imitation) and iconography (trophies, banners, floats, marches). Whole nations rally behind a "winning team." Holding a forefinger up to television cameras (We're Number One!") is to be, for one brief shining moment, in Camelot.

Observe the bumper stickers all across the land: Smile, God Loves You; I Believe in My Country; Love It or Leave It; Honk if You Love Jesus. And yell if you have your favorite team. At the basis of organized spectator sports there must be consensus, community consciousness, shared values. Every society has mechanisms to generate such feelings; in modern America, organized sports are taking over the role of organized religion. Are not our young millionaires rising not out of business and industry, but professional sports?

The sporting event itself is only the eye of the storm; the real waves are made by books, magazines, films, and reconstructions which surround it. For everyone who enjoys sports-through-vision, there are thousands who must be content with sports-through-journalism. Hundreds of sportswriters turn out thousands of words to fill this huge gap. Watch people read a newspaper–a large number begin by turning to the sports page. For more information, and more careful analysis, there are dozens of magazines, like *Sporting News, Pro Football Weekly*, and *Sports Illustrated*, with features, exposes, pictures, tables, and predictions. Here the target isn't so much the fan as the affluent leisure-time audience–which runs into the millions.

There are distinct categories for sports books, including:

1. How to–who can resist them?
2. Records and statistics–absolutely necessary to any serious or dedicated fan.
3. Biographies and revelations–to take the place of the "Lives of the Saints" and Sunday school literature.
4. Histories–here nostalgia plays a major role; the best histories serve the same purpose as (3) above.
5. Coffee-table picture books–to impress neighbors and visitors.
6. Analytical books–for those who are really "into" a particular sport or problem.

One need not depend on print for sports news and excitement. Broadcasts allow us to be absentee spectators, with the outer eye in television, and the mind's eye in radio. They enhance attitudes, impressions, and emotions of those actually *at* the game. But only on television can you see the "magic moment" again–by instant replay. Thus does the medium triumph over time.

We got our national sport, baseball, when we finally got a united nation–after the Civil War. In rules and strategy, the game was played and understood exactly the same way in the remotest corners of the Union. It was a boon to a nation that had no royal family, no threatening neighbors, and millions of immigrants who could pick up this point of reference quickly and easily.

Professional sports took the place of cross and crown in a suddenly industrialized America. In sports, success was clearly defined. Attachment to a sports figure involved little conflict with other identifications (national origin, religion, politics) that might otherwise cause discomfort.

We can make analogies to the "pluck and luck" aspects of the Success Myth. In football, the tackling and blocking imply that while there are hard knocks in the world, good guys overcome them. Instant replays suggest that time is recoverable–not lost in the flux of life. This in turn suggests immortality. Other parallels between football and religion can be made:

Religion	*Professional Football*
Saints	Superstars
Sunday Service	Sunday Game
Offering	Ticket
Ecumenical Movements	The Great Merger
Knight Seeking Holy Grail	Player Seeking Super Bowl

People need myth, ceremony and ritual which football supplies in place of organized religion. As religion "demythologizes" and becomes more and more rational, football becomes more mysterious and fantastic–with attacks and formations that function the way theology does for the religious.

America has a genius for inventing religions. There may be more religions in southern California than in any part of the world. Where would one expect to go for the Rose Bowl, except sunny southern California?

By 1900, American sports had changed dramatically from a mainly amateur gentlemen's pastime into highly commercial competitive business. A simultaneous change took place in rural people, herded into large, impersonal, often brutalizing cities. The natural impulses of generosity, elation, and heroism had to find and flow in new channels, like sports. In an impersonal, irreligious society, sports of all kinds offer an activity in which community and pride can emerge again; and in which ceremony can flourish. Sport is the art of the people. The vast public ritual of mass spectator sports is the last heroic drama of a community that has exhausted its religious heritage.

Think what sporting events mean to working-class people everywhere, as they go off to the stadium, spread out in a long line from pavement to pavement, eyes bright, yelling snatches of pop tunes. They are like children anticipating Christmas. When actuality lives up to imagination–the play, music, and sport are as good as we hoped they would be–then we are fulfilled. Sports were popular in Egypt and had strong religious overtones. The Olympic games of the Greeks (like the Pythian, Isthmian, Nemean, and Athenaic) were sacred festivals, integral aspects of the religious life of the Hellenes. They were sacred games, staged in a sacred place and at a sacred festival–a religious act in honor of the deity. Those who took part, did so in order to serve the gods. The Olympic games had their roots in religion.

Parallels between sports and religion continue everywhere. Today, music is frequently used, being one of the quickest awakeners of the corporate conscience. (What is a football game without a band?) Behind the electronic sound are ancient rites and primordial dreams. No matter how much they have been changed or cheapened by commercialism (have not rites always lined someone's pockets?), they are religious.

This use of the word "religion" offends some because our regarding religion as an *institution* sometimes prevents us from seeing the sacred or sacrosanct in everyday life. We *want* religion locked into a pietistic Sunday morning service, and we mold our language accordingly. Look at the faces of people listening to Easter sermons on the church's Super Sunday (Easter), and compare them with faces watching football's Super Sunday. Where is there more involvement, *angst, redemption*?

Everyman's metamorphosis to Everyfan is little studied or understood. Anyone can make qualitative judgments; little quantitative information is available. A stopwatch can provide new insights. There is surprisingly little action in TV's "action filled" bowl games. Pre- and postgame activities consume 20% of the TV time, advertising another 15%, comments, between-play and halftime another 40%. Much of the remaining 25% scoreboard clock time goes for huddles, decisions, and penalties. In fact, during the four-hour telecast, there is *less than ten minutes* when the football is actually in motion.

Media myths function in a manner similar to traditional mythic attitudes, providing personal identification, heroic archetypes, communal focuses, and temporal frames of reference. "In the classical manner of mythical beliefs and religious activities," Michael Real writes, "the Super Bowl is a communal celebration of and indoctrination into specific socially dominant emotions, life-styles, and values."[3]

The annual Super Bowl parallels the spectacles of Rome's Coliseum, where the spoils of imperialism were grandiosely celebrated. As a game, the Super Bowl is not a simple traditional diversion like playing a hand of cards. Football is an aggressive, strictly regulated team game fought between males who use both violence and technology to win. It propagates these values by elevating football to the level of a mythic spectacle.[4]

What is at stake in a "friendly game" is a minutely observed and monitored battle between highly skilled males who use cunning, deceit, and power to attain their ends. Does this sound like a corporation or bureaucracy? Is sports a mirror image of Life Out There?

Has not America always played the game on God's side, bound to be perennial world champions? "We're number one" is no mere exercise in arithmetic; it's a covenant with Jehovah. We're the greatest. We love our heroes and give them special names. How about "Gentleman" Jim Corbett, Stan "The Man" Musial, and "Mean" Joe Green? (Green's fusion with the Coke bottle created one of the all-time great television commercials.) After years outside the "sacred circle," blacks are admitted now. Jackie Robinson was the archetypal gentleman, and the nation so honored him during the opening ceremonies of baseball's 1972 World Series. Hank Aaron broke Babe Ruth's home-run record; and Muhammad Ali was "the greatest."

They fade fast; the last years of once-famous athletes provide materials for Greek tragedies. We strut quickly across the stage, have our moments, and disappear into the darkness.

"Super Sunday" no longer means Easter for many Americans, but the day professional football players battle for the "crown of glory" in the Super Bowl. A whole generation has been raised to honor this event.

Can we include this in a book on popular religion? How can we speak of theology–Queen of Heaven–in the same breath with popular culture? What do they have in common? Both deal with right and wrong, tears and laughter, life and death. If religion is that which we take seriously, how can we say that the Super Bowl isn't "religious?"

Football has acquired sacred songs, places (stadiums and bowls), pleas (Fight team fight!), colors (Go Big Red!), symbols (flags, banners) decorated with totems (eagles, lions, antlers).

The search for a new universe and new gods has bred a terrible urgency, even desperation, which highlights such things as revivalism, awakenings, satanism, and occultism. These things seem to have taken the place of eschatology, theology, and liturgics.

Meanwhile, back at the stadium, the Big Game is on, and players, officials, and fans have all put on special *personae*. Clothing changes: loud colors, parkas, blankets–perhaps gaudy pennants. Into the coat pocket are stuffed dollar bills, for popcorn, peanuts, and hot dogs; the most important item (the flask) is hidden, worn close to the heart. So dressed, the fan fights his way to a congested parking lot where he can inhale enough carbon monoxide to supplement his alcoholic input, and assure body reaction. There may be a parking lot party. Then he marches onward and upward, looking for the elusive seat, searching (like saints of old) for the Holy Grail, the sacred football. Eventually the flask will be dry and the scoreboard numbers blurred. Then the theophany: "Damn, I *love* sports!"

So do our national leaders, no matter what their policies or politics. For decades the president of the United States has "thrown the first ball" to open the baseball season. President Nixon's aides took advantage of "the football vote," and cultivated it. Nixon was the first president to attend a regular pro football game in the regular season. On several occasions he made televised visits to locker rooms after the game, and flew to Green Bay (professional football's spiritual capital) to attend a testimonial dinner for quarterback Bart Starr. What was the President doing when 250,000 anti-Vietnam demonstrators were outside the White House on a Saturday afternoon in November 1969? Watching the Purdue-Ohio State football game.

Then Nixon was gone and a Hollywood actor who had starred in a football film about Notre Dame's "Fighting Irish" was in the White House. By 1982, Ronald Reagan's America was mired in a grim recession; no segment of the economy had been harder hit than the automobile industry. Recessions come and go: but Super Bowls partake of the eternal. The football owners chose Pontiac, Michigan for Super Bowl XVI, played between San Francisco and Cincinnati

on January 24, 1982. All the rituals and incantations were performed as usual. San Francisco won, and cheers went out throughout the land. Once again, Super Sunday had lived up to its name.
The fans could wend their way home, tired, even exhausted. The
technicians could rewind their miles of cables and wires, and editors could go through miles of films made from a score of cameras,
to isolate "the right shots." Now everyone must work at keeping
the memory, the exhilaration, the liturgy, alive. These are the real
trophies and the commemorations. A man may lose his job, but no
one can take his religion away from him.

A new breed of "Jock Evangelist" has worked to fuse sports and
religion. Muscular Christianity is in, team prayers have become all
but mandatory. Jesus the consoler has deferred to Christ the competitor. One indication of this is the mushrooming FCA (Fellowship
of Christian Athletes) with the motto: "Until a person knows where
the spiritual home plate is, how can he get the ball over?" Dr. Louis
Evans, "Doc" Eshleman, and Tom Skinner have prospered by
sanctifying sweat and blessing bruises. Their prayers bring back the
memory of Billy Sunday: "God, if you ever helped mortal man,
help me get that ball!"

In *The Joy of Sports*, Michael Novak suggests that in contemporary America sports serve as "natural religions" (also morality
plays?); the holy trinity is baseball, basketball, and football. Spectators perform a sacramental act–paralleling that which their ances-
tors got by going to church. Both church and stadium are places of
renewal and sanctity.

Bob Hill interviewed dozens of born-againers for his book *The
Making of a Super Pro*. Rocketed into instant fame, as millions
watched their every move from different camera angles, right there
on the instant replay, they leave the locker room to face the toughest
backfield of all: boredom, loneliness, weariness, and slumps. With
more money than they ever dreamed of having, many turn to alco-
hol, sex, drugs–then to Jesus. He alone gives them a permanent
high: Jesus the perfect coach with the perfect game plan. Hence the
apt title of Bill Glass's book *Don't Blame the Game*. "It's a highly
pressurized existence," Glass points out. "Our society is drawn into
sharp contrast: if you're pagan, you're very pagan. It's either 'I'm
gonna be a committed Christian' or 'I'm gonna overdose.' "

Some pro players "tell their own stories"–with a little help from ghostwriters, editors, and publicists. Roger Staubach, star quarterback for the Dallas Cowboys, published his autobiography *(First Down, Lifetime to Go)* in 1974. A devout Roman Catholic, he won games with what writers liked to call "Hail Mary passes." NFL "Player of the Year," he had no trouble justifying the vast sums of money he hurled into fried-chicken franchises and Ronald Reagan's campaign. "I do think it's okay to have money," Staubach said in an interview. "Even the apostles weren't perfect–they were fickle. We don't have the opportunity ourselves to stick our hands into the wounds."

Nor does Everyfan get to see the human price paid for the rituals and extravaganzas he loves so well. He goes from game to game, strength to strength, just as did Everyman before him. Only poets and philosophers, like T. S. Eliot, catch the larger implications:

Go, go said the bird;
Mankind cannot stand too much reality.[5]

NOTES

1. The preeminence of spectator sports is manifest in all the media, especially newspapers, magazines, and television; so there seems no need for elaborate endnotes to this chapter. Bear in mind that spectator sports are the largest single waking activity of modern life. If one were to choose a single comprehensive summary, it might be James A. Michener, *Sports in America* (New York: Random House, 1976).

2. Max Scheler, *Selected Philosophical Essays* (Evanston: Northwestern University, 1973). An exception is the spring 1983 issue of the *Journal of Popular Culture*, which examines the inner significance of sports in our culture.

3. Michael Real, *Mass Mediated America* (New York: Prentice-Hall, 1977), p. 199. This is one of the most perceptive accounts of the relationship of sports and religion.

4. Perhaps that is why, by the time Super Bowl XXVII was "staged" in Pasadena, California's Rose Bowl in 1993, the celebration had extended beyond the game to include a whole week of pregame revelry, publicity stunts, performances by models, and talk shows.

5. T. S. Eliot, *Collected Poems, 1909-1935* (New York: Harcourt Brace, 1936), p. 89.

Chapter 9

Religion on the Airwaves

As long as the money lasts, my voice is yours.
So long as my voice lasts, I shall fight your battles.

–Charles E. Coughlin

Three o'clock, Sunday afternoon: Father Coughlin time. Those who had radios gathered round them. Those who didn't visited a neighbor, or walked down to the barbershop or Ford agency, where there was a communal receiver. Talk and laughter ceased; people seemed almost to stop breathing. Then Father Coughlin spoke. It was like the word of God.

During the Depression this obscure priest became a celebrity, a cult figure. He was idolized. "So far as audience response is concerned," said *Fortune* magazine in May 1936, "Coughlin is the biggest thing that ever happened to radio."

How big? Neither Rudy Vallee nor Burns and Allen matched him. No other program could compete. When asked to choose between their symphony orchestra and Coughlin, Philadelphia voted 187,000 to 12,000 for Coughlin. People said he could be president. Some went further: had Christ come back to save us?

Coughlin, "the Radio Priest," reached more people than all Christ's disciples combined. He not only reached them, but also their pockets. Since his radio ministry was completely tax-exempt, no one knew his income. But after asking listeners for a single dollar on a Sunday broadcast, he went to a Detroit bank on Thursday to deposit box-loads of dollar bills. Postal money orders went into the millions. Like the electronic preachers who followed him, Father Coughlin recorded the names of all contributors. By 1934 his file had over 2 million names. "I believe," he said without a blush of modesty, "I possess in them the greatest human document of our time."

Our time–that was the key. A grim lean time when America's breadbasket, the Farm Belt, was running out of bread. Farms were mortgaged, mines closed, steel mills operated at 12% capacity. The stock market collapsed, and nothing would revive it. On July 8, 1932, the market average slipped down to 58. When asked for a room in a high-rise hotel, clerks would ask, "For sleeping or jumping?" Not only were there no buyers for many crops–you couldn't even give them away. Everything nailed down was coming loose. Men moved from snug cottages to hobo jungles. Two pop songs summed it up: "Can I Sleep in Your Barn Tonight, Mister?" and "Brother, Can You Spare a Dime?"

In industrial areas like Detroit, where Father Coughlin lived, money and hope were running out. Who was to blame? He knew– and with that special self-righteousness of the religious zealot, he told the country, again and again. He ushered in the Electric Gospel and the Invisible Church.

He understood that radio was one of the great inventions of the century, since it brought the world into the living room. Radio provided sound, listeners filled in the rest with their imagination. It gave listeners the sense of having heard things exactly as they happened, when they happened. By closing the time gap, radio did something neither film nor recording could do. Radio, Coughlin began to understand, was the perfect device for his ministry. It could improve on actuality itself.[1]

He also understood the political opportunities and implications of radio, as did the president he first endorsed and then denounced, Franklin D. Roosevelt. The President's "Fireside Chats" are always cited as the media events of the early 1930s; but Father Coughlin's sermons were powerful too. His velvet voice and flair for the spoken word enabled him to spread his ideas and stir emotions as few if any preachers have done since. He helped make radio the most popular medium of the Depression years–more so than newspapers or films. A poll in 1937 showed that an American home was more apt to have a radio than indoor plumbing or a telephone. Another poll that same year found that Americans were more satisfied with radio than religion–though Father Coughlin managed to merge the two.[2]

Today Coughlin's emulators are legion, filling not only radio but television, recording studios, and satellites with their salvation salvos. For a while, many considered this priest the most dangerous man in America. Now, in retrospect, he seems more like the rock on which the radio church was built.

His origins were humble, his start inauspicious. In 1891 he was born in Hamilton, Ontario, of a Canadian mother and an American father. The Coughlins were pick-and-shovel Irish: his great grandfather helped build the Erie Canal. His father, Thomas, one of 12 children, was poorly educated and victimized by strong anti-Irish Catholic sentiment. So he went to sea, shoveled coal, and got typhoid fever. Hospitalized in Canada, he resolved to stay there and became a church sexton. He married a young seamstress who attended mass every day. Their infant daughter died at three months; their son, Charles, was raised as an only child in religious surroundings. He entered St. Michael's College, which trained priests. He was raised tough and played rough. As fullback on the football team, he finished the game even after his jaw was fractured. Eventually he graduated from the University of Toronto, took his vows, and studied for the priesthood as a novice in the religious order of St. Basil.[3]

In 1916 Charles was ordained and assigned to St. Agnes Church in Detroit. Always adept at public speaking and preaching, he wrote and rewrote, polished and practiced his sermons. The more he preached, the more people came. Handsome, confident, articulate, he was well on the way to mastering skills that would make him a weekly visitor into millions of homes.

Incardinated into the Detroit diocese in 1923, Coughlin was briefly in Kalamazoo, then back to a major church in Detroit. A super-preacher, well liked by his bishop, Michael Gallagher, he was soon given his own church in North Branch. When the Bishop returned from Rome, having attended the canonization rites of St. Therese, the Little Flower, he decided to erect a church in her honor in the Detroit suburb of Royal Oak. A poor town pockmarked by vacant lots, it was a stronghold of the Ku Klux Klan. With fewer than 30 Roman Catholic families, it would require a dynamic, aggressive, young priest. Why not Charles E. Coughlin?

Off he went to Royal Oak–to "make a missionary oasis in the desert of bigotry." The church was hardly completed before the Klan burned a cross on the lawn with this sign: "Move from Royal Oak." The Klan had misjudged their man. Coughlin would not only stay, he would make Royal Oak a shrine, a household name around America. That would take some doing.

He decided to combine theology and theater. To start, he arranged to have Babe Ruth and other Yankee baseball stars come to his shrine. The church was mobbed; Ruth and his teammates took up a collection before they allowed anyone to enter. They raked in over $10,000 (giving no change) and helped Coughlin expand his work. How could he be a national spokesman? Coughlin decided the answer was radio.

It was a brilliant gamble. Many immigrants who couldn't read English depended on the radio. So did thousands of others, recently introduced to the magic box. Optimists were even predicting that some day most American homes would have a radio. Suppose they were willing to hear a Sunday sermon without leaving home? Why not use his God-given voice, which so many admired, to reach thousands, perhaps millions, by air? If the disciples used the roads, why couldn't he use the radio?

The beginnings of the Electronic Church were modest. Founding Father Coughlin paid only $58 a week for the telephone lines which carried his broadcasts from the church to Detroit station WJR. His membership fee for the Radio League of the Little Flower–a dollar a year–seems equally miniscule in today's age of televangelism. The initial broadcast on October 3, 1926, called the "Golden Hour of the Little Flower," was aimed primarily at children. Perhaps the Electronic Church has not changed its content much in 60 years.

For three years, Coughlin's range was local. In the fall of 1929, Chicago and Cincinnati stations were linked in. The big breakthrough came in 1930 when his broadcast was carried by Columbia Broadcasting System. The Irish priest in suburban Michigan had made the big time.

In his January 12, 1930 radio address Coughlin launched an all-out attack on Bolshevism, which he said was destroying family life in Russia. This was a major theme for the rest of his career. Not only did he attack the Godless Russians, he also called upon American capitalism to eliminate the Communist appeal by providing fair wages for workers. From the first, he knew mixing religion and economics was potentially dangerous:

> I know my pilgrimage is both treacherous and narrow. On the one side there are the quicksands of idealism, of radical socialism, in whose depths there are buried both the dreams of the poet and the ravings of the revolutionist. On the other side are the smiling acres of Lotus Land, where it is always afternoon, always springtime, always inactivity.

Eventually, Charles E. Coughlin got caught between those two sides, denounced by both politicians and churchmen. But for a while, he succeeded beyond anyone's expectations. He was well trained and well grounded in Catholic doctrine–in many ways a model priest. His own bishop was extremely supportive. A major papal document–Pope Leo XIII's *Rerum Novarum*, the social justice encyclical, provided a focus for bishop, priest, and public in a time of gross economic injustice. Father Coughlin was a strong and sincere critic of capitalism, although he never advocated its overthrow. He defended private ownership and followed the standard line of St. Thomas Aquinas on the use of private property:

> The temporal goods which God permits to a man are his in regard to property. But in regard to use they are not his alone, but others' also who can be sustained by what is superfluous for him. If the individual owner neglects his social responsibilities, it is the duty of the state to enforce them.

The Catholic hierarchy was aware of Coughlin's growing popularity. Severe critics, like William Cardinal O'Connell of Boston, were offset by Coughlin's own bishop, the easygoing Michael James Gallagher, who urged Coughlin to propagate the social encyclicals. Pope Pius XI's issuance of *Quadragesimo Anno* in 1931–an updated reiteration of social doctrine on the fortieth anniversary of *Rerum Novarum*–strengthened Coughlin's hand.

Still, it was not his sources but his speaking which made the difference. If radio magic depends heavily on the speaker's voice, Coughlin used his like a musical instrument, going from high and plaintive to deep and solemn, trilling his r's, with his deep Irish brogue resonating deep in his chest, ringing like a bell. His was a voice made for promises. It was, Wallace Stegner reported, "a voice of such mellow richness, such heart-warming intimacy, such emotional and ingratiating charm, that anyone turning past it almost automatically returned to hear it again. His was without a doubt one of the great speaking voices of the twentieth century."

By 1933 listeners were contributing approximately $5 million yearly to the Radio League of the Little Flower–enough cash for Coughlin to pay all his bills and plan bold new ventures. He repeatedly reminded his audience that without contributions he would be forced off the air. Indeed, as his national network expanded to carry his message to more cities across the country, the bill for rental of radio lines climbed to $50,000 a week. With clerical staff salaries to pay and mailing costs to cover, Father Coughlin needed and got generous support. He also got a tower at his shrine: 111 feet high, made of granite and marble, costing over half a million dollars.

His motivation may have been theological–to spread the Word– but the immediate goals were political. Conversion was never Coughlin's main theme. His theological views were orthodox, not evangelical. He showed no interest in the dogmas that separated Protestants and Catholics, or ways to reconcile them. The church was his platform, not his refuge.

Always aware of key issues, Coughlin entered the lists against Prohibition. In three 1931 speeches, he gave the supporters of Prohibition the full Coughlin treatment. His sharp Irish wit was never more evident than when he belittled those more anxious to stop some from drinking than to start the hungry eating. But he chose a bigger target when he entered the mainstream of American politics in October 1931–the President of the United States. Berating Herbert Hoover for not taking effective action to combat the Depression, Coughlin spoke for countless Americans when he said the economic crisis could not be cured "by waiting for things to adjust themselves and by eating the airy platitudes of those so-called leaders who have been busy assuring us that the bottom has been reached and that prosperity and justice are 'just around the corner.'"

There were many and complex reasons for Coughlin's urban Catholic following. The Radio Priest, in channeling their anger, promoted a kind of inverted nativism. The hunted of the past could now be the hunters. Those who had suffered because, in truth or in fantasies, they had been considered unequal by the more established and richer groups, could now turn the tables on the oppressors. If, as Coughlin argued, the wealthy Anglo-Saxon Protestant elite of the East Coast were a gang of internationalists and exploiters, then his own followers were at last vindicated. They were more honest, more democratic, and more American than their enemies. And they well deserved the brand of social justice he offered.

Coughlin's strength lay in his instinctive feeling for his radio public and his ability to manipulate them. He prided himself in presenting "plain facts for plain people, in plain language." Not so. He took facts and wove them into highly opinionated conclusions; catered to the have-nots by damning the haves; and embellished his sermons with emotional phrases and flourishes. His strategy was not to inform, but to inflame.

Image-making was his potent weapon. Thus, he called Christ back "to gaze into the open window of a sweatshop," urged the Unknown Soldier "to return to visit his brother," saw the banker "turn down the sweating farmer, who put bread on America's table." These images people could understand and long remember. Listen as Coughlin appeals to the veterans, millions of whom had fought in Europe and now starved in America: "Oh, soldier boys, I ask you in the name of those thousands who today join with me in memory of your heroism, to count each tear as a precious pearl which we lay at the throne of Almighty God!"

What did Father Coughlin stand for? Authority, stemming from Mother Church, but rehired in the secular world as well. He liked the strong hand—even the mailed fist; hated socialism, Communism, and bankers; and inherited an anti-Semitism which in his generation was more condoned than criticized by the Church.

As he grew older, a new trinity of key words emerged: frustration, anger, and hate. Yet he survived. Millions inside and outside the church viewed Coughlin as the leading crusader against Communism, the deadly enemy of Catholicism. Red-baiting reached a new high as he beamed out his weekly messages over the airwaves.

When the Russians discarded matrimony, they "replaced it with a license for legalized lust." How did this affect society? "The Bolshevists wrung the lamentable but logical conclusion of Christlessness from the skull and crossbones of murdered Russian family life." Nor was this sacrilege confined to Russia. America was "seriously tainted with the purple poison of Bolshevism and its doctrines." What of the scholars and intellectuals who condoned the socialist experience? They "dig in the literary muck heap for reference data until they become dizzy with dirt, their moral sense having become confused and benumbed by the Red Fog which enshrouds them."

Thus it was that in six years–from 1926 to 1932–he helped shape the nature of American Christianity. Estimates of his radio audience vary, of course; some are as high as 30 million. We have a more accurate notion of the amount of mail he received: by 1932 he was using 106 clerks and four personal secretaries. Later on his stenographic staff reached 145; the basement of his shrine tower looked like the post office of a middle-sized city. In Detroit his own printing press produced millions of sermons and brochures to mail out. Fifty years before the high-powered televangelists of the 1980s, Coughlin knew how to combine and exploit different forms of communication. The Comptroller of Detroit reported that Coughlin was getting 25,000 letters a day, with a following "just about equal to that of Gandhi." Thousands of pilgrims came to Royal Oak. An imposing man (in 1932 he weighed 200 pounds), good-humored and charming, Coughlin exuded charisma. He never seemed self-serving. Unlike many of today's God pumpers, he did not dazzle with diamonds, or supplement baptismal fonts with swimming pools. He lived in a small house by his church with his devoted parents, his mother serving as the rectory housekeeper. The priest's inseparable companion was Pal, a huge Great Dane, who became a favorite with tourists.

This down-home quality helps explain Coughlin's rapid rise to fame and influence. The nation was in desperate straits when he expanded his national radio career in 1930. The times made the man. Like Roosevelt, whose "Fireside Chats" became a leading factor in political image-making, Coughlin understood and utilized the radio–before Roosevelt. Our television generation can scarcely realize the attraction of radio to the average American in the 1930s. It was a cherished member of the family. Favorite programs drew millions of avid listeners. Father Coughlin's Sunday talks became a weekly ritual for millions who would hush their children and hang on every word. To these people Coughlin was the one man whose views they could trust. After all, he was a priest dedicated to social justice, not a politician seeking votes. This was the word of God.

That Coughlin's ministry took on a strong political overtone—even a messianic calling–is certain. Just when this occurred, why, and how is hard to say. Well-schooled in Catholic theology and devoted to the hierarchy, he never saw himself as a rebel or apostate. But he was lured on by the power he had, and wielded. He was like Faust, who suddenly could change lives and opinions–and enjoyed doing so.

Pleased to perceive this, Coughlin decided to expand his radio operation. He approached network officials, who were leery of his explosive method and style. When refused time on the National Broadcasting Company (NBC), Coughlin decided to set up his own network. The idea worked. Within a year he had 26 stations stretching from Maine to Colorado–possibly the prototype of the Christian Broadcasting Network, which Pat Robertson set up half a century later.

The network was an ideal vehicle for his growing talents and ambitions. While assistants handled the other church business and services, Coughlin concentrated on radio sermons, obsessed with making them irresistible. He revised, refined, reworked–honing his style to a razor-sharp weapon. Every word was written to be heard, not read. The imagery was carefully selected. His vague but powerful style was used to full advantage. Radio transmitted nuances and subtle emotions denied to print. At the same time, it tended to arrest in the listener those critical impulses that would cause a reader to turn back to the imperfectly understood. Coughlin learned to manipulate his unseen audience.

His following grew larger, his technique more effective. His oratorical style became a blend of biting irony and well-ordered rhetoric, with popular wisecracks and vulgarisms thrown in along with biblical references. The use of "damn," "swell," and "lousy" added zest to his speech, his hearers enjoying them all the more because they came from a priest. These words gave warmth to his discussions of economic problems and brought him closer to his disembodied audience.

Finding that ringing assertions and righteous fury brought a far better response than the balanced and objective statement, he coined phrases designed to alarm his listeners, such as "Christ or chaos," or "Roosevelt or ruin." He even attempted to tie Communism to free love by proclaiming, "It is either the marriage feast of Cana or the brothel of Lenin!"

Listing names was another important part of his radio technique. It was more dramatic and persuasive to assail J. P. Morgan or Kuhn and Loeb than simply "bankers," and better to point at Hoover and Mellon than "politicians." He discovered that personalities were attention-getters, and soon their names were filling his speeches.

He and two contemporaries–Franklin D. Roosevelt and Adolf Hitler–changed history by mastering the microphone. For those born and raised with television, it was an achievement hard to comprehend; and it will never be repeated.

The crux of Coughlin's appeal, like that of Hitler, was not love but hatred. He sensed, and took advantage of, the neurotic anxiety all around him. He provided a conflict in which angry members of his audience could know and confront their real enemies. He focused on individuals–which he took care to name–who were devilish conspirators. Join my army, he promised, and we will overcome.

Gradually he developed not only his own rhetoric, but also a social dynamic. He named individuals, but presented stereotypes and caricatures of heartless bankers and arrogant businessmen: the anglicized arrogant Eastern elite. They would destroy the small farmer and businessman–a theme bound to appeal to the old Populist strain. Rich, well-educated Easterners were the real villains: "Congressmen from New York City," the "Wall Street attorney," "the erudition of Harvard, of Yale, of Princeton, of Columbia," and the bankers with their "grouse hunting estates in Scotland" who never traveled west of Buffalo. For poor urban Catholics or impoverished Western farmers, this was explosive material; they were often willing to turn their unrest into hostility toward individuals they were told had caused them suffering and denied them access to better lives.

Coughlin's sermons were flowery, emotional, and quotable.[4] He knew all the tricks of the propagandist, from name-calling to glittering generality. A favorite Coughlin technique was the dramatic dichotomy, in which "modern bands of exploitation" were aligned against the "little children, ill-clad mothers, care-worn fathers . . . on the bleak, blizzardy countryside." The "widows and orphans and inarticulate farmers" would be at the mercy of the "devouring hordes" of the enemy if not for Coughlin, who offered himself as the defender of ". . . servant girls, . . . laborers, (and) children." Indeed the priest never missed an opportunity to tell his followers of the great personal peril, perhaps even physical danger, he was risking by fighting their battles. He might exclaim that he had "sacrificed the right of natural . . . fatherhood to be the spiritual father . . . to thousands of boys . . . on the snow clad dunes of the Dakotas."

Using picture images to manipulate the most incendiary symbols of the time, Coughlin seduced his followers into a personal allegiance to himself as leader and savior. There could be no middle ground: "You are either with us or against us," he warned; "you can't be indifferent."

There was about him a flair for the dramatic which, in the light of his lightning-like success, became messianic. Consider the way he prepared the weekly radio addresses which were the key to his power. He retreated to the sixth floor of his Resurrection Tower, where he was secure and supreme behind the several locked doors which opened only by means of secret pressure on a hidden button. To this room, equipped with bed and stove, he would retire each weekend to write the radio sermon. With several assistant priests caring for the needs of the congregation, he could devote full time to the political and economic affairs that interested him most. For unlike other clergymen, he could not be satisfied with the spiritual leadership of the few; he had to be the political leader of the masses. The real Father Coughlin was a messiah.

He was a demagogue not only in the original sense of the word, as he would have it, but in every sense of the word. He fitted the dictionary definition of "one who acquires influence with the populace by pandering to their prejudices or playing on their ignorance." Certain that he had discovered the panacea for all the nation's ills, he was willing to use any means to achieve his ends.

Just who was Coughlin speaking for and to? The shepherd of
Royal Oak thought the answer was clear enough: "I speak for the
little man." This was no idle boast, for the hard core of his following was found among those industrial workers, farmers, and small
businessmen particularly hard-hit by the Depression. His power
centers were large ethnic groups in the Roman Catholic church–
Irish, German, and Polish. He was "one of them," and spoke "for
the faith." His focus was economic, not theological. The resentment
felt by low-status minority groups was crucial. Protestants liked his
fundamentalism. Though usually anti-Catholic, many fundamentalists were so sympathetic with his message and moved by his rhetoric that they became devoted followers. As Arthur Schlesinger
notes in *Politics of Upheaval*, Coughlin had strong appeal to those
who through years of Bible reading and fundamentalist revivalism
had become accustomed to millennial solutions. They picked up the
frequent references to God and Christ, Bible quotes, religious
hymns, and organ music. This man was "a Christian fighting
against atheism and sin," constantly talking about the Christian way
of life and calling for crusades.

Nothing fazed him. When "the mob" threatened him, the feisty
Father replied: "Let them come–the vile swine! I'll be right here at
the Shrine if they're looking for me. They won't have to track me
down!" Indeed, he even talked to criminals on his broadcast. When
the Lindbergh kidnapping shocked the nation, Coughlin spoke to
the abductors in a rhetorical *tour de force* that would do credit to
Cicero himself:

> Do you realize that you have their first baby? Do you realize
> that you are holding away from the mother's arms flesh of her
> flesh and blood of her blood; you are not injuring the baby half
> so much as you are crushing her heart in a grape press, making
> her bleed the wine of sorrow?"

This may not have affected the kidnappers; but it brought thousands
of letters (and dollars) to Royal Oak.

His appeal went far beyond religion. The disaffected of all faiths
joined him. By opposing big business, banks, and big labor, he
crossed all regional lines. The poor, unemployed, and discarded
flocked to his banner. So did the aged, who were becoming a dis-

placed group. Frequently forced from gainful employment before they were ready, isolated from traditional family roles, old people found leaders in Father Coughlin and Dr. Francis E. Townsend, whose Old Age Revolving Pension Plan was the basis of another major "movement."

Historians often place Coughlin with Townsend and other spell-binders of his day, forming with Huey Long and Gerald L. K. Smith, "The Alliance of the Demagogues." Coughlin also joined with Townsend and Smith to put together the Union Party, which tried to split the Democrats in 1936 by running William Lemke for president. These men knew the ways of demagoguery: playing on prejudices and passions, socking it to the rich; using rhetoric, sarcasm, sensational charges, and cajolery. They all sought to seduce their followers into an emotional attachment. They were only the most successful of a larger group: James R. Cox with his Jobless Party, William "Coin" Harvey with his Liberty Party, William Pelley with his Silver Shirt Legion, "General" Art J. Smith with his Khaki Shirts, George Deatherage and his Knights of the White Camellia. There was a clear and present danger to American democracy as the economy fell apart.

But none of these was as powerful, and potentially dangerous, as Father Coughlin. He had two things they lacked: the oldest church and the newest medium. And he used both superbly.

Coughlin was quick to recognize a radio rival in FDR. He also saw that Roosevelt's 1936 presidential opponent, Alf Landon, was not in their league. "Every time Landon makes a radio speech," Coughlin said, "he throws a million votes to Roosevelt." A few months later, when his own Union Party thrust itself into the 1936 election behind the populist Lemke, Coughlin couched his power in radio terms:

"If I can't deliver my radio audience for Lemke in November, I'm through." He didn't deliver–but he wasn't through. He rejoiced as over 10,000 delegates poured into Cleveland for the Union Party Convention. When he entered the packed auditorium his portrait was lowered from the flag-draped rafters. It was an old-style religious revival long after the old camp grounds had disappeared. One artist reported that in 36 hours he had sold 11,500 reproductions of Father Coughlin's portrait, done in misty, saint-like pastels.

The audience wildly endorsed a resolution proclaiming him to be "The greatest American of all times."

Amidst frantic applause, a delegate gripped with almost unbearable emotion proposed that "We give thanks to the mother of the Reverend Charles E. Coughlin for bearing him." For Roman Catholics, familiar with praise given to Mary the Mother of Jesus, all this sounded familiar.

They had heard him on the radio–one of their few luxuries and only comforts–and now they saw him, in the flesh. It is hard for us, who see our leaders constantly on television, to understand what seeing him meant. Week after week, he had explained that their Depression-born suffering was not their fault. Instead it has been caused by evil and mysterious forces personified by international bankers and brain trusters. He was their Moses; now he would lead them to the Promised Land.

Coughlin's arguments mirrored the era's isolationism. He was anti-Russian, anti-British, antiforeign. Why should we spend millions, even billions to feed Europeans, while our own people starve? Why should we bail out banks and railroads, but abandon Okies on Route 66? By Republican standards, the Radio Priest argued, God himself would be condemned for giving manna in the desert–because it was a dole. How could we justify poverty in the midst of plenty? "We are," he thundered, "actors upon the stage of life in one of the most unique tragedies which has ever been chronicled. Abundance of foodstuffs, millions of virgin acres, banks loaded with money alongside of idle factories, long bread lines, millions of jobless and growing discontent."

Such vigorous assaults openly involved Father Coughlin in national politics. The response was immediate and affirmative. When in his early years he threw his support to Roosevelt, Coughlin thought he was forming a "partnership." He envisioned a sort of backstairs influence later ascribed to Billy Graham during Nixon's presidency, and Falwell during Reagan's. That was not to be. Roosevelt privately referred to Coughlin as a demagogue, and told his advisor, Rexford Tugwell, "We must tame these fellows and make them useful to us." Eleanor Roosevelt wrote later that her husband "disliked and distrusted" Coughlin from the first.

When the money rolled in, the influence spread out. Coughlin began to see himself as keeper of the nation's conscience. He hired a secret group of Washington correspondents and experts at the Brookings Institute to prepare papers on economic topics. In addition to reports regularly provided by his brain trusters, Coughlin also heard frequently from tipsters (called "vigilantes") spread across the country. He set up a sort of mini-FBI. All this information was carefully collated and added to that which he himself culled. From all sources he collected enough material to fill filing cases in his own special reference room. As his information grew, so did his self-esteem. When some of Roosevelt's policies (such as gold revaluation) coincided with Coughlin's, he interpreted this as meaning he was calling the shots in Washington. He found it easy to fancy himself the Richelieu of the Roosevelt era. And believing that as the power behind the throne he should build popular support for the titular leader, he filled his sermons with praise of Roosevelt. Always prone to overkill, he called FDR "the Boss" or "the Chief." Coughlin told Roosevelt, "You have done more than any person in the history of America to break down the barriers of prejudice." He prepared a form letter which he asked his followers to copy and send to FDR in their own writing containing such phrases as "I stand solidly behind you," "I appreciate what a terrific sacrifice you personally are making," and "I love you." Coughlin himself wrote the president that "unless you are a success I can never be considered one."

Yet two years later this man of the cloth had turned against Roosevelt, whose Brain Trust was now "The Drain Trust," and whose New Deal was the "Double Deal." Impatient with what he considered Roosevelt's halfway measures, and realizing that he would never get in the inner circle, Coughlin decided to go his own way and wield his own power. He became as savage in his attacks as he had been sweet in praise of the Democrats. The fiery General Hugh Johnson, head of the NRA, was Coughlin's special target—"a cracked gramophone record, a chocolate soldier, a creampuff, not a red but a dead herring." Johnson struck back, likening Coughlin to Hitler: "You have not chosen the swastika, but a more sacred device. No swastikas for your Nazis—but a cross."[5]

The cross and the microphone were still potent forces; Coughlin used them to form the National Union of Social Justice. (There are interesting parallels to the Moral Majority in our own day.) Membership was open to all who believed in "the rightful necessity of social justice." Letters and fees poured in. While some people denounced Coughlin as a Fascist, others thought he represented Christ's second coming. His enemies persecuted him, but he continued to work for the poor and drive the money changers out of the temple. He was their man.

Seeking new allies, Coughlin turned to the charismatic Huey Long, who had become virtual dictator of Louisiana. While aspects of the coalition are still puzzling, by 1935 both men were considered serious threats to American democracy. A leading journalist and radio news commentator, Raymond Gram Swing, contended that the priest and the Senator were advance agents of American fascism. Swing viewed with alarm their ever-increasing popularity. If Coughlin renounced the democratic process, could he lead an army that would overthrow it?

The American press grew ever more apprehensive about the Coughlin-Long connection. So did the London *Times*, which warned that "if Roosevelt does not succeed in restoring prosperity, the American people will turn to Coughlin and Long and their quack remedies."[6]

Then Long was gunned down on September 10, 1935. Father Coughlin called it "the most regrettable thing in modern history." He also said he had received a warning of a plot to kill Long by tampering with his car. News of Long's death reached Coughlin in New York–where he was visiting with Joseph Kennedy, chairman of the Securities and Exchange Commission. As Coughlin's power declined, his xenophobia increased, merging with his moralism, nationalism, and isolationism. When his reforms were not adopted, his warnings not heeded, he moved further in the direction of bigotry and hate. The man who discovered the power of radio turned his back on the power of love. He endorsed official Nazi doctrines, although there is no proof that he had any connection with the German government. His own espousal of anti-Semitism in 1938 shocked many who had followed him. But it was not until 1942 that his church superiors suppressed him and his anti-Semitic outbursts.

Half a century later it is easy to dismiss Charles E. Coughlin as a "religious crackpot," and point out that he faded from the heavens just as quickly as he appeared. He was a media hype. The media giveth, the media taketh away: blessed be the name of the media.

As I hope to prove in later chapters, this is too simplistic a conclusion. Specific personalities may fade, but the archetypes and stereotypes remain. Racism, fanaticism, emotionalism, and demagoguery are always with us, just beneath the surface, ready to sprout up.

How then to summarize the career and impact of this remarkable man? Was he a true folk hero? Did he have a real political following, or only a devoted fan club from radio land? Did his National Union, appealing to the bitter and discontented, ever have a chance of changing the course of history? Did he and Huey Long make the threat of American fascism real?

Long's assassination certainly destroyed a powerful figure–had he lived, who knows? Were they both demagogues? Yes. But fascists? I think not. Their appeal was not rooted in a European ideology, but in their ability to meet real needs of terrified people. True, Coughlin tilted towards fascist doctrines between 1938 and 1944. But in his years of greatest power (1930-1936) his program and performance were not imported. They grew out of American soil and dealt with American problems.

He used the radio to bridge the gap between rural Protestants and urban Roman Catholics–a combination that had derailed the Democrats in 1924. This Pied Piper of the poor had his one moment in history; when it passed, so did his power.

Yet he himself was not poor. A heavy silver speculator and stock investor, Coughlin benefitted considerably from the very system he condemned–an irony we shall observe in many other pop preachers we examine. Secure in his tax-free status, he was able to buy property, make a loan to his father, publish newspapers and books, and organize political networks. The League of the Little Flower seeded many enterprises of which contributors knew nothing.

I never heard his radio programs; I never heard him preach. I only met Father Coughlin once–an old man in his late eighties, feeble and frail, waiting for death. The luscious brogue had faded; the voice made for promises had no promises left. Was *this* the man who moved millions and threatened to unseat Roosevelt? Knowing of his early triumphs, I had wondered if he was not fit material for a Greek or Shakespearian tragedy. Standing with him there in Royal

Oak, Michigan, I could think only of Willy Loman, in Arthur Miller's *The Death of a Salesman.*

This withered oak gazed out towards his church and tower on Woodward Avenue and Twelve Mile Road. For half a century he had been identified with that spot, that Shrine of the Little Flower. "Do you have any regrets about your ministry and your life?" I asked. "None," Coughlin answered. "I did the work of my Father."

Afterwards I went to his Resurrection Tower, now partly blocked by a gas station, to be on the ground where he held sway. "Let us sit on the ground and tell sad tales of the death of kings." The tower basement, converted into a nursery school, was full of childish chaos. His private office, from which most of Coughlin's broadcasts originated, was littered with pigeon droppings. His private bathroom was in decay. Inside the rusted sink and toilet bowl, the water glistened with orange rot. A sad sight. A bare ruined choir; and no birds sang.

NOTES

1. Of the many books on the history and development of radio, I have found these three to be most helpful: David Sarnoff, *Looking Ahead* (New York: McGraw-Hill, 1968); Morgan McMahon, *A Flick of the Switch, 1930-1950* (Los Angeles: Vintage Radio, 1976); and Phillip Collins, *Radio: The Golden Years* (San Francisco: Chronicle, 1987).

2. See Marshall W. Fishwick, "Father Coughlin Time: The Radio and Redemption," *Journal of Popular Culture*, (Spring 1988); and David H. Bennett, *Demagogues in the Depression* (Syracuse: Syracuse University Press, 1969).

3. There is no satisfactory biography of Coughlin. One has to be content with Louis Ward, *Father Coughlin: The Authorized Story* (Detroit: Tower, 1932); and Ruth Mugglebee, *Father Coughlin: The Radio Priest of the Shrine of the Little Flower* (New York: Garden City, 1933).

4. Some of his sermons were published, along with his main tenets and prejudices. See, for example, *Father Coughlin's Radio Discourses* (Royal Oak, MI: Radio League, 1931) and *Eight Lectures on Labor, Capital, and Injustice* (Royal Oak, MI: Radio League, 1934).

5. *New York Times*, August 16, 1936. See also Gerold Frank, "Father Coughlin's Fish Fry," *Nation*, CXLIII, no. 8, August 22, 1936, p. 208.

6. For more on this theme, see Charles W. Dunn, ed., *Religion in American Politics* (Washington: Congressional Quarterly, 1989).

Chapter 10

Star to the Stars

I'm just a little girl trying to get along.

–Aimee Semple McPherson

Religion in America has been male-dominated; but no male dominated Aimee Semple McPherson. She could and did evangelize with the best of them. Long before Women's Liberation, she was liberated. When it came to saving souls she had, and has, few equals.

"Oh, don't you ever tell me that a woman can't be called to preach the Gospel!" she told her male critics. "If any man ever went through one hundredth part of the hell on earth that I lived in, they would never say that again!"[1]

In the Land of the Self-Made Man, she was a Self-Propelled Woman. Aimee made her own bed and decided who would lie in it. Married and divorced three times, involved in one of the all-time notorious "love scandals," she was the first woman to preach on the radio and she built an auditorium shaped like a piece of pie. Aimee was a real star, not a passing meteor. Long after her death, her International Church of the Foursquare Gospel continues to thrive and grow–a major worldwide Pentecostal church.

This enterprising lady would do anything for the Lord: tour red-light districts to confront prostitutes; go door-to-door in San Francisco's Chinatown to convert the "heathen"; scatter tracts from an open biplane; or drive onto the stage dressed as a motorcycle cop, screech to a halt, and shout: "Stop! You are breaking God's law!" Charm and charisma coalesced in her attractive body. Aimee Semple McPherson (1890-1944) was the first female Pentecostal with celebrity status. She celebrated in the heart of downtown Los Angeles, in the very shadow of Hollywood.

Not bad for a lady of the road who arrived there in December 1918 with ten dollars and a tambourine. Converting thousands in the Jazz Age, Aimee still fascinates us as a precursor of so much and so many that followed–a Christian celebrity who combined qualities (sex and sanctity, pepper and poignancy) that would crop up decades later. She wore her religion like a cloak; but it never concealed the body underneath.

The incredible details of her life (especially the alleged kidnapping) read like a soap opera.[2] No need to analyze her theology–she had little. But we must take her seriously, as a person of note and notoriety. She belongs in a blockbuster movie–larger than life, in technicolor.

Born on a bleak Canadian farm in 1890, Aimee was the only child of a taciturn Methodist farmer and a Salvation Army mother, Minnie, who had married at 15. Aimee's grandmother had been a "shouting Methodist" who echoed through the generations. Unable to continue her work for God, Mother Minnie took refuge in prayer, Bible reading, and complaining. Whenever possible she went to the Salvation Army barracks in the nearest town (Ingersoll), and became a junior sergeant major. In that capacity she claimed her daughter Aimee was "prayed into being." Recalling the story of Hannah and Samuel in the Old Testament, Minnie knelt and begged God for a "little baby girl." She got Aimee. What a girl!

Courageous and headstrong, Aimee was not ashamed of her Salvation Army background and rearing. On her first day at the crossroads school she used a cheese box for a drum, a red rag for a "Blood and Fire" banner, and had the whole class marching behind her. The scene portended what she would be doing for the rest of her life.

Precocious and curious, she loved movies, novels, and ragtime. Aimee moved freely in and out of various churches. She dropped in on the Pentecostals–often called "Holy Rollers"–who spoke in tongues and did strange things. Suddenly, the preacher, a handsome tall man with blue eyes (a boilermaker named Robert Semple) rushed to the platform and yelled "Repent! Repent!" Aimee not only repented, but went home shaking and trembling, knowing she was a poor, lost, hell-deserving sinner. The eternal welfare of her soul was at stake. Would it be heaven or hell?

For the rest of her life it was the same–all or nothing, life or death, hell or heaven. This time, it was heaven. She wanted salvation, and the preacher. Once young Aimee wanted something, you could be pretty sure she would end up getting it. At 17, the adoring convert married the Pentecostal preacher. Off they went to save China. As the train pulled out of the little Canadian station, Aimee leaned out of the car window, waved at her mother, pointed upward, and shouted "Look to Jesus!"

A year later Robert Semple, whom she had divorced, was dead, Aimee was ill and penniless, and there was a newborn child named Roberta Star. Minnie wired money to get Aimee back to Canada, where she drifted from mission to mission, depressed and destitute, anxious to find a man to support her and the infant Roberta. She found one–a grocery clerk named Harold McPherson–and moved to his parents' home in Providence, Rhode Island. She tried to be a suburban housewife, but ended up depressed, sobbing for hours, "Jesus, Jesus, Jesus!" When son Rolf was born, Aimee's health failed. She was near death when a mystic voice said, "Go preach the Word!" Next Aimee heard a nurse murmur, "She's going!" and everything went black. Let Aimee tell what happened: "Then came the voice of the Lord–so loud that it startled me: "NOW WILL YOU GO?" With my little remaining strength I gasped, "Yes, Lord–I'll go!"

And she went. This mystical summons is crucial to understanding not only Mrs. McPherson, but the process we are studying. This is the threshold on which the rational, fact-minded historian must stop. How "real" was the experience, and how it affected her ministry, are questions of faith more than fact. To discredit or disclaim such events is easy but unsatisfactory. We study fundamentalists; to them nothing is more fundamental than the reality of a long-resisted, then absolute, submission to God's will. Can those who have not experienced this judge it?

Aimee literally took to the road. Waiting until her husband was out one night, she grabbed the two small children, jammed her clothes into a suitcase, and left Harold McPherson's home forever. Recriminations would follow, but she had set her course. Nothing could deflect her.

Leaving Roberta and Rolf with their grandmother, Aimee immersed herself in the ardor of a Pentecostal camp meeting nearby. She had been received back into God's grace. Then she accepted an invitation to preach to an apathetic half-dozen "saints" in a village. From that inauspicious start, Aimee forged ahead steadily–learning as she went, cheerfully enduring hardship, privation, and public disapproval, laughing at her mishaps, surmounting obstacles. She had no regularly organized support, knew nothing about the details of evangelism, lived from hand to mouth, and made mistakes; but she seldom made the same mistake twice. As with every major evangelist in American history, she had on-the-job training.

Aimee had only one message, one word: Joy. Having joy, she could convey it. Nothing was too hard for her–and nothing could make her complain. She "made do"–and people loved her. Finally she had enough money to buy a "Gospel Car," painted it with religious slogans, and took to the road. Up and down the East Coast she labored, from Maine to Florida. By the time World War I came, she was one of the better known itinerant evangelists.

Her strong points were preaching, converting, and exhorting. She did not have a good head for business. Con men gulled her. Her income was erratic, her outgo total. Hangers-on attached themselves to her caravan. She allowed them to remain, although they gave her a questionable air. Money dribbled through her fingers. Trying to make ends meet and manage her enterprise drained all her energies during the winter of 1917. She told the readers of her little magazine, the *Bridal Call*, for April, 17:

> I am very weak in body, and have to hang on to God for strength at each meeting. . . . I am alone, playing, leading, singing, preaching, and praying at the altar, besides having the Bridal Call to prepare; it is only the power of God that sustains me.

Doggedly she drove across America in her Gospel Car. There were breakdowns, washouts, turnouts, trackless deserts, snow-storms. On Armistice Day 1918, she rolled into Tulsa, Oklahoma, and just before Christmas, into Los Angeles. She remembered what Joshua had said before the walls of Jericho: "Shout–for the Lord hath given you the city!" She had found hers.

California was, and is, the last religious frontier. Historians speak of the Great American Tilt. Everything that isn't tightly nailed down slides into southern California. Some were frightened; but not Mrs. McPherson. To this sensation-craving corner, where even "Brain Breathing and the SECRET OF THE AZTECS" were taught, Aimee brought her gutsy emotional faith. All America was stepping out on an emotional binge, and Aimee was determined to lead the parade. So she built her Temple in that special spot that also harbored Hollywood, Disneyland, drive-in cemeteries, People's Temple, and assorted gurus. Here, for the true believer, the laws of time, space, and morality could be suspended.

In California revivalism is a way of life, and sometimes of death. Most groups advance specific techniques or tricks to "reach salvation" or transform the consciousness. They aren't interested in abstractions or metaphysics for their own sakes. Rather, they try to attain a new consciousness, a new state of being that is immediate and "tangible." The nature of the consciousness may be interpreted or described in a variety of ways: yoga exercises, meditation, "trips," chanting devotions to Krishna, messages, primal screams, or the "E-Meters" of Scientology. Long before all this, Aimee pioneered one of the main evangelical devices—faith healing. In the early days, before she had the trappings and stage sets in place, this was what drew people to her—the major attraction for the urban poor and rural masses who floated west.

Highly controversial in the 1920s, faith healing was for Aimee more of a stepping-stone than an end in itself. How much of it was inspired, how much contrived? Battle-hardened and road-tough, Aimee quickly perceived that (then as now) Los Angeles was full of the flotsam and jetsam of the Westward Tilt. Just look at her congregation. There were neurotics, psychotics, drifters, and those whom she referred to disdainfully as "nuts." To Aimee, all audiences were alike: crowds to work upon. What could she do to make a "family" out of such material? How could she not only win, but hold, their loyalty? By telling them they were somebody; they were the salt of the earth. She would be their Sister: and she would preach the Gospel truth.

At an Oakland revival, Sister was using Ezekiel 1:4-10, the prophet's vision of the face of a man, lion, ox, and eagle. She went on to describe Christ's fourfold ministry as savior, baptizer, healer, and coming king. "It's the only answer to man's every need," Aimee shouted. "It's a foursquare gospel." The phrase instantly grabbed the congregation, who shouted and clapped approval. Aimee knew a good thing when she saw or said it. She founded the International Church of the Foursquare Gospel.

Founded it, built it, nurtured it, expanded it. She was not only preacher but actor, director, and stage manager. Today her sermons do not read well, full of mixed metaphors, hackneyed phrases, and "sob-sister" sentimentalism: "A mother with trembling hands was stroking back the dampened yellow curls from a marble-white brow."[3]

Her most famous sermon, "The Scarlet Threat," abounds with melodrama, corny commonplaces, and cheap emotionalism. Yet she apparently had complete control over the mood of her audience. Nothing got away from her. She drove the Temple forward as a skilled chariot racer drove his horses.

Sister was always in the newspapers, on the air, on the move. Large banners outside the Temple read, "Welcome to our Sister!" Inside, countless cards, bookmarks, and pamphlets carried her picture and words. On an old copy of the church newspaper I count the number of times her name appears: 15, to the Almighty's nine. Her special gift was that she took everyone, no matter how vast the crowd, into her confidence.

Since this was her family, she must find something for everyone to do. In addition to the regular services she would organize a gigantic Bible school and youth center, with nurseries, helpers, singers, typists. She would expand the old magazine (*Bridal Call*) and start a new one (*The Crusader*). Anyone could call any time, day or night, and get the correct time: a brand-new idea. There would be a Prayer Tower (where people could kneel in two-hour relays) and her own radio station, KFSG (Kall Four Square Gospel). All this would make her corner of Los Angeles a center of world-wide evangelism.

And so, to work. In a few years the Angelus Temple was finished, seating 5,000, full of pictures, windows, sweeping ramps, balconies, a stage, and a baptismal pool scented with rose petals. Erecting such a church was astonishing. Filling it, and keeping it filled, called for Herculean efforts. Aimee threw all her virtuosity into this. Accomplish it she did, by means that some deplored and some praised, but the effectiveness of which nobody challenged. The religion she preached was the Foursquare Gospel, a nonstop outburst of Joy! Joy! Joy! There was no mourners' bench, no wailing over sin, no depressing emphasis on damnation and hellfire. The glimpses of wickedness that she introduced sparingly into her panorama of "hope and comfort now, and assured bliss hereafter" served as excitants; they titillated but did not terrify. They were the spice in the cake, the topping on the dessert, the fine print on the tickets she scattered profusely, to all who yearned to find the Happy Road to Heaven.

Many sought it hours before the service, standing patiently at the temple doors waiting for attendants to lower the ropes and let the lucky ones in. The whole scene smacked of Hollywood. There was the blare of trumpets, the roll of drums, the floodlights, the national anthem filling the sacred space. Then all eyes turned to a staircase coming down to the flower-decked platform. Gasps. Sobs. "It's Sister. She's coming down!"

Aimee descended slowly, dressed in white, holding a bunch of red roses. Her head was wreathed in a bouquet of interwoven flowers. Pink, blue, and golden lights took turns illuminating her. The band seemed to burst its brass acclaiming her–Aimee Semple McPherson! Month after month, year after year, she staged the most successful religious services in the nation.

No one could be sure what would happen next. On March 4, 1925, the *Los Angeles Times* reported that a 50-year-old blacksmith threatened to blow up Aimee's Angelus Temple–unless she let him plant "a kiss from God" on her lips. A butterfly had landed on his ear, the blacksmith said, with the message to do this. After an exchange of 30 letters, Aimee finally decided to have him arrested. He was declared insane. As he was being taken to the asylum, he shouted: "I'm just as much an emissary of God as Mrs. McPherson is!" Who can say?

At the center of her strategy was the sense of community. She liked mass movement and mass actions. If she did not become as closely identified with radio as her exact contemporary, Father Charles Coughlin, she did experiment with radio evangelism long before any other woman. Sister was fascinated with the possibility of linking various cities by radio, so congregations could hear the same sermon, open their Bibles simultaneously, and wave their handkerchiefs together. Penitents could come forward in temples and tents at the same signal. This is the first outcropping of the mechanistic conversion technique what would be a major factor half a century later.

She could and did do everything: write a hymn, play the piano, stake a tent, wash dishes, and sock a guy in the jaw. Death threats didn't faze her.

Sister took to the road–travelling Pullman class now–and proved that what she had learned on the West Coast worked in the East. She knew just where to hit the crowd. When she went to New York City for her "Holy Gospel Revival," she published (with illustrations) seven sermons offering teen girls advice on "How to Avoid the Pitfalls of a Great City." They came running–and stayed to hear "firsthand" about the whorehouses and gin mills where tender things were done in. There was not an empty seat in the house. Later on, dressed as Priscilla Alden, she preached a Thanksgiving sermon standing at the wheel of the good ship *Mayflower*. She was irrepressible and irresistible. "Praise be to God!" she proclaimed from the pulpit. "He has used even me, the least of all saints."

It was on these trips that she perfected faith healing. She began hesitantly, even timidly. The "power" made her uneasy; she wondered if it would work. "Jesus is the healer," she would say; "I am only the office girl who opens the door and says 'Come in.'"

The healing sessions attracted public attention, especially when near-riots occurred among the throngs of crippled and afflicted persons. In San Diego she filled Balboa Park, and for two days prayed from dawn to dusk for the sick who passed before her. When she duplicated the performance in Denver, the Mayor ordered church bells to ring and factory whistles to blow. People knelt in the streets to pray for Sister Aimee's healing sessions. She began dressing in a nurse's white uniform, with a military-like blue cape. And lo, the money came pouring in.

At first other churches and preachers welcomed Sister Aimee. Gradually many turned away from her, charging her with lurid sensationalism, showmanship, and even fraud. Her stunts and gimmicks were undignified; but they filled Angelus Temple and the collection buckets. She could be sentimental, flaky, garish, and vulgar, and people loved it. Having started with nothing, she had no illusions about the joys of poverty. She enjoyed–even flaunted–the good things of life. She was a celebrity, and linked in the popular mind with popular preaching. Her auburn hair, Paris wardrobe, Hollywood makeup, and addiction to beauty parlors let Sister upstage the other churches–and most of the stage shows. She supplemented sermons with tableaux and pantomimes, dramatizing stories and presenting morals in cartoon terms. Vaudeville in the Temple! Proper pastors shuddered. When it came to gathering in the sheep, she was the shrewdest shepherd.

The jealous and the skeptical suspected scandal in this gaudy show-biz sanctuary on Echo Park. But to rapt followers, the Temple was the embodiment of earthly and heavenly glamor, the emotionally satisfying, exciting hub and inspiration of their otherwise drab lives. In her they rejoiced; with her they perceived a primrose path to heaven.

Nicknames and "Aimee stories" abounded. Rumors of romantic involvement multiplied. Aimee was the Mary Pickford of revivalism, the teaser in the temple, the P. T. Barnum of religious show biz. Her alleged lovers included Al Jolson, Milton Berle, and "politicians in high places." (A later celebrity, Marilyn Monroe, drew similar charges.) The strongest case for an accusation of "illicit love" tied her with Kenneth G. Ormiston, her radio operator. Did she elope or was she kidnapped?

This much is clear: on May 18, 1926, Sister went swimming on a calm sunny day at a Los Angeles beach. She entered the water and was not seen to come out. The ensuing uproar–including her miraculous return and incredible story–was front-page news for months, triggering not only countless articles but books as well. One of the mock heroic epics of our time, no Hollywood thriller–not even *Perils of Pauline*–could match it.

Was she (we will always have to ask) "lured into a car by the story of a dying infant," smothered with chloroform, and driven off to a fate worse than death? Aimee gave every graphic detail, time and again, and stuck to her story until she died. Having lost consciousness, she was driven to a deserted shack, and told she was being held for ransom. When our sturdy Soldier for Christ refused to cooperate by communicating with her mother, they threatened and tortured her, holding a lighted cigar on her hand. Still she resisted.

Eventually, she said, she was tied hand and foot, placed in an automobile, and transported to an adobe hovel somewhere in Mexico, south of Douglas; she could not be more precise. From there her abductors had dispatched the "Avengers'" letter demanding $500,000 and enclosing the lock of hair for identification. If that should not suffice, they might cut off and send a scarred finger that her mother would recognize.

By pluck and luck, Aimee rolled off the cot, got to a discarded tin can, and sawed through her bonds. She escaped into the desert, staggered on blindly for hours, and finally saw the lights of Agua Prieta. Sister collapsed, but the Lord saw fit to spare her, and home she came—in triumph. She was carried back to the Temple on a flower-decked chair, as hallelujahs went up to heaven; indeed, her entrance into Angelus Temple was a sort of resurrection. Statements of disbelief by the newspapers, and officials who investigated the matter, were ignored.

When the country slowed down for the Great Depression, Sister Aimee picked up speed. During the winter of 1934, for example, she barnstormed through 21 states—15,000 miles, 336 sermons, live audiences topping 2 million not counting the radio audiences. Preaching as many as five sermons a day, she was the first woman ever to open the state legislature in Iowa.

But there were dark clouds on the home front. With money pouring in, the once-close McPherson family fell out. So intense was the infighting that the *Los Angeles Times* wrote an editorial:

> Let's have a new moratorium on the McPhersons. Many families quarrel, but few with the intense ardor of three generations. They have become court perennials, regular customers. The first time was a sensation. The second time it was still good. But now it is like the ninth life of a cat, about worn out.

Sister Aimee fought back, setting the Aimee Semple McPherson Defense Fund into motion. The faithful were urged to contribute cash, chains, gold coins, real estate, automobiles, platinum, silver, gold watches, diamond rings, gold rings, wedding rings, bracelets, pins, bridgework, and gold teeth. Remember that according to St. Paul, the Lord loveth a cheerful giver. "Blessed are they that protect the priests of the Lord." (That quotation, by the way, is not from the Bible.)

Almost as strong and colorful as Aimee herself was her assistant pastor, Rheba Crawford. They met when Rheba stopped by Aimee's Florida tent show in 1917. Rheba, an orphan and Salvation Army worker, had staked out her fame as a street-corner preacher. Hell and brimstone were her specialties. On a good day, when Satan stoked up the fire, she could attract thousands. No wonder she was the model for Damon Runyan's heroine in *Guys and Dolls*. Even Runyan gasped when, in real life, Rheba was arrested for causing a traffic jam during rush hour in downtown Manhattan.

Like Aimee, Rheba left her husband to preach the Gospel. When she reached California, Aimee signed up this "Angel of Broadway" as assistant pastor. She preached so well that some said it should be *her* Temple; so Aimee fired her. That set Rheba hopping. Rheba sued Aimee for $1,080,000, saying Aimee had called her a Jezebel, a thief, a hypocrite, an embezzler, a blackmailer, a Judas, and a partner of the Devil. The suit was settled out of court.

But the most embarrassing conflict occurred between Sister and her mother Minnie. When they quarrelled, Aimee pulled no punches. Her Mother had to be hospitalized with a broken nose.

Obviously such struggles took a lot out of Sister–especially an unsavory third marriage, with lurid separation details. Sister Aimee neither gave ground nor asked for it. She had become a tourist attraction, like Catalina Island or Hollywood's film studios. With such patronage she managed to keep the Temple's insatiable maw fed. Her gaudy banners were flaunted along its walls like circus heraldry, and though her platform mannerisms might become stereotyped and the accents of her voice strident, she always gave her best for a throng.

Her life was tough and turbulent. She lived and worked in a man's world; but no man was her master. Her message was simple–joy–but it did the job. Her major achievement was this: she combined the idea of "Christian" and "celebrity," right in the shadow of Hollywood. One of the infants she baptized was Marilyn Monroe, whose grandmother, Della Monroe Grainger, was a devout

Temple follower. If only the camera could have caught that moment: two celebrities, bound for the stars, then quickly for the grave. Their stories were poignant, tender, and tragic. So much for the American Dream.

Living after the great Youthquake of the 1960s, it is hard to understand what a stir the Lady Evangelist made in the 1920s. Not only in religious but in social and philosophical areas, she was a pioneer. The two words "lady" and "evangelist" seemed to many a contradiction, to some an abomination. They confronted her with scripture, admonishing women to stay in their place, and remain silent. Silent was one thing Aimee Semple McPherson wasn't. She was the godmother of female revivalism.

Though there have been successful practitioners since her day (Kathryn Kuhlman, Terry Cole-Whittaker, Marilyn Hickey, and Tammy Bakker, for example), none has equalled Aimee. With her long, luxuriant, auburn hair piled on her forehead, she carved out a permanent image in our gallery of heroines.

The legend lives on. People still remember her forty-eighth birthday party. She appeared in a gingham dress and sunbonnet, carrying a pail full of milk. She served her elders a cupful apiece and then used the bucket to take up the collection. Nearly 6,000 persons were on hand. She might have been aging, but she had not lost the old magic.

The thousands who thronged to Angelus Temple always wondered, "What next?" She might—and did—dedicate a seven-foot neon lighted cross atop the temple dome by climbing up like a steeplejack. Or she might preach a sermon on "Little Red Riding Hood," dressed in a scarlet cape, and lured on by a ferocious "wolf," properly fanged for the occasion. Why go to the movies when you could go to the Temple?

She was right at home with Hollywood show business. She probably could have joined it had she wished to. But she had a higher—or at least a more compelling—mission. She was, as she never tired of saying, "your sister in the King's glad service."

Let the record show that (according to her own lights) she *was* in His service. Her religious activity and output were prodigious. Modern religion inherits four ways to cure souls: healing, guiding, sustaining, and reconciling. Sister Aimee started with the first, but worked through all four. Aimee wrote full-length religious operas which were performed at the Temple. She founded a publishing house, a Bible college, and a radio station, in addition to the more usual ministries of the typical Protestant church of her day. Angelus Temple took part in Pasadena's annual Tournament of Roses parade on New Year's Day; its award-winning floats gave the church additional visibility. Parodied or ridiculed, but never ignored, she was a woman for all seasons. Sister Aimee always used her visibility, her "status" in the media, to reach the common man and woman with the Gospel, her own moral shortcomings–fabricated or true–notwithstanding.

Aimee believed in overkill. She wrote not one but three autobiographies, and several variants and revisions; published numerous sermons and pamphlets; made scores of records; and managed to be famous for being famous. She savored success, and said (long before Jackie Gleason), "How sweet it is!"

She took sweaty male-dominated evangelism from the gaslit tent circuit into the glamorous Wonderful World of Color. Some of her best efforts rivalled those of her California contemporary, Walt Disney. And did her Temple not foreshadow Robert Schuller's Crystal Cathedral?

She was no saint–but was she not treated shabbily by press and critics over her stormy career? The American public has a peculiar attitude towards Gospel preachers. While entertainers like Mary Pickford or Douglas Fairbanks made millions for merely providing enjoyment, an Aimee Semple McPherson or Billy Sunday dared not acknowledge a fraction as much income, even though they provided not only entertainment but also mass psychotherapy, a renewal of spirit, and perhaps even salvation in the bargain. Sister Aimee was one of the most powerful and influential women in American history. No wonder many devout admirers called her the Queen of Heaven.

How does a star to stars go out? Twinkling. In September 1944, she died without warning, lying in her own bed. Suicide? Heart attack? The coroner finally ruled accidental drug overdose. In the Temple, people sobbed, shrieked, and crawled on their knees to the pulpit. "Please send her back!" "Lord, she hasn't gone!" "Lord, have mercy on us!" "No, no, no! Brother, don't say it!" "Lord, it cannot be!"

But it was. Workmen quickly draped the 40-foot photograph above the Temple entrance in black. Papers everywhere put hallelujah in the headlines. During the three days her body lay in state, people waited for blocks, four and six abreast, to see her; despite wartime gas rationing, automobiles were double-parked for over half a mile around. Inside, her 1200 pound bronze casket was lined with quilted white satin. Her hands clasped a white Bible.

The thousands who were lucky enough to file by during the three days of mourning–many more were turned away–saw their Queen in what must have seemed to them a heavenly setting. Just inside the Temple to the left stood a nine-foot tower of gold chrysanthemums, orchids, and gladioli; on the wall, a huge globe of multicolored carnations. There was a gold chalice of flowers on the altar, and a floral replica of the Heavenly Throne. On the stage a blanket of purple orchids draped the bower of the bronze coffin. Flowers were banked on flowers–still they continued to come from all over the world. Radio broadcasters and newspapers pleaded that no more be sent. At least five railroad cars full of flowers for her funeral were never unloaded. Eulogy followed eulogy. She was compared to Huss, Wycliffe, Luther, Wesley, and Knox. But it was the down-home comment of Howard P. Courtney, the head of the Temple's foreign missions, that seemed just right: "Today we are here to commemorate the stepping up of a country girl into God's Hall of Fame."[4]

Five thousand of the faithful sang a hymn they knew she loved: "When the Roll is Called Up Yonder, I'll be There." Then son Rolf jumped to his feet and shouted: "Mother is not sorrowing! She is rejoicing with our Savior!" A motorcade of over 500 cars took the casket to a secluded spot on Sunrise Slope in Forest Lawn Cemetery. Sister was buried on October 9, 1944–her fifty-fourth birthday. At her head and feet were marble guardian angels chiseled into perpetual prayer. Aimee is finally resting.

The story does not end there. Forty years later the International Church of the Foursquare Gospel is going strong and (according to its own calculation) growing rapidly. Tied in with the National Religious Broadcasters and the National Association of Evangelicals, the church claims to "provide evangelical identification with 75 denominations and more than 3.5 million Christians." The Temple's property audit topped $300 million in 1984, and there were over 300,000 members in 48 countries. The Temple was the first to minister to the stone-age people in the Dunatine Valley of New Guinea, the first to translate the Choco Indian native sounds into a language, and the first to undertake to reach 100 Hidden People Groups by the year 1990. Aimee's radio station KFSG was still broadcasting 24 hours a day; earth satellite receiving stations were in place; and there were 288 weekly broadcasts in the U.S., as well as over 7,020 hours of broadcasting overseas. All this would have pleased Aimee. She was never one to hide her talents under a bushel basket.

NOTES

1. Aimee was keen to tell her story–in glowing terms. Her ministry was part religion, part theater. Her own version first appeared under the title *This Is That* (Los Angeles: Garland, 1923) and was reissued in 1985. Her story was pieced together after her death, claiming Aimee as the author, and entitled *Order Out of Chaos: The Autobiography* (New York: P. Lang, 1990).

2. Lately Thomas presents all these details in two books: *Vanishing Evangelist* (New York: Viking, 1959) and *Storming Heaven: The Lives and Turmoils of Aimee Semple McPherson* (New York: Morrow, 1971).

3. See Robert Bohr, *Least of All Saints: The Story of Aimee* (Englewood Cliffs, NJ: Prentice-Hall, 1979), p. 116.

4. Brad Williams is certainly justified in including Aimee in *Legendary Women of the West* (New York: David McKay, 1978), p. 217.

Chapter 11

The Aging Eagle

I am only a Western Union boy carrying God's message.

—Billy Graham

In March 1938 a 19-year-old student at the Florida Bible Institute finished his evening walk on the eighteenth green near the school's front door. (Bible institutes seldom have golf courses–this one was a reconverted country club, purchased cheaply during the Depression). "The trees were loaded with Spanish moss," he remembered later, "and in the moonlight it was like a fairyland." Suddenly he fell to his knees, and said, "O God, if you want me to preach, I'll do it."

He did it. William Franklin Graham has been heard by more people (live and through mass media) than any preacher who ever lived. For nearly half a century he has been *the* worldwide voice for evangelical Christianity; the epitome of popular mass religion.

It is easy to parody Graham, hard to fathom him. Taken out of context, single events or statements of his life are easy game for the smart set. But the total context of his life–and his continuing influence not just for years but for decades–is impressive. Presidents, popes, and pop singers come and go–Billy Graham remains. He anchors evangelism on the "Rock of Ages"–and is, for millions, the rock of this age.

"As I look back over my life," Billy Graham writes in *Angels: God's Secret Agents* (1975), "I remember the moment I came to Jesus Christ as Savior and Lord. The angels rejoiced! As I yielded my will and committed myself totally to Christ–as I prayed and believed–I am convinced that God 'put a hedge about me,' a hedge of angels to protect me."[1] Those angels have apparently done an excellent job.

Billy Graham–Grand Old Man of Televangelism. (Photo courtesy of Billy Graham Ministries.)

His origins are humble enough. Born in 1918 on a North Carolina farm, raised in a conservative branch of the Presbyterian church, Billy attended services regularly. When he didn't pay close attention to the sermon, his father whipped him with a leather belt. Young Billy listened, memorized the entire Shorter Catechism, and joined the church when he was 12 years old. His "decision for Christ" came four years later, in a temporary tabernacle where the fiery Mordecai Fowler Ham preached fire-and-brimstone in the piney woods and made the Devil cringe. But Ham's most famous convert was not ready to sell Christ—he chose instead to peddle Fuller Brushes door to door. Two lifelong friends, Grady and T. W. Wilson, remember details of this first calling. "Billy was the most dedicated salesman the Company ever had," they testified years later. Billy (by then Doctor) Graham explained: "I had become convinced that Fuller brushes were the best in the world and no family should be without them. Selling those brushes became a cause to me . . . a matter of principle." Billy's quick success as a salesman got him the right to be called upon to instruct other salesmen in the techniques of selling. To his mother he once remarked: "Women . . . need brushes and now I'm going to see that they get the chance to buy them."[2] A few years later the Wilson brothers would once again team up with Graham to sell what they were convinced is not only the best religious faith in the world but the *only* genuine faith. Millions have agreed, forming a network that reaches around the world.

Billy Graham's life is a parable of American righteousness. He represents, better than any other human being, Middle-America since World War II: high pastor of the proud and mighty in a mighty proud land. There is a library by and about him: most of it parochial, repetitive, and thin. Graham emerges as a long lanky cliché: an animated manikin. What makes Billy run?

The oft-repeated tale of that run (or, more accurately, climb up the ladder) can be quickly summarized. Pastor of a Baptist church in his mid-twenties, Graham was asked to take over a Sunday evening radio program on Chicago's WCFL. This went well, and he was asked to preach at the Youth for Christ rally. Another success—on the road he went, wearing loud hand-painted ties and carrying

Southern-style preaching deep into Yankee territory and Canada. He even toured Europe and converted thousands.

His first major city campaign in America (Los Angeles, in 1949) proved to be pivotal. Few could have predicted it. The Committee was reluctant to give him a larger tent and a $25,000 budget; but at the end of three weeks the revival suddenly caught on. Many credit William Randolph Hearst's order to his editors to "puff Graham." Others point to Stuart Hamblen, a cowboy singer and radio talk show host. When he announced his conversion on the radio show, crowds flocked into the Canvas Cathedral. So did Hearst's reporters and photographers. The Los Angeles *Examiner* and the *Herald Express* used banner headlines. Their dispatches, carried by Hearst papers across the country, were picked up by the Associated Press. Jim Vaus, a prominent underworld figure and wiretapping expert for gangster Mickey Cohen, was converted. Olympic track celebrity and World War II hero, who had since become poverty-stricken, Louis Zamperini followed shortly afterward. *Time* and *Newsweek* both featured the "new evangelist." Headlines across the country played up the conversions. The crusade finally closed on November 20, 1949. The tent, enlarged to seat 9,000, overflowed with the largest revival audience since Billy Sunday's New York campaign of 1917.

The 30-year-old sensation's preaching style was simple. Avoiding emotionalism, Graham followed the musical warm-ups with intense but flowing sermons heavily punctuated with quotations from the Bible and focused on contemporary public crises and personal problems. The atomic bomb became a favorite rhetorical device representing insecurities, and the spread of Communism was portrayed as an increasing crisis and threat in world affairs. Graham was and is in tune with the times. This intense trumpet-lunged prophet found the right chord, and has never stopped playing it. We are living in a time when God is giving us a desperate choice: revival or damnation.

On and on he rolled. In 1952, at the close of his five-week Washington Crusade, a special act of Congress enabled Graham to address a rally on the steps of the Capitol building and to have that address carried live by radio and television. He became a personal friend of Lyndon B. Johnson and Richard M. Nixon. In the same year Graham also met with President Harry Truman, attended both national political conventions, spent Christmas with American troops in Korea, and was called by President-Elect Eisenhower to meet with him privately in New York shortly before his inauguration.

By then it was obvious that while Billy Graham might have only one God, he had two faiths: Christian Fundamentalism and Christian Americanism. Not that he was "selling his soul" to his national religion–a notion that would and does shock him. Instead, he maintains the shell of Christian Americanism in order to put life and spirit into it. By supporting civil religion he hopes not only to combat both humanism and agnosticism, but also to use it as a springboard for leading people into the evangelical faith.

Graham fears the challenge of humanism. He thinks that if its influence can be held in check, he will have a better chance of converting people to what is the one and only way for all mankind. This is why he strongly supports Bible reading and prayer in the public schools. They will combat humanism and increase the probability that young people will be more inclined toward accepting the evangelical faith which Graham characterizes as "personal faith in Jesus Christ."

The success of Billy Graham's strategy is seen in the way General Dwight Eisenhower moved increasingly from a vague religion of "Americanism" to a definite evangelical faith. In December 1952 the general said: "Our government makes no sense unless it is founded in a deeply felt religious faith–and I don't care what it is." A month later he joined the National Presbyterian Church. His views became more clearly evangelical as he spoke of Christ as the Son of God and of the Deity of the Bible as the true Creator. When Graham visited him shortly before his death, the general asked how he could know that his sins were forgiven and that he would go to heaven. Graham reminded him of the biblical answer and Eisenhower responded that he was ready to die.

One reason for the enormous and continuous success of Graham's crusades is the simple, direct points he hammers out so that no one (not even presidents) can miss them. His own foreign policy (in an age of extreme complexity) is simplistic. One proposition says it all: without God, America and the free world will probably be destroyed. But if all Americans would repent and turn to Christ, whom Graham presents as America's final hope, then "we would have divine intervention on our side." There is little doubt that in the 1950s, Graham's version of Christianity included the doctrine that America was the land that God had prepared for a chosen people. Rugged individualism was considered the mark of both patriotism and spirituality.[3]

Largely uncritical of the McCarthy "Red Scare," Graham wanted to destroy "the rats and termites that are subversively weakening the defenses of the nation from within." He saw himself as the Joshua of Christian America. Like Joshua, he was afraid that when America's reputation slipped, so would God's. How could this be remedied? By doing what the Israelites did to Achan and his family: crush them with stone, then burn them with fire. Root out evil-doers.

The popular use of the word "sickness" to describe the condition of an entire nation is an appealing way to bring medicine and theology into a single focus. The danger is that it implies the need for drastic surgery–with some blood for an angry God. This bloodletting may be symbolic and mythic. Abraham Lincoln died on Good Friday and, in the minds of many, symbolically atoned for the nation's great sin-sickness. The deaths of Martin Luther King and the Kennedys are more recent atonements. Billy Graham is reported to have said in 1968, "If being shot or killed would glorify God, I'll be glad to go." Graham added that he almost hoped that he would have an opportunity to suffer for the sake of the Gospel.

At such moments, and in such statements, popular religion reflects its ability to adjust to new moods and understandings. The nation that confidently sent men to the moon could not free hostages held by a group of radicals in Iran. Men who had solved global problems seemed unable to cope with smog control and rain and school busing. Hence Billy Graham's "American Christianity" in the 1990s is quite different from what it was in the 1950s or 1960s. He has become increasingly sensitive to his cultural and social milieu at home and abroad. He no longer identifies Christianity exclusively with the West, or Communism with the East. What does not seem likely to change is Graham's conviction that he finds in the Bible the word of the Almighty. Were that to go, what would be left? If we can't trust the Bible, what can we trust?

In insisting that the Bible is the infallible truth from God, Billy Graham has added some special interpretations. For example, he holds that before coming to earth Jesus had no body, whereas now He does. Today that body sits at the right hand of God the Father. In Graham's own words, "There is a Man at the right hand of God the Father. He is living in a body that still has nail prints in His hands." On Johnny Carson's "Tonight Show" Billy Graham explained that a Christian entering heaven would be able to distinguish God the Father from God the Son by the nail prints in the hand of the Son. Whether this entails that the Father also has hands, feet, knees, beard, and other bodily parts is not clear.

What *is* clear is that Graham and Company are media-masters. Using the popular show is just one note on their extensive keyboard. Radio launched Billy as a media star; it might still be his best persona. He is heard every day on radio. Those who miss his voice can ponder his words in a daily syndicated newspaper column, "My Answer"; or they can get his magazine, *Decision*, which circulates in the millions. (Exact figures are hard to come by–my own inquiry to his headquarters brought the reply "well over 6 million.") Then there are the television crusades, films, satellites, videotapes, and everything electronically new and viable. Yet all these figures and media outlets don't answer the crucial question: how *does* the "miracle" of mass conversion take place? Watch Graham himself at work, and you get at least a partial answer: a time-tested formula, meticulous (almost military-like) planning, high theater, and endless follow-up. Just as it takes hundreds of unseen participants to stage a grand opera, political rally, or bowl game, so with a Billy Graham Crusade.

Since television has become his most extensive and effective ministry, and his telecasts can reach into nearly every American home, let's examine how Graham uses that hour, and how he actually comes across. When Graham was interviewed by the *New York Times* in 1957, he told precisely what he wanted:

I would have someone like Fred Waring's orchestra and glee club playing and singing old religious hymns. Then a five to eight minute skit emphasizing a moral or spiritual truth. And then an interview with a famous person such as Roy Rogers or Vice-President Nixon who would tell of his spiritual experience. This would be followed by a sermon. The program would be produced on the same scale as a major entertainment show.[4]

Graham's television success has been closely tied to his live crusades in both style and distribution. Graham's 1954 Greater London Crusade from Harringay pioneered the use of post office land-line relays to transmit Graham's voice to rented auditoriums scattered throughout England and Scotland. For the 1957 Madison Square Garden Crusade, the Bennett agency worked up a contract with ABC to broadcast 18 Saturday night sessions on national television. The live quality was a great improvement over the 1951 telecasts, and more than 1.5 million letters, including 30,000 decisions for Christ, came to Graham. God–and the tube–had blessed him.

No one in the organization–least of all Grady Wilson, Billy Graham's top "action man" since the Youth for Christ work in the 1940s–takes credit for all this. Billy's success is the will and the work of the Lord. Billy is clay in God's hand, the agent taking only a small commission to keep the crusade functioning. The real help comes from on high.

Much of the work has been done, and events planned to the split second, by the time the crowd gathers. The seeds have been well sown. This is harvest time.

The formula has been tested, tried, and fine-tuned. Year after year, country after country, the crusade goes on.

In his book *Mass Mediated Culture*, Michael R. Real sets out to compose an ethnography of the Billy Graham telecast.[5] He uses Claude Levi-Strauss's definition of ethnography: "the observation and analysis of human groups considered as individual entities."[6] Real taped six one-hour telecasts using time-logs, transcriptions, and patterns of regularity. A clear and regular pattern emerged. Billy Graham, averaging 22 gestures per minute, took 60% of the hour; master of ceremonies, 13%; visitor testimony, 10-17%; music, 10-17%. The "Goodbye and God bless you" comes as the last second hand hits the hour.[7]

Graham is American to the core, building on the native tradition of revivalism. He is able to mobilize and manage numbers and technology unprecedented in the history of evangelism. Most importantly, he understands the "global village," and knows how to call people everywhere into a "decision for Christ" and a life led in the spirit. He stresses divine intervention. One need not resort to the hypothesis of cultural variables to explain the remarkable success of Billy Graham.[8]

Billy Graham is a professional and a perfectionist, and he has turned his hour on television into a work of art. He proves it year after year, crusade after crusade–not only America but also Western Europe, Eastern Europe, Australia, India, Southeast Asia, Africa, and Latin America have all been fed into a complex computerized feedback system that records conversions, distributes follow-up literature, sends local churches converts' names and addresses, solicits and records contributions, and coordinates the multiple function of the Billy Graham Evangelical Association. Nothing except the "Decision" itself is left to chance . . . or should we say, to God?

A generation after the 1957 *New York Times* interview, the crusade telecasts (generally there are three a year) have changed little, though the pace is more relaxed. They open with long shots of the gigantic crowd while the sound track carries gospel hymn music (on youth nights, folk music). Then the camera pans on singers in the choir, and the audience. Titles are superimposed identifying the building, city, and state. In strides the master of ceremonies, Cliff Barrows, who exudes good cheer, welcomes everyone, and makes the opening sales pitch for Bible-study books. (Barrows, who joined the Graham team in 1949 when he was 22 years old, also directs the choirs, which generally feature more than 1,000 voices.) Then an "outsider" comes forth to endorse and localize the crusade. An early favorite for this spot was Roy Rogers, often accompanied by his horse, Trigger; but now Roy has a different calling and sells fast food. During this "warm up period" four or five songs are also performed, often led by George Beverly Shea, who has been with the organization since 1944. If they are available, "celebrities" like Jerome Hines, Anita Bryant, or Ethel Waters might do a hymn. All this is free–although Barrows reminds the audience that only "your" contribution makes it possible.

Then, the moment everyone has waited for. In strides Graham, his Bible held tightly against his chest, chin resolutely lifted, with that immaculate glamor of Sunday-morning certitude, that look of a blond prince out of a Nordic fairy tale. He stands before the master console (custom made for him by IBM) as waves of thunderous applause sweep over him. When it finally subsides, he speaks: "All the applause and all the wonderful things that are said will be stored up in Heaven and given to whom it belongs–Jesus!" Then the applause is repeated.

At just the right moment, the message comes. "It's almost as if I'm not even aware of the thousands and thousands of people out there," Graham says. "I'm preaching just to the first six inches in front of my face. I feel almost totally alone. And if nobody responded, if no one came, I would still preach."

So he *does* preach–for exactly 36 minutes, after which he asks listeners to make a total decision for Christ, and then to come forward to the foot of the speaker's platform. (It's the old "Action Seat" technique, used by Charles Grandison Finney more than a century earlier.) Then Graham folds his arms, reverently bows his head, and waits.

Not so with the team. Hundreds of well-trained counselors, keen-eyed and full of "proof texts" from the Bible, quietly move down the aisles, ready to answer any question, then accompany the convert on that difficult march forward, one-on-one. Nor is the spoken decision enough. Each convert is taken into a counseling room where he fills out a card of personal information. This is sent to his or her local church–with a copy to Graham's headquarters. Within the next 48 hours, the counselor will follow up with a visit, call, or letter. The decision made at that moment will not soon be forgotten–not so long as the computers respond.

The hour is almost up. One of the most important events has yet to take place: the call to the television watchers. Turning to the camera (watch cue cards!) Billy stretches out his arms (as Bernini did for St. Peter's in Rome, symbolically, when he designed the colonnade) to all the world. "You too can make the decision, if you will." He requests that you write to "Billy Graham, Minneapolis, Minnesota," and offers to send television converts the same material going to those who walked forward on camera. As he gives his final benediction–"God bless you"–up music, and pan the podium and crowd. Then the master of ceremonies, Cliff Barrows, comes in with a voice-over, repeating the call to the television audience. A picture of an envelope to the Graham Ministry fills the screen. Another blessing, and credits superimposed over the last shots of the arena. The hour is finished–on the last second.

Graham's team has delivered once again. They know their audience, and they have reached it: mainstream popular industrial culture, geared to contemporary needs and issues. Everything said, sung, and done has been within the framework of the dominant cultural assumptions of most listeners–and the power structure of those who make political and economic decisions. Graham provides the most powerful endorsement imaginable of the status quo by defining ultimate religious and moral issues as individual, private concerns. With him, Christ and culture go together like love and marriage, coffee and cream, or Peter and Paul.

The formula has worldwide appeal. Few places have responded as well to the Graham Crusade as Australia; nor was his work there cut off from mainstream America. The global village likes global evangelism. Billy's 1969 Australian Crusade, carried by 292 American television stations, brought in a bumper crop of converts at home as well as abroad.

The use of motion pictures, though less dramatic, has had a major impact which seems on the rise. BGEA has produced more than three dozen feature films. New ones are in the works. As a result of the media blitz, Graham receives more than 2 million pieces of mail annually, keeping the more than 400 employees in his Minneapolis headquarters hopping. They operate the BGEA on an annual budget of many millions. Billy Graham capitalizes on each mass medium in his role of preacher to the masses.

The scale and scope of all this, which increased rather than decreased during the Reagan years, is more mass than popular culture, although Graham does attempt to avoid overt signs of mass manipulation and to provide a degree of personal inspiration and supervision over his association. Nevertheless, the elements of mass culture are omnipresent in Graham's approach–a standardized product; average taste; a large, heterogeneous, anonymous audience; developed not *by* the people but *for* them by an organized computerized marketing operation.

In the early years Billy's spot as "top evangelist" and mass media counterpart was contested by another Protestant (Norman Vincent Peale) and a Roman Catholic (Fulton J. Sheen). Sheen wrote more books than Graham–he published 80–but is dead now, and Catholicism has taken new roads since Vatican II. The power of Peale's "positive thinking" languished in the nation that went through Vietnam, Watergate, and the Age of Aquarius. Who was Graham's chief media rival after 1965?

We need a good comparative study of Hugh Hefner and Billy Graham as media manipulators. Hedonism and evangelism do not have the same goals, but they certainly use many of the same devices and appeals. They are both very much a part of our age. Might they not both be reactions to, and offshoots from, deep-rooted American Puritanism?

By 1985, in any event, the bunny hoppers were faltering but the God pumpers were flourishing. Graham's Worldwide Pictures are just that–and contributions are tax-deductible. Their studios stand bigger and better than ever along a stretch of Burbank's Buena Vista Boulevard, just a stone's throw from the Walt Disney film factory. Worldwide owns its own Hollywood-style office building and sound stage packed with the latest moviemaking equipment. The people who work there are among the best in the industry and are paid accordingly. Making films for Billy Graham is considered a highly professional assignment.

How many people actually see these films? Here one must trust Graham's publicists. The relatively unknown film called *The Restless Ones* has, say its sponsors, been seen by more than 4 million people–of whom 300,000 were inspired to make "the Decision" once they left the theater. More recently, Graham's films have had glittery Hollywood-style premieres, complete with celebrities, engraved programs, searchlights, and special police details. At the 1975 opening of Worldwide's *The Hiding Place*, the prestigious Beverly Theater was filled with anxious, beaming first-nighters eager to see and be seen. In the ranks were stars and personalities with easily recognized faces, reputations, and connections. When the tumult and the shouting die, the multimillion-dollar campaign keeps on working, day after day, media after media–the richest and most powerful gospel organization the world has ever seen.

Over the organization towers Graham. Did anyone ever look more like Hollywood typecasting? Tall, thin, with piercing blue eyes and flowing hair, using dramatic gestures and sounding like the blast of a bugle, he is superb. Even Charlton Heston, who got the Ten Commandments (on film) from God himself, could hardly upstage Billy, who seems heaven-sent for the Billy Graham Crusade.

But he is not set in steel or chiseled in marble. He can and does adjust his "God consciousness"–not only his message, but his clothing (which has become much more conservative and business-like than in his early days), contracts, issues, and predictions. Only his success is monolithic; everything else is negotiable.

In the summer of 1984, the Graham team visited six English cities, drawing well over a million people (almost 3% of England's adult population). I was in England at the time and experienced the excitement. The conversion rate, averaging more than 9% of total attendance, was double the 4% at similar meetings across the United States. An average 55% of those going forward in Britain registered a "first-time commitment" (rather than a "rededication" or to "seek assurance"), a rate higher than the usual 35 to 40% at Graham meetings. Over 60% of British inquirers were under 25 years of age, a higher proportion of youth response than at Graham meetings elsewhere. Calling the mission "one of the most historic and momentous in our entire ministry," Graham said: "Never have people in such large numbers gathered in England to hear the gospel."

Even this achievement paled beside his evangelical tour of the Soviet Union. Earlier he had preached throughout Eastern Europe; in 1982 Graham attended a Moscow peace conference. Saying he found freedom for preaching and worship in packed churches delighted Russians. Graham got permission to come back to Russia in 1984–a triumphant return.

Piotr Konovalchik, the pastor of Leningrad's only Baptist church, wiped tears from his eyes as he welcomed this American. "We know what difficulties you faced in coming here, Billy Graham," said Konovalchik. "We rejoice that you are with us tonight." Many

young women in the choir, clad in orange dresses and white head-
bands, wept too. As Graham thanked Konovalchik, a clergyman
from Moscow went to the pulpit to offer a prayer: "You shed your
blood for Russia too, O Lord. We pray that a surge of revival may
start in this house of ours."

It was the emotional high point of the American evangelist's
most improbable mission since he went on the road for God: his
first evangelistic tour of the Soviet Union, a country zealously
committed to the extirpation of religion. While en route to Leningrad Graham commented: "I look on it as remarkable that I am here
at all, preaching." Lenin would no doubt have agreed.

Churches were full wherever he went–some with visitors who
had come 2,000 miles from Central Asia. In Tallinn, Estonia's capital, an overflow crowd of 3,000 stood in the streets outside the
Baptist church. Translated phrase by phrase by interpreters, Graham's sermons were generally familiar, but the words had special
power in the context of militant state atheism: "Jesus Christ is not
dead on the Cross. He is a living Christ. He can come to your
person. He can come to your family. He can come to your great
country." Graham assured the Soviets that Americans and President
Reagan desired peace. But he consistently and deftly attached his
hopes for world peace to the need for divine intervention–in his
oft-used phrase, "peace with God."

Returning to the United States, reporting on his trip, Billy
pointed out that all 50 church meetings in the U.S.S.R. were filled
to overflowing–even those in central Siberia. "They never told me
what to say. This is only the beginning of a new dialogue–perhaps
even a new peace offensive." Only the party was committed to
atheism–not the government, and certainly not the people. Graham
believed they were ready for a religious revival–which their officials understood.

Could this be the same man who, early in his career, had condemned the "Godless Communists," and been closely identified
with the Red Scare? What had happened to "the old Billy Graham?" No one, looking in from the outside, can say. He has listened, learned, and changed with the times. The young zealot has
become the mature statesman. His style has mellowed.

Might he be getting soft, Graham's critics asked? Could he have been used by the Russians as part of their propaganda program? Graham replied that the Russians weren't using him, but that he was using the Russians: to preach the Gospel and hear the word of God. "My trip opened up tremendous doors," he stated. With President Reagan having his first talk with a high-level Russian that same week, one could only speculate on whose medium was whose message.

Billy Graham's victory in the churches of Russia, and Reagan's in the polling booths of America, showed that the cult of personality, so long scorned by the counterculture and the chronicles of the "New Age," was alive in the mid-1980s. The "Crisis of Confidence" which Jimmy Carter had described in 1979, "striking at the very heart and soul and spirit of our national will," was over. Perhaps these matters are cyclical. There were "eras of good feelings" after the War of 1812, the Civil War, World War I, and World War II. Once again (with Vietnam and Watergate fading and losing their bitter taste) America was upbeat. "The very fact that we would like things to be better is what's important," wrote theologian Harvey Cox. Flag makers agreed. The Art Flag Company of Manhattan, a major national distributor, reported a sales increase of 30% for 1984.

When I saw Billy Graham at the Hartford Crusade in 1985, he was much more calm, low-key, and questioning than the fire-eater I remembered from my own student days. He was less prone to give answers, more ready to ask questions. The fire was still there but it was more controlled, even rationed. Cliff Barrows, Program Director since the first major Crusade, was still there; so was Tedd Smith, pianist since 1950. Most of all, there was the beloved bellow of George Beverly Shea, who has "sung the Gospel around the globe" for more than 30 years, and who was elected to the Gospel Music Hall of Fame in 1978. Seeing them in one evening had a déjà vu effect. The country and the world have changed so much. The Graham people have changed little, and the old-time hymns they belt out ("Trust and Obey," "His Name is Higher," "He Is My Reason for Living") not at all.

The same meticulous arrangements which have always marked the Graham Crusade are still in place. Special provisions are made for the deaf, handicapped, and elderly. Messages boards, Lost and Found, Crusade Books tables, ground crews, ushers, and concessions are fully manned. Buses park free, as do cars at the Aetna Insurance and Travelers Insurance Company parking lots. By merely filling out a convenient form, one can get *Decision* ("A monthly inspirational magazine filled with helpful articles") for a whole year free. Prayertime broadcasts and the Follow-up Ministry have been organized for months. God is in the details.

We need to understand Billy Graham because we need to understand ourselves. His changes are our changes; his hopes our hopes. Consider that central pillar of popular American religion, rugged individualism. Graham uses it less and less now; he prefers the term silent majority. Former rugged individualists now form a large block within America and see themselves as the backbone of true and genuine Americanism. In them, Christian Americanism is thought to be the heir of this great new land of Zion. They are the spirit of '76, the American Way embodied in flesh and blood and Fords. But recently this sort of Americanism has grown defensive. The old missionary zeal has cooled. Toyotas have come to town. The Lord God of hosts did not give swift and sure victory over the powers of evil in Vietnam. Sometimes it becomes difficult to draw the line between the forces of God and of evil. Furthermore, the American nation as a whole seems hesitant to succumb to another seizure of McCarthyism. Although the silent majority itself is more myth than reality, it does symbolize a new tone and base for popular theology. One high priest, Richard Nixon, has been deposed; Graham is still very near the altar.

Astute at reading the public's mood, Graham has now found a new war and a new enemy, a multiheaded monster–crime in the streets, dope in the schools, sex everywhere. In this sense he has become (consciously or unconsciously) allied with the Republican presidents Ronald Reagan and George Bush. Christian Americanism (unlike Roy Rogers or Gene Autry) is back in the saddle again.

For all their zip and zest, Graham and Reagan are not young men. In 1994 Graham turns 76, Reagan is 83. They are both poor boys who made good–true believers for whom the American Dream Machine ground out power and plenty. But do they still? Will Graham continue to be the "Unofficial Chaplain to the Nation"? He has met privately with every president since Franklin D. Roosevelt, was the close confident of Eisenhower, called Nixon a "splendid churchman," featured prominently in the John F. Kennedy funeral, and stayed over in the White House to help Lyndon Johnson launch his presidency.

In the crucial winter of 1993, when the U.S.S.R. had been disbanded and Russia was fighting for survival, Billy Graham announced a major Crusade in Moscow. He was welcomed with open arms–the most recognized evangelist in the world.

But was he, in his mid-seventies, in touch with that world? Would the old formula still work, and could he still move multitudes? The answer to that question is not clear. But this much we know: when the history of Cycle Five is finally written, the place of honor will go to Billy Graham.

NOTES

1. *Angels: God's Secret Agents* (1962) p. 18. Other books by Graham help to explain his position and the changes which took place over the years–*Peace With God* (1953), *Is God "Dead?"* (1966) and *The Jesus Generation* (1971). They were all published and distributed by the Zondervan Publishing Company in Grand Rapids, Michigan.

2. These and other youthful anecdotes appear in John Pollock, *Billy Graham–the Authorized Biography* (Minneapolis: World Wide, 1969). Two more useful biographies from which my account is drawn are William G. McLoughlin, Jr., *Billy Graham: Revivalist in a Secular Age* (New York: Ronald, 1960); and Joe E. Barnhart, *The Billy Graham Religion* (Philadelphia, United Church, 1972). All three have bibliographies.

3. Douglas T. Miller, "Popular Religion of the 1950s: Norman Vincent Peale and Billy Graham," *Journal of Popular Culture* 9(1) (Summer 1975): 66f.

4. *New York Times*, March 12, 1957, p. 8.

5. Michael R. Real, *Mass Mediated Culture* (Englewood Cliffs, NJ: Prentice-Hall, 1977), pp. 170-180.

6. Claude Levi-Strauss, *Structural Anthropology* (New York: Basic, 1963), p. 2.

7. Real, *op. cit.*, p. 180.

8. Joe E. Barnhart, *The Billy Graham Religion* (Philadelphia: United Church, 1972), p. 239.

Chapter 12

The Electronic Awakening

If Jesus were alive he'd be on T.V.

—Jimmy Swaggart

Every medium in its turn exalts the Messiah. We see this in prehistoric cave drawings, primitive masks, and Egyptian hieroglyphics. Megaliths were used to create Stonehenge; sand to depict the gods of American Indians. Writing was in many cultures a priestly function, since they dealt with the gods. When writing gave way to printing, Gutenberg's first book was the Bible, which remains to this day our bestseller. For many the Bible is no mere book, but the inerrant Word of God. Now the Word goes out by electronic impulses. Radio and television are the new media for the Messiah.

These media forms have not superceded older ones. Print remains the medium of continuity. Records, texts, and treaties must be printed. No evangelist used print more effectively than Martin Luther; he spent years translating the Bible into German. For centuries church sermons, tracts, and histories have been pivotal. Christian bookstores abound in our own time; the Christian Booksellers Association has over 3,000 stores. Thousands more are independent or denominational.

Today's religious bestsellers are often fundamental and Bible-based. At the top of the list are Hal Lindsey's *The Late Great Planet Earth* and *The 1980's: Countdown to Armageddon.* Anne Ortland's *Children Are Wet Cement,* Frances Hunter's *God's Answer to Fat: Lose It,* and Marjorie Decker's *The Christian Mother Goose Book* have sold millions of copies. *Christian Herald, Moody Monthly, Guideposts, Decision, Abundant Life,* and *Christian Life* grow while many secular magazines languish and die. Christian pamphlets, announcements, and solicitations never cease. Our mailbox runneth over.

Most of the material is junk mail. Yet surveys show that more people look forward to the mail than to watching television, eating, or sleeping; 75% of those who receive mass mailings actually read what comes. Except for such items many Americans would get no mail at all. Anything is better than nothing.

Though direct mail may oversimplify and misinform, it is a powerful medium. No group uses it more skillfully than the pop preachers, who fuel their cults and crusades with low-cost mail. Often it is carefully written, designed, and executed. In addition to letters there are ballots, surveys, photographs, flags, pins, and membership cards. Most offer something for nothing, though there is also a nongift strategy. The reader is urged to sign his name to such statements as: "Sorry, Preacher, I'm afraid I can't contribute, even though I know your ministry is saving thousands from Satan's grip." A returned signature lands your name on the computer. The message itself is often overblown and abrasive. "What are we teaching our children in grade school courses?" a direct mail letter for the National Conservative Political Action Committee asks, then answers: "That cannibalism, wife-swapping, and the murder of infants and the elderly are acceptable behavior."

Pithy, patriotic one-liners abound. "You and I can save America." "The time has come to wave the flag, not burn it." The Republican Presidential Task Force sent out 8 million letters in 1984 to "proud, flag-waving Americans like you who are willing to sacrifice to keep our nation strong." Rhetoric like that will get you everything–including the White House.

Often invective and hate lie just beneath the surface of blanket mail-outs. It is standard practice to exaggerate broadly just on or over the edge of lying. "I wouldn't quote somebody completely out of context," a major direct mailer writes. "I wouldn't write something that was blatantly untrue."

Records and tapes go for the ear, just as books and letters appeal to the eye. Profiting from the "Jesus rock" of the 1970s, the record industry has wedded secular rock to sacred lyrics. When celebrated secular performers like Bob Dylan, B. J. Thomas, Al Green, and Donna Summer "came over to Christ," AM and FM rock radio stations featured them, along with new Christian singers like Amy Grant. The market for evangelical music continues to grow in the 1990s.

Yet the heart of the Electronic Awakening lay in broadcasting. Radio brought the world into the living room—and a new form or religion, too. For many years radio was America's most popular mass medium. A 1939 poll indicated that an American home or apartment was more apt to have a radio than indoor plumbing or a telephone.[1] Another poll found Americans more "satisfied with radio than with religion."

The typical home had a large receiver in the living room and a smaller set in the kitchen. About one-fourth of all cars had a radio. In a 1945 poll, 84% of those asked said they preferred listening to the radio to going to the movies—and it was free. Radio was of great value during World War II, being the glue that held the nation together in its hour of peril.[2]

By then four radio networks shaped public opinion: the National Broadcasting Company (NBC), the Columbia Broadcasting System (CBS), the American Broadcasting Company (ABC), and the Mutual Broadcasting System. They helped nationalize the culture.

Religious broadcasters were among the first on the air—perhaps the very first, when on Christmas of 1909 Reginald Fessenden read Bible verses to ships at sea. Two years later, the first remote broadcast by a commercial station featured a church service.

From the very first, radio fascinated religious groups. The "one-to-many" aspect offered enormous outreach, and the radio soon became a household fixture in America. This was even more of a factor when television swept the nation after World War II.

Newly established radio stations gave free air time ("sustaining time") to religious broadcasting. Soon after going on air in 1920, pioneer station KDKA in Pittsburgh regularly beamed out religious services. For his Omaha-based revival services, which began in 1923, R. R. Brown became known as "the Billy Sunday of the air." He died in 1964, but his program continued until 1977. The first religious broadcaster to purchase network time, Philadelphia's Donald Grey Barnhouse, flourished from 1927 to 1969. During those years "The Lutheran Hour" became the most popular regular broadcast ever, reaching an audience of over 20 million.

The year 1927 introduced another major item into the religious scene: Sinclair Lewis's *Elmer Gantry*, a novel featuring a slick-talking evangelist who seduced church secretaries and de-robed choir girls. This stereotype has taken on a life of its own, appearing in films, TV series, and satires of all kinds. Steve Martin played the "Elmer role" in his 1992 movie *Leap of Faith*.

Another major success was Charles E. Fuller's "Old Fashioned Revival Hour," carried on all Mutual radio stations, helping to create an invisible church of unknown strength and size. Hard to measure, radio evangelism continued to be vocal and profitable through the 1980s.

Major networks tilted early towards mainline churches which emphasized broad religious truths rather than controversial doctrines or practices. This policy excluded many denominations and all fundamentalists, who founded (in 1944) the National Religious Broadcasters to right the imbalance. But the award-winning religious series of the 1950s (such as "Directions," "Frontiers of Faith," "Lamp Unto My Feet" and "Look Up and Live") were mainline. They reflected the upbeat patriotic mood of the Eisenhower years, and what Will Herberg calls civil religion.

But it was the Roman Catholics who found the decade's superstar in Monsignor Fulton J. Sheen. After two decades on radio he switched to television in 1950. His "Catholic Hour," with its classic simplicity and sincerity, became a national institution. His only assistant, a stagehand, cleaned the blackboard off camera. Sheen, who combined grace, intellect, and whimsy, attributed this to an "angel," and became known himself as the "Angel of the Airways." No other commercially sponsored religious program has ever matched Sheen's audience ratings; few have been so successful at attracting Protestants and Catholics, liberals and fundamentalists. People in bars watched him. Taxi drivers took time off for his show. A blind couple bought a TV set from his sponsor, Admiral, to show their gratitude.

Behind the seeming ease was endless labor. Sheen spent about 30 hours a week preparing each telecast, and trying it out on various audiences. He never used notes or a teleprompter. Astonished at his continuing success, reporters came to the studio to uncover his special tricks. There were none. Acknowledging his Emmy in 1956,

Sheen thanked his writers: Matthew, Mark, Luke, and John. Fundamentalists loved him too. The National Religious Broadcasters gave him a standing ovation in 1977, as did the audience in the Vatican when the Pope honored this superb televangelist.

Protestants prospered, too. Rex Humbard began his television career in 1953, Oral Roberts in 1954. When the "old time" TV format began to lose listeners, Roberts retooled, and featured a variety show that reflected changing times. His 1970 Thanksgiving Special reached 27 million people.

His success, which changed the course of televangelism, showed that religion too must fit under the mythic umbrella of television. Television has created a style, tone, and format which consumes those who use it. How can one challenge media myths and still preserve credibility with mass audiences? How does one keep the cross above the dollar, which dominates commercial broadcasting? These are questions as yet unanswered.[3]

Religious broadcasters have learned what others know: one gets his or her share of the audience by offering what people want, in a way they expect it. Marketing demands are paramount. So is momentum. With it you win; without it you lose. Christianity, one of the few remaining forces able to oppose our high speed homogenized culture, has opted to join it.

How can it be otherwise, in a capital-intensive industry where the big-time preachers must fund a million-dollar-a-week enterprise? Three things are required: simple theology, complex technology, and slick showmanship. This means developing and peddling your "brand name," as do those who sell cereals, cars, or deodorants. Oral Roberts offers Seed Faith, Robert Schuller Possibility Thinking, Jerry Falwell Moral Majority, Pat Robertson Kingdom Principles. For a few dollars you can get the mass-produced product; what is hard to get is genuine pastoral care and compassion. Old needs must give way to new trends and technologies.[4]

To understand the dramatic appeal of televangelism one must see it as a form of opposition to what took place in the counterculture (or Youthquake) of the 1960s. (Perhaps a better term for televangelism is *counter*-counterculture). Disgusted with the excessive wealth and conformity of their parents, the hold of the military-industrial complex, and the lock-step world of "Organization Men," a disenchanted group of rebellious children grew beards, smoked pot, practiced free love, and took to the open road. If the old folks were prudish, the young were profane. "Let it all hang out! Do your thing! Don't trust anyone over thirty!"[5]

Newly enthroned gurus included Allen Ginsberg, who claimed (in the long poem *Howl*) that the best young minds had been destroyed by madness. His colleague Lawrence Ferlingetti (in *A Coney Island of the Mind*) lamented that the American Dream was "mislaid among the sunbathers." We were all enslaved by technocracy–that social form in which historic and humanistic values lose their meaning.

To all this the new electronic fundamentalists shouted "REPENT, RETURN, REFORM." Repent of your sins, return to God, and reform your evil ways. This was no new message. Methodism and Pentecostalism had used these emotional appeals for years.[6] What was different was the size of the congregation and the scope of the media.

Interaction of media preachers and congregation is only one aspect of the complex picture of the flow and effect of mass communication. We still know little about such matters. Only recently have we identified a range of different variables that intervene between the speaker and receiver. Our measures of measuring and interpreting are still quite primitive.

Clearly the successful evangelist must have what we call (in a much overused word) charisma. Artists, musicians, hairdressers, cameramen, and fashion consultants all play important roles. The goal is not so much to give people what they need but to give them what they want. Pragmatism wins out for pietism. This emerges clearly when one examines the Rev. Robert Schuller's Institute for Successful Church Leadership, a highly visible wing of his operation. Churches are urged to insist on the same things that make for successful shopping malls: accessibility, surplus parking, adequate inventory, service after sales, visibility, and brisk cash flow. One can only imagine how the early church fathers would have responded to such a list.

Televangelists may manipulate but they do not control television. Like owners and managers, they survive just as long as they please advertisers, listeners, and patrons. Television must meet symbolic and emotional needs that existed long before the electric age. Radio and television are controlled by *vox populi*. Whenever a station or network moves too far from what people perceive as historically and socially appropriate, audience, ratings, and revenue will disappear.

Simple answers and happy endings are expected and demanded. Unhappy endings lead to low ratings and cancelled shows. Television is only entertainment—but the Christian gospel is not. The whole weight of Christian history, thought, and teaching is diametrically opposed to what works best on mass media.

Instead of a feeling of depth or the sense of the holy, many preachers resort to familiar phrases and code signals. They want to be "newsworthy," so they imitate the television news celebrities. Faith in democracy, traditional society, and Americanism become indistinguishable from religious faith. Like everyone else on television, preachers must know the market—as to Coke, Pepsi, IBM, McDonald's—then fight competitors to get it. In theory they get their Great Commission from the Gospel of Matthew: "Go ye therefore, and teach all nations, baptizing them in the name of the Father, and of the Son, and of the Holy Ghost." In practice they have rewritten the Great Commission: "Find a need and fill it; find a hurt and heal it." Some who see hidden messages in the sermons would add: "Find a fear and flame it; find a hate and inflame it."

The Feminist Revolution, which has altered so many aspects of contemporary thinking and society, has not been notably visible or successful in the Electric Church. Women have not had as strong a representation in the pulpit as they have had in the congregation. For years those connected with evangelism served as "sidekicks" to their husbands, seconding his plans and pleas, supplying the "homey touch." Many still do. Jimmy Swaggart has his Frances, Kenneth Copeland his Gloria, Rex Humbard (had) his Maud Aimee, Jim Bakker (had) his Tammy Faye. Women's ordination has seldom been mentioned or championed. Here fundamentalists stand closer to Roman Catholics (who refuse to ordain women, sanction birth control, or demand gender equality) than to the liberal Protestant churches which are often portrayed as the enemy. Indeed, the Christian Right and Roman Catholic Right have a great deal in common.

The great exception to all this is Aimee Semple McPherson, to whom we devote a separate chapter. Before her such influential women as Mary Baker Eddy (founder of the Church of Christ, Scientist, in 1879), Mother Ann Lee (leader of the Shakers), and Alma White (founder of the Pillar of Fire Church) made their mark. But it was Aimee who was the first woman to broadcast a sermon (in 1922). Her International Church of the Foursquare Gospel is still going strong.

Marilyn Hickey, the Denver-based "People's Theologian," edited *Outpouring*, a popular religious magazine, wrote a best-selling book entitled *Time With Him*, and founded the Marilyn Hickey Training Center, called Happy Church and described as "turned on and charismatic."[7] Her daily radio program, begun in 1972, is carried by 190 radio stations; her weekly half-hour television program on 20 television stations and two cable networks. She operates an energetic, competent, feminist international ministry. "With radio," Mrs. Hickey writes, "I almost stumbled into it because of my Bible study groups. But God really spoke clearly to me about a television-teaching ministry. Women must speak out. The world is dying and going to hell by the billions. So how can we stop now?"

And who would dare to stop Phyllis Schlafly, sweetheart of the Silent Majority and roadblock to the Equal Rights Amendment? Voted the world's third most admired woman in a 1985 *Good Housekeeping* poll, this mother of six grown children says she is the only woman who speaks daily to the Christian radio audience. "The Phyllis Schlafly Report" concentrates on Biblical morality, conservative politics, and strong families. Hers is the most powerful female voice espousing these causes.

Her predecessor was Katherine Kuhlman, the "One Woman Shrine of Lourdes" who died in 1976. Dropping out of an Idaho high school in 1927 to preach for Jesus, she spent the first three nights of her ministry in a turkey house. Things got better. Helped by what Kuhlman called the "H-o-o-o-oly Spirit," she went for faith healing. After she cured her first tumor, the crowds grew. Tall and slender, with Shirley Temple curls parted in the middle, Kuhlman held healing services for three decades. Then she left the tent for the studio. "The greatest combination for preachers is radio and television," she said in 1960. "Together they form a combination that is unbeatable." She proved her point, being the best-known woman evangelist when she died in 1976.

A decade later Kuhlman's mantle seemed to rest on the shoulders of the Rev. Terry Cole-Whittaker. The West Coast "blonde bombshell" began her services with a snappy suggestion: "Get out your dancing shoes and open your hearts 'cause here's a party with a purpose!"

The purpose combined dancing, praying, and giving. Terry was assisted by an even younger blonde beauty, who repeated her main line on demand: "I absolutely know that God's will for me is life–because I *deserve* to be happy." John Calvin, please note.

Reminiscent of young Dinah Shore, trim and throaty, Cole-Whittaker belted out her theme song, "I Gotta Be Me." She was a stand-up comic, like Carol Burnett or Joan Rivers. She liked jokes, quips, and gags When asked about abortion, she was apt to reply:

> People want to know what my stand on abortion is. [Pause, suspense, punch line:] I think the Pope should have the choice of whether he wants an abortion or not! [Laughs, jeers, roars.] I want that man to have everything he wants, bless him.[8]

She prays that we be released from all guilt having to do with sexuality, money, and power. "God *loves* you" is her standard refrain line. "He never judged or condemned you." Her TV sign-off line was: "I love you."

The Rev. Terry Cole-Whittaker does not fit the role of the liberated feminist: she has no quarrel with the male-dominated church and its patriarchal ways. What she has–and glories in–is sex appeal. She claims to be monogamous, though serially. Wed and divorced four times, breaking off a recent "close relationship" with a staff member, Terry has yet to equal her great-grandmother's record of six marriages. That venerable lady, a spokeswoman for Religious Science, passed strong beliefs down through the generations; not only Terry but all three of her sisters are Christian fundamentalist ministers. Going from Newport Harbor High School (and the "dumb blonde act"), Terry attended Orange Coast College where she was homecoming queen. Married but not graduated, she became Mrs. California in 1968, then runner-up to the runner-up for Mrs. America. Two divorces later (in 1975) she studied at the Er-

nest Holmes School of Ministry, became pastor at the La Jolla
Church of Religious Science, and married an ex-professional football player. Then in 1982 she left the husband and the church,
explaining, "I couldn't be limited by an organization. I had to be
part of something that could change instantly."

She gambled her ministry by betting on television. By 1984 her
half-hour show (part preaching, part studio-audience therapy) appeared in 15 markets including New York City, Los Angeles, and
San Francisco. She had, by a *Wall Street Journal* estimate, a $10
million annual budget. Cole-Whittaker herself was paid $180,000
in salary in 1984 exclusive of book profits.

"I tell people what they want to hear," she candidly admits.
"Who wouldn't want to know how beautiful they are?" Norman
Vincent Peale had been selling positive thinking since the Depression–but never with such glitz, intimacy, and sex appeal. For a
while she was big-time. Terry looked great on a magazine cover.
Celebrities joined her trendy flock: Lily Tomlin, Eydie Gorme,
Clint Eastwood. In 1984 stories of love-capers appeared in the
tabloids; Terry's insistence on condoning "whatever works" required some explaining. Details of her divorce from her fourth
husband, the much-younger Leonardo, made both her public and
private life unmanageable. Reporters hounded her. "It is now more
important than ever to trust yourself, your truth, and to be happy
and rejoice," she said. Then she announced she was resigning her
ministry. Like other media personalities, she came and went like a
shooting star.

No one could predict when the venerable Herbert E. Armstrong,
the 92-year-old head of the Worldwide Church of God, might resign. He was divorced (from his 45-year-old wife in 1985), but kept
on preaching. So did Rex Humbard (after divorcing Maud Aimee in
1983), even though by 1985 his Cathedral of Tomorrow looked
more like that of yesterday. They were the survivors.

Many who were once the rivals of these men had disappeared.
Among them was A. A. Allen, called by *Look* magazine in June 1969
"the nation's topmost tent-toting old-fashioned evangelical roarer."
From his Arizona headquarters Allen's operation had reached
every American state and ten foreign countries. A school drop-out
at age 11, ridiculed for being barefoot, Allen had entered "the

swirling rapids of sin." He smoked at age six, fornicated at 12, took a common-law wife at 18. He claimed to be the best sinner in Missouri. He wanted to have a coat of arms with a beer bucket and gin bottle on it. Then he was converted. He stopped selling home brew cooked on the stove. Then he got a tent and took to the road.

For a few years he swept like a thunderstorm across the nation. His radio ministry was second to none. But the Devil would not let Allen be. He died in the Jack Tar Hotel in 1970, clad only in his underwear, several vials of pills nearby. His associates played his radio tapes for some weeks, insisting that he was alive. Then suddenly–silence.

There was nothing silent about Detroit's black evangelist, the Rev. Ike. For a few years he developed a unique style, and with it, national standing. His message is clear and direct. Ike's advertisements, such as the one used in his 1985 California crusades, come right to the point:

Money! Sex! Religion!
The Three Hangups of Man!

He argues that the third, religion, can be used to get the other two. If we think, act, and live "full of grace and glory," then money and sex will come abundantly. Ike is often shown holding a handful of greenbacks in his outstretched hand, with a caption reading "You can't lose with the stuff I use!" To many who have long been losers, the appeal is irresistible. So they send what money they have to Ike.

In 1970 he shortened his real name, James Eikerenkoetter, and devised a religious program that is part minstrel show, part positive thinking put into street vernacular. His worship of the Golden Calf is so blatant that it is somehow hard to fault. His continuing success shows how many lack a morally grounded theology–even a vocabulary with which to explore it.

Many electric evangelists, like the Rev. Ike, thrive best in the cities. Others, especially those from India and the Far East, seek rural isolation. The American West is dotted with religious hideaways. That of the "Swami of Sex," Bhagwan Shree Rajneesh, caught the public eye and got national coverage in 1984 and 1985. With his *sannyasis* (disciples), the doe-eyed Guru took over the town of Antelope, Oregon, renamed it Rajneesh, and legalized nudity in public parks. When the group also imported thousands of homeless people from large cities for the purpose, some alleged, of winning elections, there was widespread publicity and resistance. To make it worse, Rajneesh announced that he was setting up another camp in rural England, built on the free love practices which made his lifestyle attractive to many.

Much is required of Rajneesh's converts. They must give up all their possessions, forfeit their savings, and work seven days a week for mere subsistence. Their chief reward comes at 2 p.m. daily, when the Bhagwan is driven in one of his 68 Rolls Royces down Nirvana Drive. Helicopters hover, and armed guards walk alongside. Dressed in the colors of sunrise, the adoring disciples chant, "Bhagwan's our master, we love life's laughter!"

Mixing Eastern religion and pop psychology, the Indian immigrant attracts mainly well-heeled Westerners interested in encounter therapy and free love. One of them, ironically, is the daughter of Leo Ryan, the California Congressman who was killed investigating Jim Jones's religious settlement in Guyana.

Though churches and cults ripen like melons in the California sun, none has yet surpassed that old master of healing–and appealing–Oral Roberts. His headquarters is in oil-rich Tulsa, Oklahoma. There he has built, over 40 years, a half-billion-dollar evangelical, educational, and medical complex. In the City of Faith (supported by $6 million a month from Prayer Partners) is Oral Roberts University, dedicated to Christian virtue in academics and athletics. Nearby is the impressive 60-story medical and research center, where patients' spiritual needs are as carefully attended to as the physical.

In a 1980 fund-raising letter, Oral Roberts told of his vision: a 900-foot Jesus had urged him to go for 60 stories. A few years later Jesus came again–to let him know that if each prayer partner sent in $240, a supernatural cancer-cure breakthrough would occur in the Tower of Faith. Where did the actual vision come? "I went to the desert," Oral replied. His former daughter-in-law (who divorced Oral's son, Richard, in 1979) explained: "When he said 'I went to the desert,' she told the press, he meant to the Palm Desert playing golf. When God talks to Oral, it's in very convenient terms for his next corporate move."

Clearly a number of different traditions, styles, races, and genders have found a home in the Electronic Church.[8] Competition has been keen and pop preachers have come and gone with some of the same unpredictability as pop singers. The presentations have been unpredictable, too. Ernest Angley, centered in Akron, Ohio, was an acrobatic healer who commanded demons to leave victims' bodies, shouting "Heal! Heal! HEEEEEEEEAL-aaa!" He not only saw the demons leave; he saw angels, too, standing by his side. God showed him millions of stars, assuring him that was how many souls he would save. But God didn't protect Angley from the recession of the 1970s, and his reputation waned.

Some of the ministries have weathered the storm, and continue to grow. Four of the leaders were in the South, home of the old Bible Belt that H. L. Mencken loved to ridicule. Had he lived to see what impressive organizations would grow up there in the 1970s and 1980s, he might have found them no laughing matter. The Confederates may have lost the War in the 1860s; but they are winning souls for Christ a century later. We shall call them Dixie's Holy Warriors, and discuss them in the next chapter.

What then can we conclude about the various media and the Messiah? Has televangelism become a church, even a religion, unto itself? No one can yet say. Some scholars insist that we have overestimated the phenomenon, its growth, and impact on traditional church-centered Christianity. Others say we have underestimated it–that it is as pervasive as the air we breathe, endemic to our electronic culture. Everyone agrees that it has changed millions of lives and created a multimillion-dollar growth industry. Salvation is big business, and that business is flourishing.

It is even harder to know how the new fundamentalism and conservatism in religion ties in with the culture in general. That we were dominated by a "progressive" and liberal ethos for half a century–from Franklin Roosevelt to Jimmy Carter–is clear enough. That the tone and mood of America has changed in many areas and places–theology, journalism, foreign policy; Congress, the courts, the White House–is self-evident. And this new "mood" is not confined to America. Many other nations have elected conservative leaders. The powerful Roman Catholic church has shelved the liberalism of John XXIII and enthroned a pope (John Paul II) who seems determined to turn back the clock. His strong stand against birth control, even in Third World countries that desperately need and approve of it, was shown in the Pope's 1985 tour of Africa. His views are endorsed by many fundamentalist Protestant groups, and have found their way into public legislation. That fundamentalist leaders have captured much of the Islamic world is another factor to be reckoned with.

Critics and intellectuals are too quick to condemn the media (especially television) per se. They give media not only a life but a personality of their own. Media are only the conduits, the channels through which ideas and personality flow. What we get may well be unreligious, even antireligious; but should genuine religion become a powerful, valid force, supported and demanded by the people, the media managers would get the message and feature it–just as they did with the counterculture of the 1960s. The fault, dear Brutus, lies not in the media, but in us.

This is not unique to our time or nation. Christ and culture have always been uneasy partners, and often dedicated enemies. Why should it be different with us now?

We end up with many facts but little understanding. The best survey of televangelism to date–the 1984 study by the Annenberg-Gallup organization, four years in the making–confirms this. Televangelism as a force seems to be levelling off–but how can we be sure? Data supplied by various religious groups and organizations is notoriously unreliable. What about the long-range effect of what is now taking place? What about the next generation of fundamentalists?

One thing is certain: mass media religion is a challenge unmet and dimly understood. If there is a villain, one suspects it isn't any medium, but the manipulators, who have themselves been eaten up by commercialism. Prophets have become pawns. Here today and gone tomorrow.

Salvation is on sale–let the buyer beware. Our cultural landscape seems devoid of deep spiritual meaning. The only corrective, so far as religion is concerned, might be in face-to-face encounters; penance; taking off the rose-colored glasses. The great need is not for more charismatic "living color" leadership, but for compassionate people who genuinely care for one another; who relate faith to experience, gospel to action.

The way to outwit the manipulators is not to be one. The Kingdom of God, Jesus said, is within you.

NOTES

1. Russel B. Nye, *The Unembarrassed Muse* (New York: Dial, 1970), ch. 5.

2. Phillip Collins, *Radio: The Golden Years* (San Francisco: Chronicle, 1987), pp. 26f.

3. Robert Abelman and Stewart M. Hoover, eds., *Religious Television: Controversies and Conclusions* (Norwood, NJ: Ablex, 1990), p. 53.

4. Steve Bruce, *Pray TV: Televangelism in America* (London: Routledge, 1990), ch. 2.

5. Theodore Roszak, *The Making of a Counterculture* (New York: Doubleday, 1969).

6. Harold Ellens, *Models of Religious Broadcasting* (Grand Rapids, MI: Eerdmans, 1974).

7. Richard G. Peterson, "Electric Sisters," in *The God Pumpers*, ed. Ray Browne and Marshall Fishwick (Bowling Green, OH: Popular Press, 1987), pp. 116-140.

8. Quentin J. Schultze, *American Evangelicals and the Mass Media* (Grand Rapids, MI: Academie, 1990), ch. 1. See also Clyde Wilcox, *God's Warriors: The Christian Right in Twentieth Century America* (Baltimore: Johns Hopkins Press, 1992).

Chapter 13

Dixie's Holy Warriors

Fundamentalists have hijacked the jumbo jet of evangelism.

—Jerry Falwell

The South has risen again–not on the battlefield, but on television. The long-ridiculed Bible Belt is no longer a laughing matter, especially for liberal politicians targeted by the Moral Majority. Now we call the Bible Belt the Sun Belt. It is the fastest growing part of the United States.

Which South shall we discuss–the South that was, the South that is, or the South that might have been?[1] Drenched with sunlight, soaked with tragedy, soiled by violence, Dixie has been loved not too wisely but too well. The faces and fields are rutted; but there is a thickness of social texture and a residue of shared experience. Religion is central to that tradition and that experience. Historians have long agreed that for well over a century this has been the most religious region of the nation.

The Great Frontier Revival never really ended for the rural South. Evangelism remains a life force, the organized church a social center. Annual revivals, full of sweat and sanctity, still crown the year–generally held in the Deep South between the time cotton bolls up and tobacco is laid by. Preaching goes on all day, punctuated with prayers and fried chicken. The community is purged. Deeply traditional, hierarchical, and religious, the South has a strong sub-culture. Food, speech, manners, and salvation often have a Southern flavor. Many of the great black preachers and politicians illustrate this. Both Father Divine and Jesse Jackson emerged from the rural South. The man many consider the century's most influential religious figure–Martin Luther King, Jr.–built his ministry on

Southern roots and rhetoric. So did the Southern televangelists who were Founding Fathers in the Electronic Awakening. My morning mail bears this out.

Who can ignore an oversized letter with red, white, and blue borders, inscribed *Urgent: Reply Requested*? On the back is a warning: *Caution: Do Not Destroy This Envelope!* The letter is from Jimmy Swaggart and he is desperate. A wicked bank is demanding the repayment of a $10 million loan. "I have absolutely no choice," Jimmy writes. "I *have* to make the deadline. The bank has left us no alternative." What will happen if we can't make the deadline? "I haven't allowed myself to think about that. I've just believed that God is going to make a way—and that He's going to touch your heart and make you respond accordingly."

Jimmy has help. His wife Frances rushes in. Her second letter has her name on the envelope in purple italics. She tells me (her "Dear Friend in Christ") there's both good news and bad news:

> March 15 is Jimmy's birthday; he'll be fifty. In past years I've asked friends to honor Jimmy's birthday by giving to projects . . . This year we have the most important project ever. We borrowed $10 million to help pay our bills. This loan must be repaid by May 31. Anyone would agree that we have to have a miracle to raise that much.

Who must help do it? Me! Whatever we've done isn't enough. Jimmy's entire ministry is at stake. Frances pulls out the stops:

> How would you like to face a $10 million deadline? We don't have one dollar to pay it. Some of you can easily send $50,000, others $5,000. Literally thousands can write a check for $500. We desperately need it.

How desperately? We are taken right into Frances's bedroom to see for ourselves:

> Night after night I've wakened and Jimmy's not in bed with me. He's up praying, seeking God. It's a burden only the Lord Jesus Christ knows. We gladly bear it, and thank God for the privilege: but were I to tell you that it is easy, I'd be untruthful. We couldn't do it at all without God's help.

They did it. Checks poured in, the bankers were foiled. Jimmy kept preaching and peddling salvation, Southern style. He was the best in the business: but monkey business brought him down.

The Lord called Jimmy when he was eight, watching a Western movie in Ferriday, Louisiana. Jimmy heard a voice. It gave him "chill bumps, and made my scalp tingle." It was "almost like taking a bath continuously." He kept the water running. By 1985 the Arbitron Rating Service estimated that 2 million households each were taking his bath–not with water but words. Old timers remembered that special Deep South style–it had carried Bilbo Talmadge and Huey Long to power and glory. Jimmy's monthly magazine, *The Evangelist*, had a million readers and his JSM (Jimmy Swaggart Ministries) had one of the largest nonprofit direct mailing operations in the United States.[2]

The Lord had blessed him real good. The JSM Operation Center was located on 100 acres of prime real estate worth an estimated $2.8 million in suburban Baton Rouge, where a collection of immaculate, computer-controlled buildings make up his new World Ministry Center.

When the first phase of the Center was completed in 1985, there were 500,000 square feet of working area, including a $5 million television studio, a $30 million family worship center with seating for 7,000, a student dormitory, and an office building. I went to see for myself, and this was what I found.

"I really don't look at it as success or failure," the muscular evangelist comments in his luxurious office adorned by his gold record albums. "It's mostly the Lord. He wants me to do what I'm doing." Singer and showman, he punctuates his program with a heavy bass beat that brings audiences to their feet, swaying and clapping. Like his two cousins, Jerry Lee Lewis and Mickey Gilley, he works the crowd like a carnival barker, whispering, shouting, sneering, and crying. He draws his illustrations from current TV ads: "If you think Miller Lite is gonna carry you home, you're wrong. If you think the President is gonna carry you home, you're wrong. Jesus Christ is your savior. Glory hallelujah!"

Populist and Pentecostal, playing to the Good Ole Boys, Swaggart draws tears and cheers before getting to the "Altar Call." This has been part of the Southern religious tradition since frontier days.

Swaggart coaxes, pleads, and cajoles as the music falls back to a slow beat. He sweats. He cries. Special ministers, trained in the laying on of hands, come forward to help. Cameras zoom in for close-ups. It's alright if you want to cry–there are strategically placed open boxes of tissue on the edge of the stage. Jimmy tries to maintain his humility if not his cool: "I'm just attempting to follow the Lord and I believe He calls me." The Lord sent ailing Zoe McDonald Vance, the wife of a Texas oil tycoon who fell under Jimmy's spell. She left him $7 million, but relatives contested the will. They argued that Vance was the victim of a systematic, sophisticated, and manipulative effort by Swaggart and his staff to take advantage of the mentally and physically weakened woman.

"It's much easier to shoot at the one who's visible than to aim at the crowd when you don't really know who you re going to hit," Swaggart says, speculating on the accusations against him. "I'm very visible, so consequently I attract gainsayers and reputation-makers." The Texas court awarded Swaggart 70% of the estate, the remainder going to a memorial medical fund. When journalists explored the controversy, Swaggart was quick to explain: "I know that even a halfway competent reporter or journalist can make something sinister out of the Sermon on the Mount," he says. "It's easy to do."

Swaggart's outspoken brand of religion also has made it necessary for tight security at the ministry's headquarters. "We've received some hate mail and had a few kooks out here." Visitors must wear identification badges, and security guards are never far away.

Swaggart dismisses Roman Catholics as "poor pitiful individuals who think they have enriched themselves spiritually by kissing the pope's ring." He attacks John Calvin's doctrine of predestination and the belief that God's will is the cause of all evils, calling it "a lie." He brands the Roman Catholic Mass and most major Protestant services as "liturgical, religious monstrosities." While two Atlanta television stations dropped his show in 1983 when the Catholic Archdiocese charged he was slandering priests, others in the fiercely Protestant South picked it up for the same reason. In a carefully calculated Bayou Country drawl, Swaggart announces: "I've got to preach the truth as I see it. That doesn't set well with some kinds of religion. Sometimes I say things that people don't like."

Behind superstar Swaggart looms not only a mother but a grand-mother who enjoyed drinkin', smokin', hellin', and gamblin' before she "got religion." She also knew how to play the piano—and taught young 'uns. One was Jerry Lee Lewis, whose "Great Balls of Fire" was a 1950s pop hit; another was Jimmy Swaggart. They both dropped out of school and "ran in with the law" before finding the media. Lewis has remained bad, bad, bad—and successful. Jimmy continues to pray for him, and "will not be satisfied until I know Jerry Lee has entered the Kingdom of God." Meanwhile, Jimmy switched from his "Camp Meeting Hour" on radio (1969-1973) and found his real home on television. All of Jimmy's television programs are produced and dubbed into five foreign languages at his new Vance Teleproduction Center, which houses some of the finest technical equipment available.

Ministry officials say the 44,000-square-foot facility is in opera-tion virtually 24 hours a day to meet the increasing demands of production schedules. Swaggart has expanded his message to in-clude politics and politicians as his popularity has grown. "The Bible is actually the Constitution of the United States," the evange-list says. "The Bible is really the unsung, hidden Constitution."

JSM, like most other major televangelistic efforts, is a family affair. Wife Frances, Jimmy's "God-sent helpmate," has played an ever-increasing role in the crusades, looking and acting like the prefeminist housewife. Son Donnie is also blossoming, the heir apparent. They live well, on a lavish plot of about 20 acres in Baton Rouge. The land is enclosed by a tall fence strung between posts two feet thick. Local mortgage office records show that Swaggart and his family paid about $400,000 for the property in 1981.

Swaggart's home is a sprawling two-story structure of 7,500 square feet of living space and designed along the lines of a planta-tion home, according to building records in Baton Rouge. His son's home is slightly smaller. In a newspaper advertisement complaining about unfair treatment by a local television station, Swaggart said in 1983 that 14 relatives and members of his family are employed within the organization. Southerners don't mind. The family is al-

ways first with them. Jimmy looks after his own. Maybe that's why
God looks after Jimmy. Glory Hallelujah!

Life looked rosy for the Swaggarts in 1983. But–as we shall
see–all that would change a few years later.

To the north of Louisiana, but still in the South, two other
evangelical empires sprang up in the 1970s and 1980s–those of
Jerry Falwell and Pat Robertson, both in Virginia. They mixed
religion and politics, and became forces on the national scene.
Others had done this before them: Father Coughlin in the 1930s and
Billy James Hargis in the 1950s, for example. But Falwell's Moral
Majority and Pat Robertson's Christian Broadcasting Network
(CBN) wrote a whole new chapter in the history of popular religion.

For a decade, Jerry Falwell became the leading spokesman for
fundamentalism. The movement had long awaited a charismatic
leader who could bring the scattered but unrepentant forces into a
mighty army. They found one in Jerry Falwell.

Falwell's empire is centered in Lynchburg, Virginia, an ultraconservative piedmont town that was ransacked by the Yankees and
surpassed by upstart Roanoke, 50 miles west. The "Hill City"
nickname does not mirror the incredible success of its most famous
preacher. Once a tobacco center, then a canal port, then a railroad
junction, it sleeps now on its "Seven Hills," which no one mistakes
for Rome. The canal barges have disappeared, and the old steam
locomotives have rusted. Up and down the streets Victorian store-
fronts display "For Lease" signs. The long concrete staircase in
Lynchburg's center leads up to Court Street, and prim mainline
churches. At the top stands a Confederate soldier, bayonet fixed,
waiting stoically for the Yankee's next attack. The whole scene has
about it the silence of death.

Not so Falwell's Liberty Baptist Church, located in a low-income
neighborhood teeming with life. Two sets of classical revival columns decorate the handsome, new octagonal building, flanked by
acres of parking space for hundreds of cars. Far off one sees 30 or
40 yellow school buses waiting to bring in the sheep to heed the
shepherd. This is where the action is: the Bible-believing Thomas
Road Baptist Church. When not on the road, Jerry might be in the
pulpit, cultivating the down-home look and grass-roots connections

Jerry Falwell. (Photo courtesy of Public Relations Office, Liberty University.)

that are his secret weapon. People like Jerry "real good." And they pay for the privilege. I heard him in action.

When I returned in 1993, little had changed in terms of style and content. The well-designed, immaculate new church seats 3,500 people, and has TV cameras and speakers in strategic places. Smiling ushers show you to your seat, and a whole table of literature awaits in the vestibule. The mighty organ roars, and the well-trained choir sings. The Falwell formula still works well.

"Has Don recovered from his fall off the ladder, Joe?" he asks. (Not even a sparrow falls without Jerry's noticing.) When a red-headed lad named Stephen comes forward with the American flag, Jerry recalls that he was at the hospital when Stephen was born, ill with spinal meningitis. "We joined hands around his bed and prayed. He passed through the crisis. That's when his hair turned red." Bursts of laughter. Jerry's not just a preacher–he's a stand-up comic.

While praising the Lord, he gets in a few good words for his own institution, Liberty Baptist College. Their football team, "The Flames," has one of the state's best ends. The girls' volleyball team has won first place in a tournament. That's enough to make the ushers pass the collection plate. The Lord loveth a cheerful giver.

Falwell uses friendly, easy-to-remember "gimme" gimmicks: Stake Your Claim, Silver Anniversary, and Memorial Brick families. When you join Jerry you become a Faith Partner; the computer does the rest.

Falwell exudes confidence. His blue tailored suit has an expensive look; his gold rings and quartz watch sparkle underneath television lights. He has beads of sweat on his forehead, and a large comfortable grin on his face. He is a pro. Cables from multiple TV cameras snake up and down the aisles. Fluorescent lights bathe the church in an eerie glow that lights up the dandruff on men's shoulders. Behind the Pastor is a choir of 60 photogenic people in powder blue with not a theology but an ideology–a picture of the world to guide and inspire them. The essentials of the good and Godly life are being threatened by various "enemies of the Lord" who control much of the world today. Rather than change the message of the Gospel to meet the ever-changing needs of society, the fundamentalists believe the secular world and modern ways must be changed to fit the Gospel. They lament the runaway divorce rate, the pornography plague, the banning of God from the schoolhouse, and the spread of homosexuality–all tied to the rise of "secular humanism." The answers to the problems facing the world today lie in the revealed truth of the Bible. This translates to what Falwell likes to call the "old-time" traditional American values–including monogamy, law and order, and free-enterprise capitalism. How would this come about? Through a renewed emphasis–a more apt word might be crusade–on the divine destiny of the American democracy of the Founding Fathers. It's time to go home again.

Three dominant social attitudes characterize his church: (1) an overriding social and political conservatism, (2) a strong individualism and bourgeois mentality, and (3) acceptance of traditional American values. Evangelists who championed these attitudes in the 1970s became the vote-getters of the 1980s. To "make it on TV" they put frosting on the cake–glamor, pageantry, exaggeration, and sensationalism. But the cake itself was baked from a time-tested American recipe.

Falwell has built a coalition of fundamentalists and evangelists to "reshape the forces of conservative Christianity," and "return our nation to its spiritual and moral roots." Such statements give Jerry both credibility and publicity. He, if anyone, has moved fundamentalism from the underground to the foreground. Over 200,000 students are preparing for Christian vocations in conservative schools. The Christian school movement is estimated to have 15,000 schools with over 2 million students.

The figures are inflated, critics say. The fear of blacks, not of the Lord, inspires many of those private schools. Perhaps; but we err if we downgrade the figures, then walk away. Fundamentalist preachers, Falwell in particular, have clearly demonstrated–on all levels, in all regions–that they have appeal and know how to use it.

Millions who want school prayer, strong families, and "decent communities" free of hippies, oddballs, and porn have heard Falwell and said, "Now, *there's* our man!" Mainline churches waffled. Jerry said it straight.

Hence his "new" following confirms a standard media axiom: attitude change is most effective when the "new" attitudes are merely extensions of old existing ones. This is how Jerry builds. As the number of discarded, disfranchised, and lonely grow, so will his church.

Most Americans identify Jerry Falwell with the Moral Majority. Founded earlier by Richard Viguerie, a Roman Catholic layman, the group sought aid from Falwell's computer lists of "Old Time Gospel Hour" donors in 1979. Gradually Falwell became the spokesman, and most visible symbol, of the group that combines patriotism, politics, and fundamentalism. As part of the strategy, Falwell held "I Love America" rallies in 50 states, setting up parachurch organizations and regional offices. Membership figures are disputed. Falwell claimed 800,000 in 1980, a figure which was said to include 70,000 ministers. The majority were from the Baptist Bible Fellowship and Southwide Baptist Fellowship. Many nonreligious groups joined in, attracted by the fight to "Preserve the traditional American way of life." The group's influence on the 1980 and 1984 elections gave the Moral Majority new hope and greatly expanded its program.[3]

Not all Americans were pleased with the attitudes and interventions of the Moral Majority. New bumper stickers turned up on cars: "Member of the Immoral Minority," and "The Moral Majority is *Neither*." Media writers formed a group to oppose the Moral Majority–"People for the American Way." Its leader, Norman Lear, had produced such innovative television series as *All in the Family*, *Maude*, and *The Jeffersons*. In a letter to President Reagan, Lear pointed to the President's growing allegiance to the new Christian right and the seeming inability of Reagan and proponents of a stricter separation of church and state to reach agreement.

The President, defending his position, said in one letter: "I am not using this office as a pulpit for one religion over all the others, but I do subscribe to George Washington's remark regarding high moral standards, decency, etc., and their importance to civilization and his conclusion that to think we could have these without religion as a base was to ask for the impossible."

"Obviously," he continued, "when I'm addressing an audience who share my own religious beliefs–indeed, a religious group–I see nothing wrong with talking of our mutual interests. I can recall no instance where I have ever tried to proselytize others or impose my beliefs on those of other faiths."

Lear, responding that the correspondence had been "enlighten-ing, but alas, not encouraging," concluded: "Perhaps we must sim-ply agree to disagree."

Those following the controversy noted that 20 years earlier Jerry Falwell had held a totally different view. In a 1965 sermon called "Ministers and Marchers" he had said:

> Believing in the Bible as I do, I would find it impossible to stop preaching the pure saving gospel of Jesus Christ and begin doing anything else, including fighting Communism, or participating in civil rights reforms. Preachers are not called on to be politicians but to be soul winners. Nowhere are we commissioned to reform the externals.

By then the mainstream Protestant churches–Methodists, Episco-palians, Congregationalists, Presbyterians, and the like–had turned from trying to make the nation "a Christian commonwealth" to supporting civil rights, opposing the Vietnam War, and making active efforts on social issues, usually on the side of political liber-als.

At the same time, the political system was undergoing a basic change. The major political parties, which once assimilated and assigned priority to issues, were being replaced by a host of individ-ual interest groups that competed directly for government assistance and recognition. For years fundamentalists stayed out of politics. Then, on short notice, they jumped in with both feet. They found common cause with the Republicans, picked winners, and made winners. Their day had come.

While the fundamentalist churches have been gaining members and resources, partly through television broadcasts, mainstream churches have had no such growth. They have been involved in internal disputes over their positions on political issues: how far they should go, for example, in condemning Reagan's foreign policy and in criticizing the practices of capitalism and nuclear expansion.

Indeed, the whole religious scene has become bewildering to the average churchgoer. New groups, communes, crusades, sects, and "freaks" have become so jumbled that many critics ended up con-demning them all. Especially in the 1960s, when there was a new

Eleventh Commandment (Do Your Own Thing!), confusion reigned and sympathy waned. Even participants and apologists had trouble sorting things out. A plastic-wrapped, shine-and-glow, show-and-tell society mixed cynicism with hope, means with extremes, and sense with nonsense. The path the 1960s took was a whirlwind of high moral purpose combined with the centrifugal forces generated by creating new directions in an atmosphere of terrifying freedom.

So bring on your flower children, love-ins, lock-outs, group encounters, and gang bangs; the assassination of leaders, race riots, unwanted wars, and ecology's dance of death. Take the magical mystical tour through strawberry fields and marmalade skies of psychedelia. Try astrology, kinky sex, Ouija boards, tarot cards, and I Ching. *Do Your Own Thing!*

Jesus People roamed the land, headed for places like the Areopagus House in California, the Lighter Side of Darkness House in Illinois, or the Love Inn in New York. By 1967 there were more than 800 "Christian Houses" functioning, 200 in California alone, and an up-to-date "Jesus People Directory." One convert, Arthur Blessitt, dragged a cross 3,500 miles from California to Washington, D.C., preaching along the way. That's a hard act to follow.

Members of the Process Church of the Final Judgment wore three-horned goathead symbols and silver crosses. They worshipped three Gods–Jehovah, Pan, and Satan. The Holy Order of MANS chose an acronym for mystic terms which the group would not reveal; but they stressed reincarnation and extrasensory perception. The Children of God preached complete disregard for authority and for all laws. In their communes mail from home went into a bag marked "Egypt," the synonym for bondage. The days of "Home Sweet Home" on the living-room wall seemed over. At that point Jerry Falwell and the fundamentalists emerged. Liberalism seemed bankrupt. It was time to get out the Bible.

There is little that distinguishes Falwell as a theologian. He is a fundamental Southern Baptist, using the phrases and cliches of his faith. His God is a righteous ruler who demands vengeance. His prophet is Elijah, who wants to see the chaff burned with unquenchable fire. One of Jerry's favorite gestures is the forefinger pointed at the sinner. He seems not to notice that three fingers are directed back at him.

He excels as a promoter-salesman. He knows God is in the details; that lots of little items bring in big bucks. Any edition of his *Moral Majority Report*, for which he claims a million subscriptions, confirms this.

Look at the ads. Buy a comfortable slipper ("It won't slip out from under you!"); lower your blood pressure without prescription drugs; stand or sit without help in a "cushion lifting chair." Help yourself to sleep better, with an "inflatable sleep incliner wedge–" only $4.88. Or buy a pair of professional toenail clippers for $2.99. Try a new Electronic Pain Killer, which relieves muscular backache, headache, even pain of tennis elbow, arthritis, and bursitis! (It's on sale for $29.95.) Perhaps you'd rather have "The Complete Words of Francis A. Schaeffer," or the old-time records of Kate Smith or Nelson Eddy.

Of course, there is a large assortment of Bibles and plastic relics–to say nothing of a religious quartz clock. Patriots can buy the "Double Eagle" Ronald Reagan commemorative coin ($10 plus $3 for mailing). For fishermen there is a spinning reel for only $4, and for health buffs a book entitled *Vitamin Side Effects Revealed*. Get-rich-quick schemes abound: "Retire before fifty–Clean with Duraclean!" "Sell part-time, make full-time income!" "Make $1,000 a month with just a hacksaw."

But the main thing that Jerry sells, after salvation, is education. The centerpiece is his Liberty Baptist College, founded in 1971 with 141 students to "train champions for Christ." Growth was phenomenal. Falwell was soon urging the flock to watch the Macy's Thanksgiving Day parade on TV and see the band "from America's fastest growing college"–his, of course. True enough, there was the Marching Flames Band from LBC. At first, classes were held at the church, with church staff serving as faculty. By 1982 the College had 4,000 students and plans to develop 200 acres of the 4,200 acre tract Falwell bought on hills outside Lynchburg. Most of the funding came from monthly contributions of $15 to $20, solicited through Falwell's church and television audience. Operating expenses for 1982 exceeded $21 million. In 1985, with an enrollment of over 5,000, the college officially changed its name to Liberty Baptist University.

By then the buildings on Falwell's tract had 75 academic majors,

including schools of religion, education, arts and sciences, communications, and business. Projecting an enrollment of 50,000 by the
end of the century (including master's and doctoral programs), his
university, said Falwell, would be "the Fundamentalist Harvard in
academics and the Fundamentalist Notre Dame in athletics." The
University was also challenging its graduates to start 5,000 new
churches in North America by the end of the century.

All this gives the faithful reason to rejoice, but the atmosphere on
campus is far from festive. The tone is Puritanical. The motto might
well be "Resist the sins of the flesh." Only born-again students are
accepted. They may not dance or attend movies. Girls must wear
modest dresses; boys, coats and ties. Sideburns cannot go below the
earlobes. Proctors tell students when to study, when to pray, and
when to go to bed. Church and chapel attendance is mandatory. No
beards or mustaches. Hair must not touch the shirt collar. No country or rock music (not even Christian rock), no smoking or drinking,
and a daily room check. Married male students must, "as heads of
the household, see that wives dress with appropriate Christian modesty." Dating is permitted–but freshmen and sophomores must
double-date. Most of the students I interviewed said they liked the
campus and the codes. They feared they "couldn't handle" the
freedom (they prefer to call it license) of "worldly universities."
Jerry knows what is best. We remember George Orwell.

Those who shudder and see in all this a new form of mind
control, perhaps even Big Brother, should realize that fundamentalism has positive appeal. It champions strong marriages, clean living, and moral responsibility. That all are in short supply provides
Falwell with wonderful targets. He gives Southern paranoia full
license, combining theater and technology with masterful effect. He
has learned much from his political mentor, Ronald Reagan, but
Falwell always looks out for Falwell. Noting the rising tide against
Reagan's visit to a German military cemetery in 1985, Falwell
spoke out against it. He makes a point of knowing where his sheep
are, and how they think. Then he can lead them.

Gradually Falwell has attained international attention. In 1984 he
was chosen to "represent" America's policy in a debate at England's Oxford University. In 1985 he visited South Africa, during a
period of racial unrest and crisis, to get firsthand information on the

problem. Returning to the United States, he appeared on national television and denounced black Bishop Desmond Tutu, Nobel Peace Prize winner, as a "phony." He even pledged the support of the Moral Majority for the white South African government. Twenty years earlier Falwell had chastised white American preachers for joining civil rights marches. Then, too, thousands rallied to his side.

The Rev. Jerry Falwell is a perceptive, ambitious man, and for a while his power waxed. Then, suddenly, it began to wane. Events after 1987 cut deeply into his empire, and caused the demise of the Moral Majority. We shall explore some of the reasons in the next and last chapters.

Pat Robertson, Falwell's evangelical Virginia neighbor, fared better. He had a more substantial and credible background and education; and he grasped, better than anyone else, the power of television. He could boast of a series of "firsts"–first religious TV station, first religious network, and first evangelist to use a talk-show format. Perhaps most impressive of all, he was the first to have worldwide connections (through the American Forces Radio and Television Services) and to run for the Presidency. He was prominent at the 1992 Houston Convention of the Republican Party, and seems to have the most promising future of all the major tele-vangelists.

Son of a U.S. Senator, Phi Beta Kappa, graduate of the Yale Law School, Pat Robertson presides over the "Video Vatican" at Virginia Beach. Trained as a minister, anxious to serve the poor, he fled a Pentecostal parsonage in Brooklyn, purchased a defunct television studio, and launched the nation's first Christian television station (WYAN) in 1961. To rally the faithful under the banner of the "700 Club," Robertson used telethon and telephone volunteers with the goal of getting 700 people to pledge ten dollars a month. And lo, the hundreds became thousands. Viewers enjoy his "celebrity-meets-celebrity format," as Robertson interviews fascinating people who write bestsellers, lead the Hit Parade, and roam the Corridors of Power. All have one common denominator: they are born-again Christians, who make their pitch and thus bolster Robertson's Christian Broadcasting Network.

This multimillion-dollar operation involves four television sta-

Pat Robertson. (Photo courtesy of Christian Broadcasting Network.)

tions, a recording company, a 24-hour-a-day programming service available to more than 3,000 cable systems, a complete news network, a university, and satellite earth stations. Its daily audience is estimated at over 7 million. How well does it all work? In a single 1985 short telephone campaign, CBN raised over $77 million. Robertson's appeal was typically low-key but persuasive: "I'd like us to get all that's ours in the Kingdom," he said night after night. Apparently he got it.

A direct spin-off of CBN is PTL, founded by ex-CBN employee Jim Bakker in 1974. He set up his own electric base in nearby Charlotte, North Carolina. By 1978 he had over 200 television stations nationwide: more affiliates than the entire ABC network. Young, toothy, and teary, Jim and his wife, Tammy, had learned their lessons well.[4]

But like the youthful Alexander the Great, Jim yearned for other kingdoms to conquer. Heady with the success of PTL ("Praise the Lord"–or as critics suggested, "Pass the Loot"), he bought a vast tract of land and set out to build the first Christian theme park to serve as headquarters for his worldwide evangelism and electronic campaigns. With the omnipresent Tammy and children, Tammy Sue and Jamie Charles, he constructed a vast multimillion-dollar "Twenty-First Century Fellowship Center" with a Grand Hotel featuring "turn of the century elegance." (The contradiction of entering the next century by reverting to the style of the last is a hallmark of contemporary evangelism.) The park is modeled on Disney World, which is further down the road in Florida. There is a cutesy-folksy Main Street ("a delightful, old-fashioned potpourri of quaint shops and cafes, all beneath a soaring climate-controlled cyclorama ceiling that creates its own weather moods"), a Grand Palace Cafeteria ("the largest cafeteria of its kind"), a Seminar/ Conference Center (home of PTL's Total Learning Center Workshops, and the great Hall of Agreement), and Heritage Grand Towers. Much more was planned: a projected Heritage Island, "one of the world's finest, state-of-the-art water fun parks," complete with Christian atmosphere, upbeat music, and live entertainment. Passes would be "good for all day in the sun and fun." Here was Christian competition for Disney World. The Bakkers, it seemed, had found their own highly profitable El Dorado.

How can one explain the incredible growth and influence of Dixie's Holy Warriors? They were warring against an ancient foe— modernism; but others had done so with far less success. Certainly the new technology helped, but there were other factors at work. As early as 1949, Billy Graham raised the question that millions would ask in the years ahead: "Will we turn to the leftwingers and atheists or will we turn to the right and embrace the cross?"

The rise of the counterculture, the drug culture, and the hippies was alarming enough; but when the U.S. Supreme Court prohibited prayer in public schools and allowed abortions, open warfare broke out.

"By 1975," Professor R. D. Petty writes, "the trigger had been pulled, and fundamentalism had been propelled into the *Social Unrest* phase."[5] The trigger was Jimmy Carter, a born-again Southern president, and the fundamentalists rejoiced. "We have enough votes to run the country, and we're going to take over," Pat Robertson boasted on his CBN; and when the Moral Majority was formed in 1979, it seemed as if he might be right.

In those peak years for televangelism, how large was the audience? Dr. Ben Armstrong, who coined the phrase "Electric Church," claimed over 100 million. The *Wall Street Journal* is credited with the highest estimate, 130 million. Others claimed it was far less. No one doubts it was large and powerful.[6]

Nor can anyone dispute the rapid outreach and growth of the electric church. By 1987, 20 religious radio stations and two religious TV stations were opening every month.

But the glory days were soon to end. The whole movement would move abruptly from the Garden of Success to the Garden of Excess. The Year of Scandals was about to begin.

NOTES

1. Of the writing of books about the South and religion, evangelism, and fundamentalism, there is no end. A good place to begin is with W. J. Cash's classic *The Mind of the South* (New York: Knopf, 1941). My own thoughts on these matters are set forth in *Virginia: A New Look at the Old Dominion* (New York: Harper and Row, 1960). For early religious trends see Wesley M. Gewehr, *The Great Awakening in Virginia* (Durham: Duke University Press, 1930); Charles A. Johnson, *The Frontier Camp Meeting: Religion's Harvest Time* (Dal-

las: Southern Methodist University Press, 1955); and Donald G. Mathews, *Religion in the Old South* (Chicago: University of Chicago Press, 1977).

2. See Steve Bruce, *Pray TV: Televangelism in America* (London: Routledge, 1990), ch. 4; and Christa Arnold and Dean Fedely, "Sex, Sin, Satan and Swaggart," (Paper delivered at the annual convention of the Popular Culture Association, New Orleans, April 8, 1993).

3. See David Snowball, *Continuity and Change in the Rhetoric of the Moral Majority* (New York: Praeger, 1991).

4. Charles E. Shepherd, *The Rise and Fall of Jim Bakker* (New York: Atlantic Monthly, 1989).

5. R. D. Petty, "Bibles, Ballots, and Beatific Vision," in Robert Abelman and Stewart M. Hoover, eds., *Religious Television: Controversies and Conclusions* (Norwood, NJ: Ablex, 1990), p. 201.

6. Stewart M. Hoover, "The Religious Television Audience: A Matter of Significance of Size?" *Review of Religious Research*, 29(2) (December 1987), pp. 28-33.

Chapter 14

The Chicken Little Panic

With God in His heaven and Reagan in the White House, every-thing was coming up roses for the televangelists in the mid-1980s. Then everything started to fall apart. The year 1987 might be called the Chicken Little Panic for popular religion–the sky was falling down.

At the center of the debacle were superstars Jim and Tammy Bakker: Southern, smug, and sweet as candied yams. Leaving Pat Robertson's CBN in 1972, Bakker set up his own PTL ("Praise the Lord"), the first network to broadcast Christian programs 24 hours a day to all of North America.[1] Heritage USA, a flashy religious theme park, became one of the spectacular successes of the day, as millions poured into the Bakkers' till. Tammy was a master fund-raiser. "We've done everything we can to pay our bills," she would sob on television. "We've given everything we have. Literally everything." After one such plea, it was discovered that the Bakkers had just bought a $450,000 home and two new cars–a Mercedes and a Rolls-Royce.

Yet it was not greed but sex that brought down the blue skies. On March 19, 1987, Jim Bakker admitted he had been involved sexually with 20-year-old Jessica Hahn, and was resigning his ministry. That opened the floodgates: a mighty deluge followed. Under oath, Hahn said she had been the victim of a double rape, and had been black-mailed to keep quiet.[2] The juicy details went to the top of the chart, in such publications as *Time*, *Newsweek*, and *Christianity Today.*

And how juicy they were! Here is Jessica's account of how Jim Bakker treated her:

> He started almost from the top of my head and didn't stop for what seemed like an hour and a half. He did just everything he could do to a woman . . . and he wouldn't stop . . . He had to keep finding new things to do. I just wanted to pull his hair.[3]

At the end he forced her to have oral sex. Then Bakker's side-kick, John Wesley Fletcher (another Pentecostal evangelist), forced her to repeat all this with him.

This would never do. The other televangelists rushed in to protect their good names. Heavy artillery came into play. Suddenly the critics of the "Holy Rollers" could sit back and enjoy what came to be known as the Holy War.

On March 26 Oral Roberts and Robert Schuller entered the fray. (Roberts had announced earlier that if more money was not forthcoming, God would "take him." Apparently God gave him a reprieve when all this happened.) Lesser figures vied for a place in the sun. Evangelist John Ankerberg went on national television, claiming that Bakker was serviced by prostitutes, undisturbed by wife-swapping on his staff, and involved in homosexual practices.

Enter Jerry Falwell, who agreed to "take control" of the messy situation. Why did Bakker allow this? Because, he said, he was the victim of a hostile takeover from a fellow minister in the Assemblies of God, Jimmy Swaggart.

But Jimmy, it came to be known, had problems of his own. Sometimes known as the Scourge of Sinners (he had, for example, helped defrock and bankrupt another TV evangelist, Marvin Gorman), Swaggart broke down and confessed his liaisons with prostitutes and long-standing obsession with pornography. Stand by, Chicken Little.

Always one to take the initiative, Swaggart faced his millions of TV viewers, confessed, and burst into tears. All this took place on February 21, 1988. Finally he addressed God:

> I have sinned against you, my Lord, and I would ask that your precious blood would wash and cleanse every stain until it is in the seas of God's forgetfulness, never to be remembered against me anymore.[4]

Then he skillfully shifted the focus from himself to the universal need for forgiveness. His hand was placed on the Bible. "This Gospel is flawless even though it is ministered by flawed men." He begged his wife, son, and son-in-law for forgiveness. As the audience clapped and cried, the begging was expanded, to include his church, his college, the Assemblies of God, and all the television audience.

The confession was rhetorical and effective but the damage had been done. The Swaggart Ministries lost TV coverage when 200 stations dropped his weekly program; ratings declined 69%; revenues fell from $3 million to $1 million.

The fate of the Bakkers was even more devastating. An official body of the Assemblies of God banished them from PTL, and defrocked Jim Bakker. Waging a counterattack, Bakker went on national television and blamed Jerry Falwell for stealing the ministry. Falwell rallied, condemning Bakker's immorality, dishonesty, and greed. The clouds got darker and darker. PTL filed for protection under federal bankruptcy laws, and Jim Bakker, having stood trial, went off to jail.[5]

Swaggart also went from bad to worse. In October 1991 he was caught in the company of a prostitute named Rosemary Garcia. He was forced to resign and seek medical help; his TV studios were shut down, his equipment sold. *Res judicata*–the matter has been decided.[6]

What has not been decided is how much the scandals (and there were other less-publicized ones) will affect not only televangelism but conservative Christianity in general. Apparently no lasting damage has been done in the eyes of core constituencies. Preachers may betray, but not the Bible. Another factor is that in fundamentalism there is an imperative to forgive. The most popular speakers on the "born-again" circuit (such as Chuck Colson, the Watergate fixer, and Eldridge Cleaver, the radical black) had to be "forgiven," and made handsome profits from the process. Those who had always suspected and derided the televangelists felt confirmed, of course; and all the comedians added Bakker and Swaggart jokes to their repertoire.

Many scholars did not find it a joking matter, characterizing what had occurred as "The Rape of the Vulnerable." They suggested that religious fervor tends to follow the vagaries of capitalism, captivated by wealth, lust, greed, and power. Ray Browne raised these questions after the Chicken Little Panic: "Will the televangelists continue to prosper, or have the affairs lowered the value of their stock on the Heavenly Stock Exchange? Are the explosions merely a part of a Great Religious Franchise War?"[7]

It is too early to tell; but we have certainly seen an incredible splintering of the forces that make up popular religion in the Ec-static Eighties: not only with the televangelists but also the Moonies, Jesus freaks, body mystics, India gurus, crusading funda-mentalists, hands-on healers, out-of-body tourists, tongue-speakers, proud witches, and trembling exorcists. Are we headed for a Great Awakening or chaos?

Certainly chaos took over in a fundamentalist compound near Waco, Texas in March 1993. Led by David Koresh, who claimed to be Jesus Christ, the barricaded group shot and killed four Federal agents, then destroyed themselves by fire. A shocked nation looked on in disbelief, and political ramifications rocked the administration in Washington. How could this happen?

No one has given a better explanation than Michael D'Antonio, who immersed himself for two years in the Christian Right. He believes that more and more people feel lost in the ever-more modern high-tech society, and yearn for the security that has been lost. He agrees with H. L. Mencken, who said in 1925 that conser-vative Christianity is a fire still burning on a far-flung hill. Who could have anticipated the firestorm at Waco? And how many fires will break out as we approach the millennium?[8]

Scandals in the religious sphere have been matched in recent years by scandals in the political and social arena. Trust in our basic institutions, and those who govern us, has reached an all-time low. This, in turn, has caused many conservative Christians to band together to meet what the Book of Revelation calls the final battle. Chicken Little concerns are endemic. In the 1990s Colorado Springs, for example, has become a center for the religious right, with over 40 evangelical groups based there. Many residents of this city of 280,000 fear that the city is becoming a haven of intolerance, and some of them started Citizens Project in 1993 as a "counter-voice" to the evangelicals. They were alarmed when a school in the nearby town of Woodland Park was sued for teaching Greek and Roman mythology, on the grounds that if these were taught, so should Christianity. Other schools cut back on Halloween celebra-tions following loud protests that this holiday had pagan origins.

The largest of the evangelical groups, Focus on the Family, moved to Colorado Springs from Los Angeles in 1991 after having received a $4 million grant from a local foundation, El Pomar.

Another highly visible group, the New Life Church, has 3,300 members who (according to *The New York Times*) respond with exuberant clapping and shouts of "Amen!" and "That's right!" The fundamentalist groups constantly tell members how to exert their influence in areas from public schools to federal legislation. How communities like Colorado Springs will respond will make an interesting chapter in the saga of popular religion.

But if support in North America was sagging, it was increasing mightily in South America. In 1987 about one-eighth of the Latin American population was fundamentalist, Pentecostal, or evangelical.[9] Growth was even more spectacular in East Asia, which had less than 2 million Christians in 1900 and over 80 million in 1987. The vast majority of these (one estimate was 80%) were Pentecostal or charismatic. Much of this growth was in the new megacities of the Third World, such as Mexico City, Buenos Aires, Saõ Paulo, Bombay, and Seoul. New values and attitudes emerged, and religions with new hope prospered. This was the same kind of appeal that Methodism had in England during the Industrial Revolution, and it seems to be growing stronger as we prepare to enter the twenty-first century.

Worldwide evangelical radio continued to expand. By 1990, a missionary radio station in Quito, Ecuador was broadcasting 24 hours a day, with programs in 13 languages. The larger TransWorld Radio, begun in 1954, was covering the entire globe and broadcasting in 75 languages. Some saw this to mean that popular religion has emerged from its postimperial self-doubt, and is ready again to Christianize the heathen, from Greenland's icy mountain to India's coral strand. Clearly the Christian message was being reinterpreted to meet local needs. It was the conservative, not the liberal, churches that were the gainers.

Conservative Protestants were willing to spend money for these missionary efforts, at home and abroad. Thought to be terminally ill at the turn of the century, conservatives not only survived the closing years of that century, but were in better shape than the mainstream churches.[10] Go around any American town–mine, for example–and you will see that the newer buildings and most ambitious expansion plans belong to the conservatives.[11]

So do a number of new universities and training schools–Oral

Roberts University, Jerry Falwell's Liberty University, Herbert W. Armstrong's Ambassador Colleges, Robertson's CBN University. They are producing not only pastors, but Bible-oriented graduates in law, medicine, communication, business, and journalism. Their impact will not be felt for some years, but it will be considerable.

So will the "changing of the guard" which occurred in 1992 when the Reagan-Bush era ended, and the Clinton-Gore baby boomers took charge. The new President was young enough to be the son of either of his predecessors; his worldview was so different from theirs that it was not just a change but a sea change. Moreover, Clinton was a Baptist from the traditional Southern Bible Belt. And the discredited televangelists were regrouping for another battle.

Take heart, Chicken Little. The sky may not be falling down after all.

NOTES

1. Joe E. Barnhart, *Jim and Tammy: Charismatic Intrigue Inside PTL* (Buffalo: Prometheus, 1988), ch. 1.

2. Steve Bruce, *Pray TV: Televangelism in America* (London: Routledge, 1990), ch. 10.

3. Barnhart, *op. cit.*, p. 162.

4. Bruce, *op. cit.*, p. 207.

5. John Stewart, *Holy War: An Inside Account of the Battle for PTL* (Enid, OK: Fireside, 1987).

6. Christa Arnold and Dean Fedely, "Sex, Sin, Satan, and Swaggart," (Paper delivered at the annual convention of the Popular Culture Association, New Orleans, LA, April 8, 1993).

7. Marshall W. Fishwick and Ray Browne, *The God Pumpers: Religion in the Electronic Age* (Bowling Green, OH: Bowling Green University Press, 1987.) Browne believes the public will be deceived "as long as the public does not have some definite purpose in mind, some national and personal goal."

8. Michael D'Antonio, *Fall from Grace: The Failed Crusade of the Christian Right* (New Brunswick: Rutgers University Press, 1992).

9. David Martin, *Aspiring Flames: The Explosion of the Protestanism in Latin America* (London: Basil Blackwell, 1993), p. 51.

10. W. C. Roof and W. McKinney, *American Mainline Religion: Its Changing Shape and Future* (New Brunswick, NJ: Rutgers University Press, 1988).

11. *Ibid*, p. 245.

Chapter 15

Big Mac and Big Jesus:
Brave New McWorld

We have been so mesmerized by sex and scandal in the pulpit that we may have missed the real threat to Christianity: the McDonaldization of the church.

The alarm has already been sounded by George Ritzer in his book *The McDonaldization of Society: An Investigation Into the Changing Character of Contemporary Social Life.*[1] The issues were stated even more succinctly by Benjamin R. Barter in a seminal article entitled "Jihad vs. McWorld."[2]

Ritzer defines McDonaldization as the process by which the principles of the fast-food restaurant are coming to dominate more and more sectors of American society as well as the rest of the world. It shows every sign of being an inexorable process engulfing seemingly impervious institutions–such as the church.

Barter puts the matter even more clearly in religious terms, using the Islamic term *Jihad* (holy war) contending with the new mass culture, labeled McWorld. He thinks the key word is *fast*: fast food (McDonald's), fast computers (Macintosh), fast music (MTV), pressing nations into one commercially homogenous global glob: one McWorld, kept on course by televangelists. The planet is falling precipitantly apart and coming reluctantly together at the very same moment. O brave new McWorld!

There are striking parallels between the rise of Big Mac and Big (Electronic) Jesus. The first McDonald's opened outside Chicago in 1955, when Billy Graham's ministry was making national headlines, and television was becoming evangelism's medium of choice. The goal was products–customers for food chains, converts for evangelists. The key to success had been spelled out in the 1920s by the German social theorist Max Weber: standardize, mechanize, rationalize. The rational systems would surely increase efficiency; but, Weber warned, they would also dehumanize. That is exactly what has happened. The Protestant Ethic and the spirit of capitalism have merged.[3]

Success hangs on the administration of things–with people among the chief things to be administered. In both the secular and sacred areas, McWorld, aided always by high tech, swears by laissez-faire market principles and worships a new trinity: efficiency, productivity, and beneficence.

If one goes strictly by the numbers–or should we say the bottom line–Big Mac may have outdistanced Big Jesus.[4] By 1993 there were 12,000 McDonald's serving Big Macs, as 100 other fast-food chains tried to catch up. They had all been McDonaldized. They had increased their efficiency, predictability, calculability, and control.

The land of the free is also the land of the "Mc." Not only is this true at McDonald's (where Big Macs, McNuggets, and McLeans prevail) but in dozens of other places. We have McDentists, McDoctors, McChild Centers. The highly successful *USA Today* has become our McPaper, serving us "News McNuggets"; and when the paper launched a TV program modeled on the newspaper, it was quickly dubbed "News McRather."

There is more. Leave off the "Mc," and note the scores of businesses that use "Mc" principles and tricks pioneered by fast-food chains. The spokesperson of Toys "R" Us says they want to be thought of as a sort of McDonald's of toys. The same could be said of others using McModel: Jiffy-Lube, Midas Muffler, H&R Block, Pearle Vision Centers, AAMCO Transmissions, AT&T, Kampgrounds of America (KOA), and Kinder Care (also known as "Kentucky Fried Children").

Endless advertising and forced pleasantries ("Have a Nice Day!") would have us believe all this is a vast improvement–nowhere else in the world can one find such efficiency, economy, predictability, and productivity. And "they do it all for you." This might be translated, in the world of popular religion, as Amazing Grace.

Big Mac and Big Jesus have other things in common. Both offer not only a "product," but also entertainment. Fast-food restaurants are a kind of amusement park for food; televangelist's church services, an amusement park for religion. There is color, smiles, variety in both places. McDonald's has pretty young waitresses, the televangelists, pretty young sopranos. They both offer a kind of public theater, offering not so much a private experience as a public spectacle–and a superbly orchestrated sales campaign.

We have learned to "sell" hamburgers or salvation with a carefully conceived program using the three Ps: promotion, packaging, and profit. We know it has sold billions of hamburgers. Only God knows how many souls it has saved. But televangelists have millions of names to work with. Recall that back in the 1930s, Father Coughlin had to employ 106 clerks and four personal secretaries just to handle the mail. All that was B.C.–before computers. With salesmen for Big Jesus, they are state of the art. I know, because I have gotten on the mailing lists and have seen the results. This is high tech persuasion at its best–or should we say at its worst?

The tendencies towards mass-produced efficiency at the price of dehumanization spread far beyond the religious or economic sphere. Bill Clinton was labeled the first "McDonaldized" president in 1993, and all the official rhetoric did not quell fears about his medical and health reforms. It seemed as if the chief task of the presidency had become not governing but selling.

When religion becomes an accelerated sales campaign, conversion may well become a pseudo event. Of course there are genuine conversions, healings, savings–yet we wonder how many are staged for the media? Perhaps one of the perennial fears of Christians for centuries is coming true in ours: that religion has become captive of the culture and its values; that it has not only copied but wedded the culture, an unequal partner willing to love, cherish, and obey. Then the top dollar becomes the bottom line. Not truth but profit is supposed to set you free.

If this becomes the case, religion in America will have cut itself off from the very forces that might redeem and reconstruct it. We will have won the battle and lost the war. Big Jesus never planned it that way.

NOTES

1. George Ritzer, *The McDonaldization of Society: An Investigation Into the Changing Character of Contemporary Social Life* (Newberry Park, CA: Pine Forge, 1993). Ritzer points out that many of the trends he discusses were first analyzed half a century ago by Max Weber.

2. Benjamin R. Barter, "Jihad vs. McWorld," *The Atlantic Monthly* (March 1992), pp. 53-63.

3. Max Weber, *The Protestant Ethic and the Spirit of Capitalism* (New York: Scribner's, 1904-5/1968) and "Religious Rejections of the World and Their Directions," in *From Max Weber: Essays in Sociology,* H. H. Gerth and C. W. Mills, ed., (New York: Oxford University Press, 1915/1958). For work by a neo-Weberian, see Ronald Takaki, *Iron Cages: Race and Culture in 19th Century America* (New York: Oxford University Press, 1990).

4. Marshall W. Fishwick, ed., *The World of Ronald McDonald* (Bowling Green, OH: Bowling Green University Press, 1983); and Max Boas and Steve Chain, *Big Mac: The Unauthorized Story of McDonald's* (New York: E.P. Dutton, 1976). The spectacular success of McDonald's in Russia and the Pacific Rim has been widely heralded. McDonald's expects more than one half of its revenue to come from abroad after 1994.

Chapter 16

Some Final Thoughts

Tongues of fire with strange words and nowords . . .

–Harold Bloom,
The American Religion

Watching the inauguration of Bill Clinton, America's forty-second president, on January 20, 1993, one could have no doubt that religion was popular and prominent. On such occasions as this, the doctrine of the separation of church and state seems to disappear.

There was the Aging Eagle, Billy Graham, giving his blessing as he had with every president for half a century; conceding that "the nation is reaping the whirlwind of crime, racism, immorality and social injustice," and urging the nation to turn to "the Mighty God, the Prince of Peace." He closed his final benediction "in the name of the Father and the Son and the Holy Ghost."

President Clinton's Inaugural Address abounded with religious references, and pleaded for God's help. He quoted from the New Testament (Galatians 6:9), using the King James Version so dear to conservatives and fundamentalists. Maya Angelou's official Inaugural Poem was in the same vein, referring to the Creator and listing religious groups in the plea for national unity.

A few days later the new president announced immediate integration of gays into the military, and set off a firestorm of protest and outrage. Both the Old and New Testaments condemn homosexuality–a key plank in the Christian Right agenda. Clinton soon found out how true this was. Pat Robertson sounded a clarion call to his weekly audience, estimated at 15 million. He warned that "very very radical groups . . . who just yap, yap, yap" were behind this dreadful decision. What should a good Christian do? Call the Congressional switchboard–he kept flashing 202-224-3121 on the screen–and let them know what you think.

They did. By 5 p.m. on the first day more than 434,000 calls (ten times the daily average) had been made, most of them opposing the ending of the ban against gay military service. Meanwhile, Jerry Falwell was sending out the same plea on his "Old Time Gospel Hour," as were other major conservative figures such as James Dobson and Paul Weyrich.

Not only Congress, but also the Washington press, were impressed. The *Washington Post* documented the outburst, attributing it to evangelical groups whose members were largely poor, uneducated, and easy to command (February 1, 1993). Now it was the *Post's* turn to be deluged. "They were very angry," said Joann Byrd, the paper's ombudsman. "They felt insulted." The Christian rock fills the air, and religious news takes up columns of our newspapers and magazines. Still, the crucial question haunts us. Are we "saved?" Is America more religious than it was ten or 20 years ago?[1]

Since we cannot see inside human hearts, we cannot know. The externals may or may not point that way. Pollsters report that when asked about the role of religion, most Americans think it is "more important to them"–whatever that means. They also confirm a "Back to the Bible" mentality, and a greater willingness to confront political problems from a religious viewpoint. "You hear less about science being able to save us," sociologist Robert N. Bellah of the University of California noted in 1985. "The mood is changing, especially in the universities." As a university teacher, I agree. The fundamentalists are plainly the big winners. The National Council of Churches, a kind of ecumenical umbrella for liberal churches, has lost ground and support, and now has little influence with the White House.

Why have so many liberals and intellectuals been ineffective against the fundamentalists? Perhaps because they too are insulated and isolated, victims of their own preconceptions. We are the true individuals, the free ones, liberals insist–while demonstrating in speech, dress, politics, and lifestyle that they are often frightened conformists. The myth of the autonomous individual has filled our universities with scholars who are slaves to security, status, and tenure.

Academics talk of holocausts and crusades, while waging petty battles for crumbs from the table. They take refuge in pointless questions and measurable results, labeled "advanced research." Reality becomes what is realizable in these petty kingdoms. Pompous and proud, they turn all the world into an extended battle over semantics.[2]

Liberalism may not be dead but dormant. All this may be part of the cycle. The gods, very old and very powerful, are not easily discarded. They wait patiently for a new day.

Not so, some say, in the age of televangelism. The notion that new media can destroy religion is a fiction. Media are more apt to revive and extend religion–to bring about a cultural fission. That may be the most important achievement of the 1990s.

Not so, evangelists would argue. The great achievement is salvation–the deliverance from the power and effects of sin. (The root word is *salver*, to save). No one can say when another is born again, redeemed, saved. But we can observe how the media works and affects its audience. And we can apply the old biblical measuring rod: "By their deeds ye shall know them." Words are not enough. Paul urges us not just to *say* the truth, but to *do* the truth.

What do we see in Cycle Five? High tech America has invaded religion, and the camera and computer have become crucial.[3] Technology has triumphed over theology. Modern equipment can reproduce sound and vision in a degree of detail unavailable in older churches or meeting halls. Letter-writing machines and prayer phones create a false sense of intimacy. Television is not only a reflector of mass culture–it is becoming a culture in its own right. In that culture fundamentalism seems to flourish.

What worries us about fundamentalists is the note of absolute certainty–and absolute disdain for the opposition. They are right, and they *know* they are right. But what if they are wrong? Confidence is a great virtue in saints; but hardening into unheeding dogmatism, it can produce terrifying sinners. Saint Paul was sure he understood the Gospel–so was Jim Jones. Charlemagne rallied Europe to his own Holy Crusade; so did Adolf Hitler. One of the fundamentalists' chief tenets is that the Bible is "the Word of God."

But the book itself is subject to all manner of translations, interpretations, and misreadings. Listen to the "exegesis" that takes place, day after day, on radio and television, and recall the Tower of Babel.

Popular religion is not as deep as a well. It thrives on buzz words, simple solutions, and quick fixes (spiritual, physical, and mental). Too often it offers magical rather than truthful answers. Roots, heritage, basics, morality, and old-time religion are "in." Seldom stressed are discipline; quietude; and the extent of human fallibility (let alone original sin). Ours is the land of the free and the home of the 30-second commercial, the 9-second sound bite, and the one-liner. When Christianity embraces this ethos, the result becomes a caricature of the gospel.

From all sides we hear that ours has become a Godless nation, and that we must espouse the old-time religion. Perhaps we have not too little but too much religion–much of it a hype. We have too many heroes, superstars, and godlets–not to be confused with the One True God of the Old and New Testaments. This is no new thing. The problem of idolatry was well known when Moses received the Ten Commandments, and when Jesus conducted his ministry. The attraction of the Golden Calf is perennial.

When critics tell us that religion in America is diffuse, fragmented, and internalized, they are certainly right. So is American life. Instead of being great weaknesses, these qualities may turn out to be strengths. They are the platform on which democracy works. Churchill may have been right when he said democracy was the worst form of government–except for all the others.

Post-Reagan-Bush America has many problems to solve, many shortcomings to remedy. We have failed too often to take care of either the physical or psychic needs of our aging population. Welfare and medical programs stumble. Those fortunate enough to have funding send the elderly to "homes" or sanitized profitable retirement "communities" with assuring names like Heritage Hall and Friendship Manor. But are they not in a kind of mechanized Brave New World, their very lives dependent on how much money Congress votes for Social Security and Medicare? And do not Jerry or Terry or Oral or Jimmy, appearing regularly on TV and radio when no one else turns up, become their *only* "hope and salvation?"

Friends are hard to come by in mass culture; TV preachers want to be friends. Recently a lonely, elderly woman whose heat had been turned off by the utility company took her own life in the bleak mid-winter, preferring that to freezing to death. She left a suicide note–to her TV set. "Goodbye, dear friend," it read. "You're the only one who stuck by me to the end."

The American Way of Life leads us to seek and expect quick, easy solutions. There are few. The human condition in which we find ourselves has been shaped over millions of years–it will not change when the next Congress or U.N. Security Council meets. We won't "improve" the religious life of our nation by changing the media and offering better programs. Just the reverse is true. We must change people if we want the media changed. The media succeeds by holding the mirror up for us to see ourselves: it *is* us. "Fans" like pro football, beauty contests, game shows, sitcoms, and gooey religions. By their ratings ye shall know them. When the fans change, so will the media.

The true enemy may not be religious television, but television itself. More and more Americans are addicted to televised sports, soaps, and pseudo-events. That is why they settle for pseudo-conversion. Hypnotized by television's potential and the millions of dollars it brings in to their ministries, televangelists may have lost sight of religion's central mission.[4]

The Electric Church is a contradiction in terms. The one essential for worship–total presence–is absent. The implied intimacy is dishonest. This is one-way communication with no way of talking back. The congregation listens to celebrities, waiting only to be told, like so many sheep, when to bleat together.

What about all those toll-free (800) numbers? Each call is categorized by the "counselor," then fed to the computer. Once you are in the proper category (salvation, prayer requests, Holy Spirit baptisms, answers to prayers, etc.) the computer can set up the proper mailing program and solicitation. When you phone you become as programmed as the program. Personal advice? You might as well talk to a parrot.

The great words and concepts of religion (indeed, of life) have been misused and chewed to death by singers, ad men, pop preachers, and the whole schlock world. We waste verbal and conceptual resources and fill our minds with rubbish as freely as we foul our environment. Since we have instant information, we expect action– and solutions. We expect instant coffee, instant sex, instant improvements. A key word to the 1980s was *quickie*. Has salvation become a "quick fix?"

Or perhaps a hype? Some say this new pop term is derived from the hypodermic needle, source of the "fix"; others say it is derived from hyperbole, in rhetoric an extravagant exaggeration. Hypes have long dominated advertising and TV commercials. Now, it would seem, fundamentalism has become wedded to the "powers and principalities" of mass media. What millions see on TV must be both important and true. Why and how could the miracle of TV lie to us? TV anchorman Walter Cronkite used to sign off every evening: "And that's the way it is." How could it be otherwise? Pray TV is "hype."

This is not to charge the major practitioners with insincerity (they may well be sincere) or to criticize their joviality (we can stand some in such grim times). Their great lack is failing to present the Christian Gospel as it has come down to us. Instead of demanding repentance and conversion, they mouth the words, then settle for positive feelings and a happy smile. They'd rather be rich than right.

Their brand of Christianity is glittering and prepackaged–happy, happy people loving the Lord, and paying for the privilege. Beautiful blonde models, glamorous stars, and muscular athletes beckon us forward. Flicking the dial, one chooses a "crusade" or "ministry" the way one chooses a polyester sports shirt, a mouthwash, or designer blue jeans. Wrong size? Change channels and choose another.

Have we sold our priceless birthright of compassion and community for a potage of publicity and hype? The fearful thing isn't the power of the Word but of TV itself–part of our life-support system, more influential than any network, program, preacher, or crusade. The cryptic platitude of the much-maligned Marshall McLuhan comes back to haunt us: the medium *is* the message.

Common themes link contemporary televangelists. All are charismatic and patriarchal. Wives and children "know their place," and recite biblical verses in support of their secondary roles. All are theatrical and pragmatic: they know how to grab you, shake you, change you. Some lose the touch, yet hang on too long (Oral Roberts and Norman Vincent Peale are examples). They are religion's Willie Lomans.

All mix salt and pepper: sin and salvation, horror and humor, laughter and tears. They cut deep. Some who heard Jonathan Edwards went home and cut their throats. Three centuries later, those who followed Jim Jones drank Fla-vor-aid mixed with cyanide.

All know that secularism is on the wane, humanism on the defensive. They sense (but cannot always articulate) the exhaustion of modernism and tedium of the unrestrained self. "There is a reaction against extreme individualism and self, a preoccupation with and a search for Roots with a Capital R, which takes people back to religion," says Robert N. Bellah. "Tradition is back on the agenda with a positive force."[5] Not just students, but the academic community in general, long a haven for skeptics, is now giving religion a second look. "There is the sympathetic entertainment of religious belief in intellectual circles that you wouldn't have detected ten years ago," says Peter Steinfels, executive editor of the Roman Catholic lay periodical *Commonweal*.

But the most important common link might be their toughness–televangelists are, in a cutthroat world, survivors. In a real sense, they are "singing for their suppers"–and if they are off-key they go hungry. Their colorful journeys through Medialand are hardly less perilous than those of the early apostles around the Mediterranean–and their critics are just as savage. There is an earthy vaudeville flavor to preachers like Billy Sunday, Aimee Semple McPherson, Jimmy Swaggart, and the Rev. Ike that is "street smart." By comparison, the preaching and exhorting of most mainline ministers seem pallid and uninspiring.

This zest and enthusiasm speaks to many young people. While enrollments in some colleges and universities decline (the "baby boom" generation has bottomed out), the number attending "Christian colleges" has risen dramatically. These colleges have even invented news degrees, such as MM–Master of Media, which prepares television crews and writers for evangelical service.

It is easy to uncover deficiencies in the conduct and doctrines of God pumpers, both in churches and on the media. There is no such thing as a TV pastor, since there is no human contact. Yet millions watch TV, and listen to radio, in order to be saved. They have needs which many institutional churches did not and do not meet. Into the void stepped a new type of church. In the 1970s and 1980s there was much talk of the "New Christian Right," a term used by the media for a merging of conservatives opposed to such "liberal" changes as abortion, gay rights, affirmative action, and busing. The most successful example was the Moral Majority; but the Christian Voice, Religious Roundtable, and a host of smaller groups got a hearing at the national level. Did all this signal deep shifts in American religious life? Or was it the old yearning for simple truth, divine assurance, and "amazing grace?"

The deep paradox in American religion won't go away. We yearn for old-fashioned Bible stories, built on supernaturalism and revelation, while insisting that we remain the world's most advanced technical and scientific nation. The lines were drawn in the eighteenth-century Enlightenment–we knew that pure, sweet reason would save us, as we left the dark superstitious past behind us. Hell was dismissed as a relic of barbarism, and a menace to health and happiness. Science was salvation. Such thinking changed one set of myths for another; neither has proven adequate. The laboratory has tried to serve the function once met by the church. But in our time, many people are not buying "better things for better living through chemistry." They yearn for transcendence. Instead of saving us, a dependence on science seems about to do us in.

Empirical methods, cell-counting, statistics, and objectivity do not supply a sense of the sublime, of the holy. Into the vacuum went fundamentalism. The movement had long awaited charismatic leaders who could bring the scattered flock together. Clearly one such leader was Jerry Falwell, who hid his complex sophisticated ministry behind the disarming title of "The Old Time Gospel Church." The moving force behind Moral Majority, he held press conferences, spoke for his "invisible army," debated senators, and sat at Reagan's right hand. He targeted liberal senators, and promised to knock them off the way back-country hunters shoot quail. He did: as ex-Senators Frank Church, John Culver, Birch Bayh, George McGovern, Warren Magnuson, or Gaylord Nelson could testify.

Then he made a monumental blunder. He visited South Africa in 1985 and returned to denounce Nobel Prize recipient Bishop Desmond Tutu as a "phony." The national and international reaction came immediately. How could Falwell, after a quick visit, know the Bishop was a phony? To make it worse, he sent out a hysterical letter to his computerized friends. "Since my return from South Africa," it said, "Communist terrorists are openly threatening to kill my family and me." Due to "vicious media coverage," his contributions had plummeted. "Please help us through this crucial time by sending your sacrificial gift of $100 today." He talked like a captain whose ship was sinking. It was. In 1989 he announced the closing of the Moral Majority, "since its work is done."

One of Falwell's Virginia neighbors, who was a much better political analyst, wasted no time in filling the leadership gap. Pat Robertson's tendency to mix religion, politics, and foreign policy peaked in the 1992 elections. His "Christian Coalition" distributed 40 million copies of a voter guide just before the elections. The guide defined a "good Christian" as one who opposes abortion, gay rights, and condom distribution in schools; and favors the death penalty, school prayer, a balanced budget amendment, and separation of church and state. His efforts backfired. He did so poorly in the early primaries that he was forced to drop out of the race.

Still, he had made a major contribution to the conservative Protestant cause in 1988, when his run for the presidency was the most visible form of grass-roots activism. By insisting that he would run only if three million people asked him to by signing petitions, he was able to get not only the signatures but also to raise $10 million even before announcing his candidacy. Before suspending his campaign in April 1988, he had raised and spent $27 million. He had also got over 40% of the vote in three state caucuses (Hawaii, Alaska, and Washington) and over 18% in five state primaries (Oklahoma, South Dakota, South Carolina, Arkansas, and Louisiana). He had raised the prestige and self-image of a whole segment of Americans that had been ignored, or even ridiculed, for years. He had brought a new sophistication to the Christian Right.

Nevertheless, most American intellectuals, liberals, and spokespersons for mainline churches tend to dismiss, or at least downplay, today's version of what their grandfathers called "Holy Rollers."

Elitists always tend to devalue the popular, forgetting that ours is "a government of the people." This is especially true of European writers like Steve Bruce, who dismisses the religious TV audience as "largely found among less well-educated older women who are already conservative Protestants," and vows he will expose the televangelists' "hype."

America's various Awakenings have always been labeled "hypes" by the unawakened; yet those awakenings (which I have tried to describe and analyze) have been the shaping force of American culture from its inception. The first settlers to British North America were part of the great Puritan Awakening in England which provided the core of our culture and the impetus that led to our independence. It was the evangelical tradition that championed other crucial causes, such as antislavery, public education, feminism, and social legislation. One must ponder the words of William G. McLoughlin when he writes: "The story of American evangelicalism is the story of America itself in the years 1800 to 1990"; and in the same book, "To understand it is to understand the whole temper of American life in the nineteenth century."[6]

That "understanding" has been put forth largely by theologians and humanists, like McLoughlin. They tend to attribute awakenings and revivals to strain or crisis; to people seeking personal meaning and control. In recent years social scientists and anthropologists have given other explanations. George M. Thomas, Clifford Geertz, John Walton, and Sylvia Thrupp (among others) believe these awakenings and movements are routine aspects of social life. Any social movement must be interpreted in terms of the cultural knowledge on which it is based, not on some supernatural inspiration or intervention. A religious movement must work on the cultural frame. It is the carrier of a particular worldview or ontology. These movements compete with established organizations to promote their own beliefs. Long-term trends within Christianity spring from the rhetoric of the external culture. Their main emphasis is on individualism and nationalism.

Working on this theory, the new school stresses institutional models, market penetration, the political-economic context of revivalism, and quantitative analyses.[7] We should welcome these new insights and methods, and factor them into the complex question of just how popular religion does function in a diverse and democratic society.

Now, at the end of the twentieth century we are confronted with this question: why has Protestant evangelicalism flourished so remarkably since World War II and especially since the mid-1960s?[8] Why are the mainline churches shrinking, while such evangelical groups as the Southern Baptists, Assemblies of God, Church of God, Mormons, and Pentecostals are flourishing? Perhaps because the evangelical church is much more than a place of worship. In this Age of Inner Isolation, it serves as a community for its members. They talk now of a "total church living complex." How might this change our culture?

America is made up of two religious cultures which thrive on tension and cyclical change. The Reformation culture remains the basis of American experience. The liberal ethos, which came into power after the Civil War and dominated the country from the 1920s through the 1960s, seems now in retreat. In *A Guide for the Perplexed*, E. F. Schumacher points out that periods of growth highlight the quest for freedom; periods of depression are characterized by the search for order.[9] In the 1990s we seem to be in the latter phase. That may explain the growth of conservative religion that we have documented. The Democrats under Bill Clinton have promised that the 1990s will be a time of renewal. Clinton speaks as a Baptist, replacing the Episcopalian Bush. That act should not be overlooked. Mass media, evangelism, and popular culture are forming a new trinity, and it will change the face of American religion. As yet we cannot recognize this new beast, shuffling towards Bethlehem to be born. But as a new century and a new millennium begin, we know this: we cannot ignore it.

That is the admonition of Harold Bloom, in *The American Religion*. He believes the Mormons, Southern Baptists, and Pentecostals are the three most vital ongoing movements today. They are "the religion of our climate," pointing to what a "purified and amalgamated form of the American Religion would be."[10]

Religion never exists in a vacuum, or in a church, or in a medium, but in the whole culture. Sometimes religion seems to be outside, above, or against the culture. This is an illusion: the culture absorbs even those who oppose or reject it.

Religion cannot be equated with churches or networks. Christianity is not Churchianity. Whenever yesterday's answers fail to meet today's needs, any institution (including the church) ends up being a safe deposit box where archaic images and embellished documents are stored. When the dynamic dies, the institution becomes a museum.

When one moves around the global village and comes to see that Christianity is a minority concern for a world that is two-thirds nonwhite, one realizes that Americans are, for all our wealth and power, remarkably provincial. Four out of five non-Christians alive today may never have any contact with Christianity, or meet anyone advocating it. The nineteenth-century dream of extending the Kingdom to every shore disappeared with the notion of the White Man's Burden.

As we conclude our study, we must beware of dogmatic conclusions. Our definitions, categories, and criteria have been far too inexact for that. When we speak of popular religion, for example, are we speaking of mass religion, controlled by mass media, or religion "of the people," controlled by the people themselves? When we measure growth or impact by Neilsen ratings, box office receipts, polls, and graphs, are we dealing with substantive data, or surface scratchings? Does popular culture have a theology and rituals of its own?

Religion has always been a mighty force in our land before and after we became the United States of America. We have thought of ourselves as chosen people–exceptionally blessed. This notion still holds at the end of the twentieth century, when we are the most churchgoing (if not the most religious) nation in the Western world.

Our churches, synagogues, and mosques dot the landscape, but the nature of our attendance and doctrine is changing–from mainline to evangelical; from liberal to fundamental; from personal to electronic. As we approach the millennium, we seem to be involved in yet another Great Awakening. Who knows where it might lead?

There is something presumptuous in thinking we can have God on our terms, instead of His. Conversion must never be reduced to a pseudo-event, brought about by gimmickry and trickery which impress the gullible but cheapen the revealed Word in the Bible. The spirit of truth and wisdom should not be cloaked in nonsense and contradictions.

We have been so fascinated with what we want that we seldom ask what God wants. Self-centeredness is the original sin; and it is everywhere about us. Disguising it under catchy slogans and masquerading it as entertainment does not change the essential sin. Looking for saviors and saucers in the sky will not bring salvation.

We must learn to be honest and humble. We must be lamps unto ourselves. Only then can we look forward to the kind of world envisioned by the great Roman Catholic theologian Teilhard de Chardin:

> Some day, after mastering the winds, the waves, the tides, and gravity, we will harness for God the Energies of love. And then, for the second time in the history of the world, we will have discovered fire.[11]

NOTES

1. The intriguing question is often asked, and draws many different answers. For a sample, see George Marsden, *Evangelicalism and Modern America* (Grand Rapids, MI: Eerdmans, 1964).

2. One of the strongest recent attacks is Ray Browne, *Against Academia* (Bowling Green, OH: Bowling Green State University, 1990).

3. Like many others, I can see both positive and negative results from this "invasion." I have studied the televangelists for 20 years, and for most of them I have had strongly negative reactions. While they are still there, I have come to see that my judgments may have been hasty, and not grounded in a long look at popular religion. I hope I have found a more tenable middle ground.

4. That is the opinion of Gregor T. Goethals, *The TV Ritual: Worship at the Video Altar* (Boston: Beacon, 1981). For a more balanced view, see William F. Fore, *Television and Religion: The Shaping of Faith, Values, and Culture* (Minneapolis: Augsburg, 1987); and Jerry D. Cardwell, *Mass Media Christianity* (New York: Lantham, 1984).

5. Robert N. Bellah, *Varieties of Civil Religion* (New York: Harper, 1980), p. 98.

6. William G. McLoughlin, *Revivals, Awakenings, and Reform* (Chicago: University of Chicago Press, 1978). The quotations are from chapter 1, pp. 1 and 3, entitled "Awakenings as Revitalizations of Culture."

7. George M. Thomas, *Revivalism and Social Change* (Chicago: University of Chicago Press, 1989), chapter 1. See also Clifford Geertz, *The Interpretation of Cultures* (New York: Basic Books, 1973), and Russell Kirk, *The Politics of Prudence* (Bryn Mawr: Intercollegiate Studies Institute, 1993).

8. Grant Wacker asks this question in an essay entitled "Uneasy in Zion: Evangelicals in Postmodern Society," in *Evangelicalism and Modern America*, George Marsden, ed. (Grand Rapids, MI: Eerdmans, 1984), ch. 2. See also Matthew C. Moen, *The Transformation of the Christian Right* (Tuscaloosa: University of Alabama Press).

9. E. F. Schumacher, *A Guide for the Perplexed* (New York: Harper and Row, 1977), p. 127.

10. Harold Bloom, *The American Religion* (New York: Simon and Schuster, 1992), p. 256.

11. Teilhard de Chardin, *The Future of Man* (New York: Harper and Row, 1964), p. 246.

Further Information

National Council of Churches
475 Riverside Drive
New York, NY 10115-0050

World Association for
   Christian Communication
357 Kennington Lane
London SE11 5QY
England

National Citizens' Committee
   for Broadcasting
PO Box 12038
Washington, DC 20003

Museum of Broadcasting
1 East 53rd Street
New York, NY 10022

Journal of Communication
Oxford University Press
16-00 Pollitt Drive
Fair Lawn, NJ 07410

Christian Broadcasting Network
CBN Center
Virginia Beach, VA 23463

Old Fashioned Gospel Hour
 PO Box 10324
Lynchburg, VA 24506

Centre for the Study of
   Communication and Culture
221 Goldhurst Terrace
London, NW6 3EP
England

Media and Values Quarterly
1962 So. Shenandoah Avenue
Los Angeles, CA 90034

Further Reading

Ahlstrom, Sydney A. *A Religious History of the American People*. 2 vols. New York: Doubleday, 1975.

Allen, Robert J. "Catholic Social Doctrine in National Network Catholic Television Programs in the U.S., 1951-68." PhD dissertation, New York University, 1972.

Anderson, Gerald H., and Thomas F. Stransky. *Evangelization.* New York: Paulist, 1975.

Armstrong, Ben. *The Electric Church.* Nashville: Thomas Nelson, 1979.

Attfield, Robin. *God and the Secular.* Cardiff, Whales: University College Cardiff Press, 1978.

Bachman, John W. *The Church in the World of Radio-Television.* New York Association, 1960.

Barna, George, and William Paul McKay. *Vital Signs: Emerging Social Trends and the Future of American Christianity.* Westchester, IL: Crossway, 1984.

Barr, James. *Fundamentalism.* Philadelphia: Westminster, 1977.

Benson, Dennis. *Electric Evangelism.* Nashville: Abingdon, 1973.

Berger, Peter, and Richard Neuhaus, eds. *Against the World, For the World*. New York: Seabury, 1976.

Bestic, Alan. *Praise the Lord and Pass the Contribution.* London: Cassell, 1971.

Bethell, Tom. "The Common Man and the Electric Church." *Harpers*, April 1978, 86-90.

Bloesch, Donald. *Essentials of Evangelical Theology: God, Authority, Salvation.* Vol. 1, 1978. *Life, Ministry and Hope*, Vol. 2, 1979. New York: Harper and Row.

Bloom, Harold. *The American Religion: The Emergence of the Post-Christian Nation.* New York: Simon and Schuster, 1992.

Bruce, Steve. *A House Divided: Protestantism, Schism, and Secularization.* London: Routledge, 1990.

Buddenbaum, Judith M. "The Audience for Religious Television Programs." MA thesis, Indiana University, 1979.

Christ, Carol and Judith Plaskow. *Womanspirit Rising.* New York: Harper and Row, 1979.

Clabaugh, Gary K. *The Protestant Fundamentalists.* Chicago: Nelson-Hall, 1974.

Coleman, Richard. *Issues of Theological Warfare: Evangelicals and Liberals.* Grand Rapids, MI: Eerdmans, 1972.

Cross, Whitney R. *The Burned-over District: The Social and Intellectual History of Enthusiastic Religion in Western New York, 1800-1850.* New York: Harper, 1965.

Daly, Mary. *The Church and the Second Sex.* New York: Harper and Row, 1968.

_____ . *Beyond God the Father: Toward a Philosophy of Women's Liberation.* Boston: Beacon, 1973.

_____ . *Gyn/Ecology: The Metaethics of Radical Feminism.* Boston: Beacon, 1978.

D'Antonio, Michael. *Fall from Grace: The Failed Crusade of the Christian Right.* New Brunswick: Rutgers University Press, 1992.

Diamond, Edwin and Stephen Bates. *The Spot: The Rise of Political Advertising On Television.* Cambridge: MIT, 1984.

Dollar, George W. *A History of Fundamentalism in America.* Greenville, SC: Bob Jones University Press, 1973.

Douglas, Ann. *The Feminization of American Culture.* New York: Knopf, 1977.

Dunn, Charles W., ed. *Religion in American Politics.* Washington, DC: Congressional Quarterly, 1989.

Dussel, Ennique. *Ethics and the Theology of Liberation.* Maryknoll, NY: Orbis, 1978.

Edwards, George R. *Gay/Lesbian Liberation: A Biblical Perspective.* New York: Pilgrim, 1984.

Ellwood, Robert S., Jr. *Alternate Altars: Unconventional and Eastern Spirituality in America.* Chicago: University of Chicago Press, 1979.

Engel, James F. *Contemporary Christian Communications.* Nashville: Thomas Nelson, 1979.

Falwell, Jerry ed. *The Fundamentalist Phenomenon.* Garden City: Doubleday, 1981.

Fern, Dean William. *Contemporary American Theologies I: A Critical Study.* New York: Seabury, 1981.

_____ . *Contemporary American Theologies II: A Book of Readings.* New York: Seabury, 1982.

Finney, James B. *Autobiography of James B. Finney; or, Pioneer Life in the West.* Edited by W. P. Strickland. Cincinnati: Methodist Book Concern, 1853.

Fishwick, Marshall W. *The Hero in Transition.* Bowling Green, OH: Popular, 1983.

_____ . *Common Culture and the Great Tradition.* Westport: Greenwood, 1984.

_____ . *The Seven Pillars of Popular Culture.* Westport: Greenwood, 1985.

Flowers, Ronald B. *Religion in Strange Times: The 1960s and 1970s.* Mercer: Mercer University, 1984.

Frank, Ronald E., and Marshall G. Greenberg. *The Public's Use of Television: Who Watches and Why.* Beverly Hills: Sage, 1980.

Friendly, Fred W. *Due to Circumstances Beyond Our Control.* New York: Vintage, 1968.

Geertz, Clifford. *The Interpretation of Cultures.* New York: Basic, 1973.

George, Carol V. R. *God's Salesman: Norman Vincent Peale and the Power of Positive Thinking.* New York: Oxford, 1992.

Georgianna, Sharon. *The Moral Majority and Fundamentalism: Plausibility and Dissonance.* Lewistown, NY: Mellon, 1989.

Hadden, J. K. and A. Shupe. *Televangelism: Power and Politics on God's Frontier.* New York: Henry Holt, 1988.

Harrell, D. E. *All Things Are Possible: The Healing and Charismatic Revivals in Modern America.* Bloomington: Indiana University, 1975.

Haught, Robert. "The God Biz." *Penthouse,* December 1980, 102-6, 250-7.

Henry, Carl F. H. *Evangelicals in Search of Identity.* Waco, TX: Word, 1976.

_____ . *God, Revelation and Authority: God Who Speaks and Shows.* 4 vols. Waco, TX: Word Books, 1976, 1979.

Herberg, Will. *Protestant-Catholic-Jew: An Essay in American Religious Sociology*. Garden City: Doubleday, 1955.

Hofstadter, Richard. *The Paranoid Style in American Politics*. New York: Random House, 1965.

Hoge, Dean, and David Roozen. *Understanding Church Growth and Decline, 1950-78*. New York: Pilgrim, 1979.

Holt, B. Russell. "Superbowl Christianity." *Ministry*, May 1980, 19.

Hoover, Stewart M. *The Electronic Giant: A Critique of the Telecommunications Revolution from a Christian Perspective*. Elgin, IL: Brethren, 1982.

Horsfield, Peter G. *Religious Television: The American Experience*. London: Longman, 1984.

Jewett, Robert, and John Shelton Lawrence. *The American Monomyth*. New York: Doubleday, 1977.

Johnson, Charles A. *The Frontier Camp Meeting: Religion's Harvest Time*. Dallas: Southern Methodist University Press, 1955.

Judah, J. Stillson. *Hare Krishna and the Counterculture*. New York: John Wiley and Sons, 1974.

Kahle, Roger. "Religion and Network Television." MA thesis, Columbia University, 1970.

Kelley, Dean M. *Why Conservative Churches Are Growing*. New York: Harper and Row, 1972.

King, Martin Luther. *Why We Can't Wait*. New York: New American Library, 1964.

Kuhns, William. *The Electronic Gospel*. New York: Herder and Herder, 1969.

Kung, Hans. *On Being a Christian*. New York: Doubleday, 1976.

La Barre, Weston. *They Shall Take Up Serpents: Psychology of the Southern Snake-Handling Cult* (New York: Schocken, 1969).

Latourette, Kenneth Scott. *A History of the Expansion of Christianity*. 6 vols. New York: Paternoster, 1971.

Le Bon, Gustave. *La Psychologie des Foules*. Paris: Presses Universitaires de France, 1973.

Lecky, Robert, and Elliott Wright. *Black Manifesto: Religion, Fascism, and Reparations*. New York: Sheed and Ward, 1969.

Lewis, Norman. "A Harvest of Souls." *Independent Magazine,* 1 (April 1989): 20-8.

Liebman, Robert, and Robert Wuthnow. *The New Christian Right.* New York: Aldine, 1983.

McFague, Sallie. *Metaphorical Theology: Models of God in Religious Language.* Philadelphia: Fortress, 1982.

Mann, James, with Sarah Peterson. "Preachers in Politics: Decisive Force in '80?" *U.S. News and World Report,* September 15, 1980, 24-26.

Marsden, George. *Fundamentalism and American Culture: The Shaping of Twentieth Century Evangelicalism, 1870-1925.* New York: Oxford University Press, 1980.

Marty, Martin. "The Electronic Church." *Missouri in Perspective,* March 27, 1978, 5.

_____ . *The Improper Opinion: Mass Media and the Christian Faith.* Philadelphia: Westminster, 1961.

_____ . "The Invisible Religion." *The Presbyterian Survey,* May 1979, 13.

_____ . *A Nation of Behaviors.* Chicago: University of Chicago Press, 1976.

_____ . *Pilgrims in their Own Land: 500 Years of American Religion.* New York: Little, Brown, 1984.

Mavity, Nancy Barr. *Sister Aimee.* New York: Doubleday Doran, 1931.

Mehta, Gita. *Karma Cola: Marketing the Mystic East.* New York: Simon and Schuster, 1979.

Merton, Thomas. *Mystics and Zen Masters.* New York: Dell, 1961.

Monaco, James. *Celebrity: The Media as Image Maker.* New York: Dell, 1978.

Morris, James. *The Preachers.* New York: St. Martin's, 1973.

Moseley, James G. *A Cultural History of Religion in America.* Westport: Greenwood Press, 1981.

Needleman, Jacob. *The New Religions.* New York: Doubleday, 1970.

_____ . *A Sense of the Cosmos: The Encounter of Modern Science and Ancient Truth.* New York: Doubleday, 1975.

Nelson, John Wiley. *Your God is Alive and Well and Appearing in Popular Culture* (Philadelphia: Westminster Press, 1976).

Niebuhr, H. Richard. *Christ and Culture.* New York: Harper and Row, 1951.

Northtrop, F .S. C. *The Meeting of East and West: An Inquiry Concerning World Understanding.* New York: Macmillan, 1960.

Novak, Michael. *All the Catholic People.* New York: Herder and Herder, 1971.

Osborn, Ronald E. *The Spirit of American Christianity.* New York: Harper and Bros., 1958.

Owens, Virginia Stem. *The Total Image; or, Selling Jesus in the Modern Age.* Grand Rapids, MI: Eerdmans, 1980.

Panikkar, Raimundo. *The Intra-Religious Dialogue.* New York: Paulist, 1978.

Park, Jeff. "PTL Encounters the FCC: Truthful Probe or Witch Hunt?" *Action,* March 1980, 10-14.

Pavols, Andrew J. *The Cult Experience.* Westport: Greenwood, 1982.

Peel, Robert. *Christian Science: Its Encounter with American Culture.* New York: Henry Holt, 1958.

Peterson, J. W. *Those Curious New Cults.* New Haven: Keats, 1975.

Phy, Allene Stuart. *The Bible and Popular Culture in America.* Philadelphia: Fortress, 1984.

Pierard, Richard V. *The Unequal Yoke: Evangelical Christianity and Political Conservatism.* New York: J. P. Lippincott, 1970.

Pollock, John. *Moody: The Biography.* Chicago: Moody, 1983.

Porterfield, Amanda. *Feminine Spirituality in America: From Sarah Edwards to Martha Graham.* Philadelphia: Temple University Press, 1980.

Quebedeaux, Richard. *The Young Evangelicals: Revolution in Orthodoxy.* New York: Harper and Row, 1974.

_____ . *The New Charismatics: The Origins, Development and Significance of Neo-Pentecostalism.* New York: Doubleday, 1976.

_____ . *The Worldly Evangelicals.* New York: Harper and Row, 1978.

Ranaghan, K. *Le Retour de l'Esprit.* Paris: Les Editions du Cert, 1972.

Raschke, Carl. *The Interruption of Eternity: Modern Gnosticism and the Origins of the New Religious Consciousness.* Chicago: Nelson-Hall, 1980.

Real, Michael R. *Mass Mediated Culture.* Englewood Cliffs, NJ: Prentice-Hall, 1977.

Rockefeller Foundation Conference Report. *The Religion Beat: The Reporting of Religion in the Media.* New York: Rockefeller Foundation, 1981.

Rogers, Jack. *Confessions of a Conservative Evangelical.* Philadelphia: Westminster, 1974.

_____ , ed. *Biblical Authority.* Waco, TX: Word Books, 1977.

Ruether, Rosemary, ed. *Liberation Theology.* New York: Paulist Press, 1972.

Ruether, Rosemary, and Eleanor McLaughlin. *Women of Spirit: Female Leadership in the Jewish and Christian Traditions.* New York: Simon and Schuster, 1979.

Russell, Charles Allyn. *Voices of American Fundamentalism: Seven Biographical Studies.* Philadelphia: Westminster, 1976.

Ryan, Michael D. *The Contemporary Explosion of Theology.* Metuchen, NJ: Scarecrow, 1975.

Sabato, Larry J. *The Rise of the Political Consultants.* New York: Basic, 1982.

_____ . *PAC Power: Inside the World of Political Action Committees.* New York: W. W. Norton, 1984.

_____ . "Mailing for Dollars." *Psychology Today,* 18 (10), (October 1984): 38-52.

Salisbury, W. Seward. *Religion in American Culture.* Homewood, IL: Dorsey, 1964.

Sandeen, Ernest R. *The Roots of Fundamentalism: British and American Millenarianism, 1800-1930.* Chicago: University of Chicago Press, 1970.

Scharpff, Paulus. *Geschichte der Evangelisation.* Basel: Brunnen-Verlag, 1964.

Schneider, Michael. *Neurose und Klassenkampf.* Germany: Towohlt, 1973.

Segundo, Juan Luis. *Our Idea of God,* vol. 3. Translated by John Drury. Maryknoll, NY: Orbis, 1974.

_____ . *Liberation of Theology.* Maryknoll, NY: Orbis, 1976.

Sheen, Fulton J. *Treasurers in Clay.* New York: Doubleday, 1980.

Sholes, Jerry. *Give Me That Prime-Time Religion.* New York: Hawthorne, 1979.

Shriver, George H. *American Religious Heretics.* Nashville: Abingdon, 1966.

Southey, Robert. *The Life of Wesley and the Rise and Progress of Methodism.* London: Bell and Daldy, 1864.

Stewart, John T. *The Deacon Wore Spats: Profiles from America's Changing Religious Scene.* New York: Holt, Rinehart, and Winston, 1956.

Strober, Gerald, and Ruth Tomczak. *Jerry Falwell: A Flame for God.* Nashville: Thomas Nelson, 1979.

Suenens, Cardinal L. J. *Une Nouvelle Pentecôte?* Brussels: Desclee De Brouwer, 1974.

Suzuki, Shunryu. *Zen Mind, Beginner's Mind.* New York and Tokyo: Weatherbill, 1973.

Tabor, Charles. *The World Is Too Much With Us.* Mercer, GA: Mercer University Press, 1991.

Talbot, Peter. *The Jesus Movement.* New York: National Board of YMCAs, 1972.

Thomas, George M. *Revivalism and Cultural Change.* Chicago: University of Chicago Press, 1989.

Thomas, William. *Assessment of Mass Meetings as a Method of Evangelism.* Amsterdam: Rodopi N.V., 1977.

Toynbee, Arnold. *Civilization on Trial.* New York: Oxford, 1948.

Van Allen, Roger. *American Values and the Future of America.* Philadelphia: Fortress, 1978.

Van Dusen, Henry P. "Third Force in American Christendom." *Life*, June 9, 1958, pp. 38-41.

Verkuyl, Jan. *Inleiding in de Nieuwere Zandingswetenschep.* Kampen: J. H. Kok, 1976.

Wagner, C. Peter. *Latin American Theology: Radical or Evangelical? The Struggle for the Faith in a Young Church.* Grand Rapids, MI: Eerdmans, 1970.

Weisberger, Bernard A. *They Gathered at the River: The Story of the Great Revivalists and their Impact Upon Religion in America.* Boston: Little, Brown, 1958.

Wells, David F., and John D. Woodbridge, eds. *The Evangelicals: What They Believe, Who They Are, Where They Are Changing.* Nashville: Abingdon, 1975.

"What's Wrong with Born-Again Politics?" *Christian Century,* 97, (October 22, 1980): 1002-4.

Wilcox, Clyde. *God's Warriors: The Christian Right in Twentieth Century America.* Baltimore: Johns Hopkins Press, 1992.

Williams, William Carlos. *In the American Grain.* New York: Morrow, 1925.

Wills, Gary. *The Kennedy Imprisonment: A Meditation on Power.* Boston: Little, Brown, 1982.

Wirt, Sherwood Eliot. *The Social Conscience of the Evangelical.* New York: Harper and Row, 1968.

Wood, Robert W. *Christ and the Homosexual.* New York: Vantage, 1960.

Woodward, Kenneth. "A One Million Dollar Habit." *Newsweek,* 98, (September 15, 1980): 35.

Wylie, Irvin G. *The Self-Made Man in America: The Myth of Rags to Riches.* New York: Free, 1954.

Zweier, Robert, and Richard Smith. "Christian Politics and the New Right." *Christian Century,* 99, (October 8, 1980): 937-42.

_____ . *Born-Again Politics: The New Christian Right in America.* Downers Grove, IL: Inter Varsity Press, 1982.

Index

Notes:

Book titles and reference sources are indexed under authors' names. *Further Information* and *Further Reading* sections are not indexed.

"n" indicates an end-of-chapter Note, and numbers in parentheses are text discussion locators; e.g., 37n3(27): page 37, Note 3, discussed page 27.

Readers are advised to consult the Index and cross-reference all names and subjects of interest.

applied to sports professionals, 117-118
creation of, and regarding Jonestown tragedy, 64
function of, 117-118
mythic umbrella of television, and as independent cultural entity, 179,180-181,188, 223,224,225,226
media state, U.S. as, 113
media writers, opposition to Moral Majority by, 200-201
Mehta, Gita, 108
Mellon, Andrew W., 132
Melville, Herman, 101
Mencken, H.L.
    on conservative Christianity, 214
    ridicule of Bible Belt and fundamentalists by, 78,80, 187
    of Baptists, 80
    of William Jennings Bryan, 89
    of Billy Sunday, 52,88
Mennonites, 10
messiah, messiahs
    exaltation of, historically, 4,175
    self-proclaimed prophets and, cult leaders as
        Father Coughlin, 123,131,133, 136,138
        Father Divine, 89,90-91,93
        Jim Jones, 69-70
        David Koresh, 214
        Sun Myung Moon, 63
Methodism, Methodists
    appeal of in Industrial Revolution England, compared to current convervatism, 215
    dominance in U.S., 34
        during Frontier Awakening, 28
        geographic concentration circa-1800, 23
    emotionalism of, 180
    in early American congregations, 22

European, relation to U.S., 10-11
    to first awakening, 13
Father of American Methodism (Francis Asbury), 2,23-24, 25n6,34
social justice issues supported by, 201
United Methodist Church, 1980s membership status, 84
Meyer, Donald B.
    The Protestant Search for Political Realism, 38n10(36)
Michner, James A.
    Sports in America, 121n1(113)
Milk, Harvey, 73
millenarian sects, 104
millenarianism, defined and expansion of, 85-86
Miller, Arthur
    Death of a Salesman character Willy Loman, comparisons to, 140,227
Miller, Douglas T.
    Popular Religion in the 1950s, 173n3(162)
Miller, Perry, and Thomas H. Johnson
    The Puritans, 18n2(9)
Miller, William, xiii,35
Millerites, xiii,35
minorities. *See* African-Americans; civil rights; immigrants; Native Americans; women
missionaries, missionary work
    conservative Christian, twentieth-century, U.S. and worldwide, 215
    liberalism integral in, 82
    Mormon, 96
    nineteenth-century proliferation, 27,34,232
    of radio evangelism, worldwide, 215
    secularization of the church by, 27
Mitford, Jessica